Best wishes,
Opal Clark

A Fool's Enterprise

THE LIFE OF CHARLES PAGE

By Opal Bennefield Clark

Dexter Publishing Company

Revised edition.

Dexter Publishing Company
1055 Douglas St.
Sand Springs, Oklahoma 74063
(918) 245-4271

Manufactured in Oklahoma, in the United States of America, for the Dexter Publishing Company.

Cover photo by Beverly Clark Klopfenstein.

Library of Congress Catalog Card Number: 88-51538
ISBN 0-9621444-0-1

In memory of my dear departed husband, Jimmy.

Dedicated to Beverly, Lori,
Lynn, Susan, and Karen
who tolerated my constant
preoccupation with writing.

Contents

The Early Years

The Dream Takes Shape

Not A Vision Anymore

Introduction

Charles Page is Dead and Two Cities Mourn

So READ THE FRONT PAGE HEAD LINES OF *THE TULSA TRIBUNE*, DECEMber 28, 1926. Few people knew that Charles Page had been fighting a diabetic condition. His doctors had warned him that overwork could be fatal, but he had an obsession to secure the future of his "kids." That's what he called us. And we called him Daddy Page.

On the evening of December 18, 1926, Charles Page went to Tulsa to attend a meeting with the Tulsa Chamber of Commerce. He had a severe cold and his wife begged him to stay home and take care of himself.

"I have to go to this meeting, Lucy," he had exclaimed. It's about a steel mill I'm trying to get for Sand Springs. Think of all the jobs it will make for my kids."

Mr. Page called his dog, Jim, his constant companion, and together they went on their way. It was a bitter cold night and the fourteen mile ride to Tulsa and back in an unheated car turned his cold into the flu. When he got home he went right to bed. A doctor was called the next morning but he continued to grow worse. His body was too exhausted to fight the disease and he went into a diabetic coma. Within eight days he was gone.

His death came as a surprise to the people and they were in shock as they stood in groups, discussing the demise of the man whom friend and critic alike, had once called a fool. They now spoke of his greatness.

Ballads and poems honoring him were written by sophisticated news editors and just plain folks. One likened him to a mighty oak that had been cut down in its prime and strength. Will Farrell, in his poem "The Broken Wheel," depicted Charles Page as the "bull wheel" of an oil derrick, when he wrote,

> "The bull wheel is broken, the derrick is still.
> There is dust on the bailer and frost on the sill.
> A world he had built with a zeal all his own.
> Now the artisan sleeps on his pillow of stone.
> A spirit — not dead — but alive and aflame.
> Deathless in purpose and deathless in name . . .

All Oklahoma news media carried the story of this unique man *The Tulsa Tribune* devoted several pages of pictures and tributes from his friends. They bordered the columns in black.

Thousands came from near and far to pay their last respects to the man who, like Abou Ben Adhem, had loved his fellow man. The man who had fed the hungry of Tulsa and Sand Springs and contributed so much to the lives and to the building of both Sand Springs and Tulsa.

The funeral was held at 2:00 p.m. Thursday afternoon in the large living room of his children's home. Most businesses closed so that all might be able to attend his funeral.

Both Sand Springs and Tulsa police officers directed the continuous flow of traffic along the highways as thousands came to pay their last respects to the man who had done so much for so many.

The press of the crowd was so great that my sister and I were never able to get inside the door of the Home where we were reared. We were pushed back with the surging crowd that overflowed halfway down the west lawn.

I shall never forget that day. Church bells rang and factory sirens gave a mournful wail as the wheels of industry in both Sand Springs and Tulsa came to a halt for ten minutes in his honor.

As my sister, Beulah and I stood weeping, strangers around us spoke in hushed whispers of his greatness. We had never thought of him as they pictured him. We knew him only as Daddy Page.

Newsmen came from the east to get his story. It read like a work of fiction. They wanted to know about his childhood, for it surely had played a part in making him the way he was. For this they went to his family and friends. For the latter part of his story they went to his friend and cohort, Mr. Brinton Flint Breeding, who was with Mr. Page from the beginning of the controversial project dubbed "A Fool's Enterprise" and later "Charles Page's Folly."

His "Fool's Enterprise" earned for him a statue in the town of his creation — a library, a school and a highway in his name, as well as a place in the pages of *Who's Who, Who Was Who In American, The Americana, Ripley's Believe It or Not,* and numerous other publications.

I have told his story from its beginnings. I have had the help of Mr. and Mrs. Breeding; Mrs. Charles Page and her daughter Mary; Charles Page's niece and nephew Mildred Chapman; and George Campbell; and other relatives and friends who were there when it happened. I have done my best to document the facts in this biography of Charles Page. Names have been changed in three incidents to save embarrassment.

As a child I sat on his lap as he talked of his childhood. I knew Charles Page well, for I was one of his children.

Opal Bennefield Clark

Acknowledgments

THIS BOOK WOULD NOT HAVE BEEN POSSIBLE WITHOUT THE HELP OF MRS. Charles Page and Mary; Mr. and Mrs. Breeding and their daughter Margaret; George Campbell; Mildred Chapman, Mr. Page's niece; Joe Williams, Bill Brown, of the Sand Springs Board of Trustees; and especially La Nell Zahn of the Home Interest offices for proofreading, and supplying many photographs. Bobby Davis and Patrick Chalmers of the Sand Springs Railway Co.; Mary Ward and Beryl Ford for photographs to add to my collection. Miss Dobozy and Miss Margaret Lindsay for information and photographs. Joy and Paul Galloway who assisted in Mr. Galloway's story; Betty Lewis for her story; Lute Bond; Martha Coon; Estell Hughes; Hilda Paden; Dorothy Roberts Hollon; My dear Tulsa Junior College instructor Suzan Jarvis, and classmates who advised and encouraged me. Mary Beuby; Wesley Burditt; Neal Hallford; Sammy Harmon; Laquinta Wheeler; Norma Lockwood; Brian and Sandy Miller; Pat Palmer; Pearl Patterson; Renee Wilson; Tony Flanary; Loretta Carlson; Lucy Saeger; Dorothy Baker; Henry Bailey; Chris Casey; Kay Finch; Shirley Ives; Dwayne Pass; Kathy Youngen; Dianne Holcomb Clayton; May Kyler Avey, former Home girl; Sarah Davis Barber, one of the original 21 orphans; The Charles Page Library, The Central Library, and Tulsa World Library. Photographers Whitey Vallet, Lynn Klopfenstein and Beverly Clark Klopfenstein. Susan Coman, Karen Slankard and Pat Dock who assisted in the book production. And to Mary Obrian for encouragement. I thank you all.

Opal Bennefield Clark

The
Early Years

1908. Tulsa's Frisco depot was on Third street

The Young Man
Repeated Vows
Tulsa in 1903
The Salvation Army Comes to Town
The Big Scotsman
A Girl Named Lucille
Oklahoma Becomes a State
The Depression Versus the Dream

The young Charles Page.

1

The Young Man

CHARLES PAGE, THE SEVENTH CHILD IN A FAMILY OF EIGHT CHILDREN, was born June 2, 1860, in Arnott, a new settlement on the outskirts of Stevens Point, Wisconsin.

Although his home environment and life were much like that of other boys of that time, Charles himself was different. This difference manifested itself at a very early age, to the extent that it was discussed among the members of the family. He was born with a sense of responsibility and a feeling of love and compassion for others. Charles was comfortable to be with, and when any of the other children had to go to the dentist or doctor, it was Charles whom they wanted to accompany them. He was big like his father's people, possessing great physical strength and a sense of protectiveness. He always tried to carry the burdens of those around him, even in his early years.

Charles Page's parents, like most pioneers of this country, were sturdy, honest, Christian people. His mother, Mary Ann Gottry, was from Alsace Lorraine, France. She was eight years old when her German father and French mother came to America. The Gottry family left their wealth in grape vineyards along the Rhine river, near Strasbourg Germany, under French rule, rather than lose a second son in the French army. One night they smuggled their eighteen-year-old son on board ship in a box and set sail for America.

Not knowing their "Atlas," as Mrs. Gottry called it, they had no idea that America was so far away. The hardships of that voyage cost them their two-year-old son, who became ill and died. He was buried at sea.

Soon after they arrived in the United States the eighteen year-old son they had tried to save from war was killed in a cave-in accident while working in an excavation ditch in New York.

Only five of the ten Gottry children remained — Elizabeth, Kate, Anthony, Fanny and eight-year-old Mary Ann.

Mary Ann, mother of Charles Page, worked her way through college. She spoke French, German and English, although her tyrannical German father forbade any language other than German to be spoken in his presence.

Mary Ann married James William Page, a rather severe and puritanical man, of French-Scotch parentage. Born to that union were William Henry,

Catherine Alma, Mary Christine, Chloe Alice, James Ephrim, Elizabeth Rhoania, Charles Edward and Edwin Adalbert.

Although Mary Ann had been reared a Catholic, she accepted the Presbyterian faith of her husband. The children were taught the simple but enduring faith of that generation.

Before Charles was a year old, the rumblings of turmoil and strife in the United States erupted into the Civil War. Charles' brother, seventeen-year-old William Henry Page, fought in that war. He was stationed at Fort Sill, Oklahoma, then Indian Territory. His commanding officer, Dewitt Brown, was married to Mary Ann's sister, Fannie. Aunt Fannie, a nurse, followed the men into the army camps.

One evening while returning from battle the troops were ambushed. William was shot, but he rode on into camp.

"Aunt Fannie, I'm shot," he said, as he slid from his horse. He died in his Aunt's arms. He was buried in Fort Sill.

Charles' father was unable to serve in the army because of the loss of one eye. He fought his battle with the soil of his farm as he assumed the responsibility of feeding five families of women and children whose men-folk were serving in the Union Army.

Charles was five years old when the Civil War ended. About one year later he entertained himself after a rain by building a small town in the damp sands of his father's farm. He was very proud of his town and took his father to see it. His father, pleased with his son's creativity, asked his neighbor to see the child's masterpiece.

Soon after, older neighborhood boys came along with sticks and knocked his city down.

"Some day I'll build a real town that you can't tear down," Charles cried in childish bravado.

They laughed. "Where would you ever get money to do that?" From then on they called him a dreamer.

Charles' vow was one of the many tales told when the family got together and began remembering. They teased him and called him "The Dreamer." But Charles didn't mind. He knew that dreaming was nothing more than setting a goal and working toward that goal. He had the kind of optimism that made him believe man was capable of almost anything, if he set his mind to it. The world was big and full of promise. Man's possibilities were limitless if one was willing to work hard, save his money and press toward that a goal. He intended to be just such a man.

"You've just got to keep your thinking right and be on the alert to every opportunity that comes along," he often said, and "Think Right" became his motto.

Aspirations to make money were evident in Charles even as a child. Charles could make willow whistles which had a very nice sound to them. He often traded his whistles for something he would rather have. But when he came home with a dog sled and told his mother that he traded a willow whistle for it, she looked at him sternly.

"Nobody would trade you a dog sled for a willow whistle!" she scolded.

"Well, Ma, I didn't exactly swap the whistle for a sled. I swapped it for a puppy. I have a dog, but I figured I could get a better swap out of a puppy than I could a whistle. I traded a healthy puppy for this old broken down sled, Ma."

"Well, it still doesn't sound very honest to me," said his mother.

"Ma, it ain't dishonest if everybody is satisfied with the trade," Charles replied.

Mrs. Page accepted his explanation as reasonable, but she still wasn't sure about the honesty of it.

Charles mended his broken sled, and hitched his dog to it. Driving his dog sled into town, he went to the stores and to the townspeople, asking if they would be interested in buying rabbits to eat. He soon had more customers than he could supply, but he wasn't worried. He told his friends that he would give them five cents for every rabbit they caught. He sometimes worked far into the night, by lantern light, cleaning rabbits, which he sold to his customers for ten cents, making a nickel profit on each rabbit sold.

The Page family moved from the pioneering farm village of Arnott to Stevens Point, Wisconsin, so that the children could go to school.

Mrs. Page, an educated woman, always boarded the village school marm, hoping to give her children an extra learning advantage.

Mr. Page went to work delivering freight from boat docks to the Stevens Point stores. However, his health began to fail. When he became too ill to work, it was Charles, age ten, who took his father's place in the seat of the big freight wagon.

Charles' mother objected to his quitting school, as she had paid his tuition for the entire year. But he was headstrong. "I'm not a book boy, anyway," he argued.

Sadly, his mother admitted that the family needed the money. Charles was permitted to work, providing he derived all the benefit he could from having a teacher in the home.

Proudly Charles maneuvered the double team of horses. He soon became adept at backing them up to the boat docks, loading the merchandise into the freight wagon, and delivering the goods to the Stevens Point stores.

Mr. Page died in 1871 after suffering with cancer for a year. The family's grief was magnified by the desperate financial situation the family was in.

The Wisconsin Central Railway had come into Stevens Point about this time, and goods came cheaper by rail. The horses had to be sold to pay his father's doctor bills, and Charles was suddenly out of a job.

The three older girls were already married and had families of their own. They offered to share their homes with their mother, but she refused to burden them. She assured her daughters that she would find a way to support her four remaining children.

She made arrangements for sixteen-year-old Elizabeth Rhoania to do housework for one of the teachers. The girl earned a small wage for her services as well as tuition so she could continue her studies. Fourteen-year-old James Ephraim, started working as a dentist's apprentice. This left Charles, now age eleven, and Edwin Adalbert, age nine, to be looked after.

Charles helped all he could, chopping wood and doing the few odd job he could find to do. One cold dreary day, not long after his father had died, Charles came in with an arm load of wood, which he tossed into the wood box. He removed his gloves and held his hands before the fire to thaw them a bit, so he could unwrap the burlap strips from around his worn shoes. He kicked his heels and toes alternately against the wood box to restore the circulation to his near-frozen feet. Edwin sat beside the fire reading a book.

Charles looked toward his mother, bent over a tub of clothes. She had tried to keep her children from knowing how worried she was about their finances. The cold wintry weather added to her depression and her sadness over the loss of her husband. Charles' mother was weeping silently. Her tears falling into her wash tub. His big heart swelled within him. He put his arms around her. "Ma, never you mind," he said wiping his tears on his sleeve. "I'll help you all I can. When I get to be a man you won't have to work. I'll take care of you." He nodded his head in earnest. "I'll take care of other poor mothers and their children, too. Just wait and see."

Seeking something she could do to earn a living, Mrs. Page spoke to the Wisconsin Central Railroad authorities. There were no restaurants near by, and she offered family style meals to the men working for the railroad. She was told that some of the men also needed a place to stay. She had a nice big home, built for a large family, so she accepted the challenge.

However, Mrs. Page made it clear to the men that she would not tolerate rough talk, spitting tobacco, drinking, playing cards, nor any music other than church music.

Mrs. Page mothered her new tenants. She sat up with them when they were sick, doctoring them until they were well. She was the same way toward her friends and neighbors. Everyone was soon calling the sweetly indomitable woman "Ma Page."

Charles was the most devoted of all his mother's children. He helped her all he could, even with the cooking. He became a very good biscuit maker.

One day Morland Monsell, one of Mrs. Page's boarders mentioned that the Wisconsin Central Railroad Depot needed a dispatch boy. Charles was quick to respond. Pulling himself up to his most commanding height, he applied. The job required that the dispatcher have a horse. Charles talked them into letting him use his dog and sled to deliver messages through the winter months.

Charles worked hard and saved what money he could. He soon had enough money to buy the horse he needed. But he remained constantly on the alert for anything that would bring in money.

Charles' next job was clerking in the general store. He sold his horse and bought seven head of cattle at a bargain price and sold them for a neat profit. This was his first big investment experience. He became a quick appraiser of values, a ready purchaser and a willing seller if the offer was good.

The Wisconsin Central railway company was a line that pierced the timber country of the badger state of Wisconsin. Hearing the railroad men who boarded at his mother's house talk of the big country they traveled through, gave Charles a thirst for adventure. He was sixteen when he and a friend Tom Carence joined the ranks of railroad operators and traveled the great northern states. He became one of the crew of trainmen.

But seeing was not enough. The big outside world was calling him. He was about seventeen when he went into the rugged timber country of the north. Told that he was too young to be a lumberjack, Charles signed on as cook's helper, eager for the opportunity to prove to the boss that he was capable of doing a man's job and earning a man's wages.

Charles was sending part of his wages home to his mother, and saving what he kept for himself against that day when he could invest and double it. He wanted more money.

"I've been chopping wood practically all my life," he said. Furthermore, he boasted the ability to chop a tree down as fast as the best man in the camp. Of course, when put to the test, Charles didn't win, but he did well enough to be advanced to a full-fledged lumberjack.

But this didn't satisfy Charles for long. He was in a hurry to get rich. He was always asking questions and learning. He studied the method the men used in maneuvering the double yokes of oxen, pulling the big logs down hill and into the Mississippi river, where they were floated to a St. Louis sawmill. He questioned the men and found that the loggers were paid more than wood cutters. He also learned that those who owned the oxen they drove, got pay for the use of the oxen as well.

Charles told his boss he had driven a double team of horses pulling a big freight wagon at age ten, and that he was sure he could drive a yoke of oxen. By now, the men believed the young fellow could do what he said he could. Anyway, it was a diversion to let him try. One man had just hooked his team to a long log. He handed Charles the reins.

Charles began slowly and patiently maneuvering the oxen to get both team and log headed in the right direction. Going in and out, around and through the forest of trees with the big log was harder than it had looked. But he got the log down the hill and into the river. The men cheered. They liked the ambitious young Charles, and talked the boss into advancing him.

Before long Charles had saved enough money to buy his own double yoke of oxen and was drawing pay for his work, as well as for the use of his oxen.

The men always went to town on Saturday and stayed until Sunday evening. Tom Carence still worked for the railroad and lived in the town. He and Charles remained friends and would get together on Saturdays when Charles was in town.

One Saturday a prize fighter and his manager came to town, challenging anyone who wanted to fight. The men at the lumber camp, amazed at Charley's strength, hunted him down and talked him into getting into the ring. Always eager to earn that extra buck, Charles agreed. He won the fight, but he wasn't happy about it. He feared he had injured the prize fighter for life.

The crowd cheered, challenging others to fight Charles. Charles refused, saying he didn't want to maim a man for life who was just trying to earn a living as best he could. Such an attitude was hard for his fellow workers to understand. But as Charles told Tom Carence, he didn't worry about the opinions of others.

It wasn't long before Charles had his own logging operation with men working for him.

Charles' jobs were as varied as his adventures, which took him throughout the north and western states. Occasionally he went back to Wisconsin to visit his mother. He especially liked going home for Christmas. When he did, it was a big occasion. All of Mrs. Page's children and grandchildren gathered at the Page home. There were so many grandchildren that some had to sleep on the floor, or four in a bed. It was like having a slumber party and the children loved it.

There were always cookies, candy, and a great tree strung with popcorn and colorful peppermint sticks. The night before Christmas Aunt Fannie, Mrs. Page's sister, would slip out of the room and put on a Santa Clause suit then come running into where the children were, with a merry "Ho, ho ho." This she had done since Charles and his brothers and sisters were small.

The children couldn't understand how Santa knew so much about them as he called them by name and told them one by one things that they had done during the passing year. Finally Santa had them all to kneel and solemnly promise to do better next year.

When Santa left to visit other boys and girls, Uncle Charley, the honored guest, handed out the presents.

The next day the family went to one of the girls' houses in the country. Charles donned an apron, went into the pantry and made the biscuits. His sisters smiled as Charles tried to tell them how to do the rest of the cooking.

As Charles said good bye to the family, he would slip a silver dollar into each little palm.

Charles was still in his teens when he became a member of the police force in Ashland, Wisconsin. He had no qualms about using his strength and agility in keeping law-breakers under control.

However, beyond the rough-and-ready exterior of the young man still lay a heart of compassion. When he found someone in need, he tried to help him. When he left Ashland, he left his furniture in his leased apartment and gave the keys to some homeless men, who then made the place their home.

From Ashland, Wisconsin, Charles Page went to the "rough and tough" town of Tower, Minnesota, where he became Chief of Police. He was barely twenty years old.

One night when he went into a saloon in Tower to arrest a man, somebody shot out the lights, plunging the room into darkness. Shooting continued but Chief Page emerged with his man. He also had two bullet holes in the shoulder of his coat.

The ability he displayed as an officer of the law got him a position with the famous Pinkerton Detective agency. Charles was assigned the task of tracking down a dangerous killer. He trailed the man to Cincinnati, Ohio, before he caught up with him. He had traveled with the man a week when one night, while reminiscing over a camp fire, the man admitted his guilt. Charles brought him in.

But Charles didn't like this kind of work. He liked people. He felt sympathy toward some of the men and didn't like bringing them in to be punished. He quit that job and headed back toward Wisconsin.

In 1881, while Charles was working in Duluth, Minnesota, he met a young widow with a four-year-old son, Willie. After a short courtship he and Lucy were married.

Charles soon moved his family to Ellensburg, Washington, where he had a job as a colonization agent for the Northern Pacific Railroad, opening up new territory. He invested five hundred dollars in timber property in Tacoma, Washington, to start a real estate venture of his own. He made a deal with a sawmill company to swap logs for lumber to build houses, and was doing fine when Lucy, who was pregnant, became ill.

"Charley it's the baby! It's coming, I'm sure!"

Charles was alarmed and excited. "It's not time for the baby," he said, "and Aunt Fannie isn't here to help you."

"Babies often choose their own time," said Lucy, grimacing with pain.

When the men in the logging camp heard, they were worried. "She'll never make it," said one. "It's thirty-five miles to the nearest doctor. A wagon would take forever and be dangerous, bumping over the rough terrain." They shook their heads fearing for Lucy's life. They knew nothing about birthing babies.

"Charley, what are we going to do?" cried Lucy, wringing her hands. "What are we going to do?"

Charles had been pacing the floor. Suddenly he grabbed his hat and hurried out the back door.

Charles proved his ability to make quick decisions when he speedily saddled his horse and told one of his men to hand Lucy up to him.

"Charley," Lucy exclaimed, "I can't ride a horse!"

Charles took no time to explain. "Hand her up to me," he repeated. As Lucy was handed up to Charles, she looked back at her little son, Will. "He'll be all right," said Charles. "These guys will take care of him." Then cradling his wife in his arms to shield her from the bounce of the saddle, Charles made a thirty-five-mile dash through the vast timberland to the hospital.

FAMILY GROUP No. _____

Husband's Full Name **James William Page**

This Information Obtained From: *Mary Annes Bible*	Husband's	Day Month Year	City, Town or Place	County or Province, etc.	State or Country	Add. Info. on Husband
	Birth	2-6 1817	Lake Chaplain			French + Scotts
	Chr'nd					
	Mar.	10-17-1843				
	Death	1871-Cancer	- Stevens Point, Wisconsin			
	Burial		Union Cemetery - Stevens Point, Wisconsin			
	Places of Residence					
	Occupation *fur freighter*	Church Affiliation *Presbyterian*		Military Rec.		
	Other wives, if any, No. (1) (2) etc. Make separate sheet for each mar. *none*					
	His Father			Mother's Maiden Name		

Wife's Full Maiden Name **Mary Anne Gottry**

	Wife's	Day Month Year	City, Town or Place	County or Province, etc.	State or Country	Add. Info. on Wife
Compiler	Birth	10-7-1825	Alsace Lorraine, near Strassburg		Germany	
Address	Chr'nd					
City, State	Death	1891	Stevens Point, Wisconsin			
Date	Burial		Union Cemetery -- Stevens Point, Wisc.			
	Places of Residence					
	Occupation if other than Housewife *She Kept Boarders*	Church Affiliation *Presbyterian*				
	Other husbands, if any, No. (1) (2) etc. Make separate sheet for each hus. *none —*				She was German + French	
	Her Father			Mother's Maiden Name		French

Sex	Children's Names in Full (Arrange in order of birth)	Children's Data	Day Month Year	City, Town or Place	County or Province, etc.	State or Country	Add. Info. on Children
	1 **William Henry Page** Full Name of Spouse* *never married*	Birth	27-10-1844	Rock River, Jamesville, Wisconsin			
		Mar.	never mar:	ambushed while in battle. —			
		Death	1862 at age 17 - during Civil War - Fort Gibson, Okla.				
		Burial	at Fort Gibson, Okla.				
	2 **Catherine Alma P.** Full Name of Spouse* *Horace Warner*	Birth	28-10-1846	Rock River, Jamestown, Wisc.	4 to that union		
		Mar.			Edith,		
		Death			Sylvia		
		Burial			Horace Myrtle		
	3 **Mary Christine P.** Full Name of Spouse* *Neal North McLeod*	Birth	15-4-1894	Rock River, now Jamestown, Wisc.	4 children		
		Mar.			1. Reota Flora,		
		Death	27-3-1890		2. Marian Esther		
		Burial		3. Georgiana 4- Neal			
	4 **Ice Alice Page** Full Name of Spouse* *Jerome Kingsberry*	Birth	23-6-1851	Marquette Co. Near Markson, Wisc.			
		Mar.		five children			
		Death		1. Mark 3. Faye 5. John - father of Wayne			
		Burial		2. Author 4. Beatrice			
	5 **James Ephraim Page** Full Name of Spouse*	Birth	14-1-1885				
		Mar.					
		Death					
		Burial		before 1926 Buried in Woodland Cemetery, SS, Okla.			
	6 **Elizabeth Rhoania** Full Name of Spouse* *Morland Monsell*	Birth	7-11-1857	Portage, Co. Town of Sharon, Wisc.			
		Mar.		3 children - 1. Elizabeth who married			
		Death		Dr. Campbell, parents of George Campbell			
		Burial					
	7 **Charles Edward P.** Full Name of Spouse* 2nd - *Lucile Rayburn*	Birth	2-6-1860	near Arnott, Wisc.			
		Mar.	1881 To Lucile. -3 Duluth, Minn. 2nd. marriage				
		Death	27-12-1926				
		Burial		Woodland Cem. in Sand Sprs. Okla. 1 child MARY			
	8 **Edwin Adalbert P.** Full Name of Spouse* 1. Libby — son Carl 2. Luise 3 children	Birth	13-12-1862	near Arnott, Wisc.			
		Mar.					
		Death					
		Burial		Woodland Cemetary, Sand Spr. Okla.			
	9 Full Name of Spouse*	Birth					
		Mar.					
		Death					
		Burial					
	10 Full Name of Spouse*	Birth					
		Mar.					
		Death					
		Burial					

*If married more than one (1) No. each mar. (1) (2) etc. and list in "Add. Info. on children" column. Use reverse side for additional children, other notes, references or information.

2

Repeated Vows

THE BABY WAS STILLBORN. CHARLES, GRIEVING, BLAMED HIMSELF FOR the death of his little son until the doctor assured him that the baby had died earlier, and that his quick thinking had saved Lucy's life.

"Moreover," warned the doctor, "your wife is not a strong woman. She can't endure the hardships of frontier living. Most important of all, Mr. Page, she should not have any more children."

Charles tried to keep a brave front for Lucy's sake. But outside the hospital his shoulders sagged and his breath caught in his throat. Wearily seating himself on the retaining wall on the hospital grounds, he held his head in his hands and wept. He loved children. He wanted lots of children, but his big concern was for Lucy.

"Dear Lord," he whispered, then hesitated. "I'm not worthy of your help. I've never really done anything for you. I don't even know what you expect of me. But if You'll show me what You want me to do I'll try to do it . . . But please, God, it's Lucy I'm asking you to help. She's awfully sick and discouraged."

Charles sat, unaware that it had started to snow. The snow was falling on his hat, covering his shoulders and piling up around his feet. His thoughts were on Lucy. What to do? The doctor had said that she shouldn't live in rough surroundings. He would have to give up his project, sell everything and find work where she could live in the city.

Suddenly Charles became aware of the snow. He was shivering. He pulled his coat collar up and, with eyes blurred and watery, hurried down the street as large snowflakes whirled past him. His back and shoulders ached. The long ride holding Lucy aloft was taking its toll. He rubbed his shoulder, wondering if this were the kind of suffering old folks went through when the cold winds blew against their bones. He had heard his mother complain of aching bones during the winter.

Charles walked, shoulders hunched against the driving snow for what seemed an interminable amount of time. To make matters worse, his stomach felt drawn together like a pouch with a pulled drawstring. Darkness was beginning to settle around him, and he hadn't eaten all day. He paused to get his bearings. Where was he? He knew the town well, having policed it in his youth. He looked down the street. Squinting his eyes against the lashing icy particles that stung his face, he became familiar with his surroundings.

There was Mrs. Barber's house. He recalled his policing days, when they brought her husband home to her. Mr. Barber had been killed by a wild stallion he was trying to break. Mrs. Barber must be very old by now, thought Charles, remembering that she was a very kind woman.

A man driving a buggy hurried past, anxious to get out of the sudden blast of winter weather, and caused his thought to turn momentarily from Mrs. Barber, until he heard a door open. He turned back to see Mrs. Barber come out of her house clutching a shawl around her stooped shoulders. She picked up a few pieces of wood from the small stack on her front porch. Then, without looking up, she went back into the house.

Charles looked at the small stack of wood and wondered if that was all the wood she had against the cold winter ahead of her. Were her bones aching with the cold? Impulsively he reached into his pocket and drew out a twenty dollar bill. All was quiet when he stepped up on her porch. Silently he slid the twenty dollar bill under Mrs. Barber's door and left.

Later, in a hotel room that night, he pondered his actions. What made him do what he had done? Was it God, giving him a "nudge," to help the elderly widow? For a few moments he had forgotten his own problems and helped somebody else. Ma would like that, he thought, because that's what she would have done.

As he lay listening to the staccato rhythm of the sleet pelting the windowpane, his mind returned to Lucy. What would he do? Finally he closed his eyes and went to sleep.

Charles sold his land, and when Lucy was out of the hospital he bought a hotel in Tacoma, Washington. There he settled Lucy comfortably, and arranged for Aunt Fannie, who was now a widow, to live with them and watch over his frail wife.

Mr. Page's hotel at 1124 Pacific Avenue catered to such influential and lasting friends as former Governor Hardy of Washington and J. Hamilton Lewis from Illinois, who practiced law in Seattle, and later became a senator.

In Tacoma, Charles invested money in what seemed a sure thing. In his first attempt at a financial coup, he tried to corner the prune market and was soundly trounced for his inexperience.

He heard about a gold rush in Canada. This was his chance for the big money. He went into the Okanogan district of British Columbia, and was working like a mule when he got word that his mother was seriously ill, and calling for him. He left everything and headed for home.

As the result of a fall, Mrs. Page had broken her hip and complications had set in. True to his word, Charles had kept in touch with his mother, sending money as regularly as he could, thus providing many comforts she might not otherwise have had.

He never left her bedside during that time but endured the long nights, as he watched his indomitable mother grow weaker with the dawning of each day. He regretted not having been with her more. The influence of his mother's character on his life and the bond of understanding and affection that existed between them was intensified. Saddened by the suffering which preceded her death, and remembering the hardships of his courageous mother, Charles held her frail hand and renewed his vow to help other widows and orphans whenever he could. Nothing that his mother had said or done during her lifetime could have impressed her teachings and her wishes so firmly in Charles' mind as did those last four days as she told him of her hopes and dreams for him. She died in 1891. It was Charles who tried to comfort the family, although they all knew he suffered greatly. He was still a kind, understanding person to cling to for comfort, wiping the tears from the faces of the sorrowing grandchildren. Pressing a silver dollar into each little hand he told them that their grandmother was up there with God where she could smile down upon them.

When their Uncle Charles went away again they wouldn't hear from him as often as they had before Grandma Page died. Christmas, the season for family gatherings, was never quite the same.

The Stevens Point News reported that Mrs. Page's funeral was the largest the town's people had ever had. A friend to all, she had never been known to turn a hungry man from her door. There was hardly a time when she didn't have someone who needed a home staying with her. At her death Mrs. Page left behind over one hundred "tintype" photographs of children she had assisted into the world.

After his mother's death, Charles went back to his diggings on the west coast. He tried his luck in various areas from Washington to Idaho and back again, but had little success in his mining ventures. Luck had not been with him for four or five years, and it continued. In 1892-93 there was a depression, when banks all over America went broke, and Charles Page lost all the money he had saved. All he had left was a piece of forest land near Everett, Washington, that he had purchased while in the colonization business. He had no alterative but to take his wife into the rough country again where he could make a living from his land by cutting trees and selling them to a sawmill. However his Aunt Fannie who was a nurse agreed to go along to take care of his frail wife. He was clearing the land to start a building program when he heard that gold had again been found in Cripple Creek, Colorado, dubbed the "BOWL OF GOLD" in 1859. It lay like a large bowl, surrounded by the sloping mountains not far from the 14,110 foot "Pikes Peak." It had been the liveliest, most publicized of all the mining camps.

The gold rush had flared up and then faded; then flared once more in 1887, only to die out again. The recent news was that a new vein of gold had been found and millions of dollars were being made from it. The stampede of 1895 drew Charles Page into the gold rush. He sold everything he had. At thirty-five years of age, if he were going to make it rich, this would be the time. He left money to take care of his family, and headed for Cripple Creek, Colorado.

Seeing a housing shortage, and having faith in real estate, Charles decided to combine his real estate experience with his mining. He did well in the real estate business, but the profits he made in real estate was absorbed by his mining losses.

From Cripple Creek Charles went back to Victoria, British Columbia. Four or five years passed with nothing but discouragement. Lucy was in the hospital and he was out of a job. It seemed that Charles met with failure in everything he tried. He was standing on the street corner pondering his predicament when there came a sudden cloudburst. He swung around the corner in a hurry to get out of the rain, when he bumped into a young Salvation Army lady who was pressed against the building to escape the downpour. He apologized and she smiled, rattling her tambourine in his face.

"Do you want to give something to the poor?" she asked.

"I'm broke," he said, and drew his hand from his pocket with a silver dollar, a nickel and a dime. "That's all I have. What do you think I should give?"

"Give your tithe," was her reply.

Charles asked, "What's a tithe?"

"Tithes are one tenth of all your income," the young woman explained. "God truly gives us all we have. He only asks that we give one tenth back to Him to carry on His work. This makes you partners with God."

"Humm," said Charles. "I don't see how a fellow could ever go broke if he's partners with the Big Fellow." He tossed the fifteen cents into the tambourine. Then he went on his way with nothing to click against the silver dollar in his pocket, but he had a lot to think about.

Charles got a job the next day and from his first pay he put his tithes into the Salvation Army tambourine.

Later, looking for a house in Victoria so that he could send for his family, he ran into an old friend. Jeff had been Charles' bookkeeper when he was in the lumber business.

"Charley, I'm broke," said Jeff. "Have you got any money?" Charles only had thirty dollars, but he handed Jeff ten dollars and went on into the real estate office.

A few days later Charles met Jeff again and told him of his good luck.

"When I left you the other day I went into the real estate office," said Charles. "While I waited, a man came in and asked the realtor if he knew who owned certain oil leases. The realtor said no, that they didn't handle oil leases. Well, as I always say, if you keep your ear to the ground, you'll know what's coming down the road. I figured this realtor was overlooking an opportunity that I wasn't going to let get away. I trotted after the man as he left the realtor's office.

"Mister," I said, as I caught up with him. "I think I can get you those options." I had a little talk with him and finally he said for me to go to it. To make a long story short, I hustled around and within a few hours I had my hands on what he wanted. As a result, I pulled down a three-hundred-dollar commission." Charles handed Jeff thirty-dollars.

"What is this for?" asked Jeff.

Charles told Jeff of his decision to tithe ten percent of his income to help the Big Fellow take care of those in need. "You said you were broke. I know what it's like to be broke and out of a job." said Charles. "I've been hungry lots of times. The thirty dollars I gave you is ten percent of my three hundred dollars commission. We'll just say it's from God."

Charles stayed in Victoria for awhile, making money buying and selling mining leases and claims.

From there Charles went back to Colorado. He liked Colorado, so he decided to embark upon another real estate venture. He became partners with a builder by the name of White, in Colorado Springs, and together they developed what was called the "Page-White" addition. His dream city was on its way, and making him quite wealthy by the standards of that time, when he noticed that people were getting rich on a new discovery, a product called "rock oil." Some called it "liquid gold," or "black gold."

Mr. Page left Colorado Springs and went to Boulder, where he pioneered in developing several shallow oil wells. From there he went to Fort Collins, a new oil town. He drilled a dry hole. The well was drilled as deep as methods would permit at that time. Later, deeper drilling would develop a major pool with large wells surrounding his dry well.

Mr. Page bought the Fort Collins Light and Power Plant and later the power plant at Boulder, Colorado. With the money he accumulated from their operation he drilled another well, but he didn't get any production.

About this time Lucy became ill again, and Charles took her to a Sanitarium at Battle Creek, Michigan, for treatments. While there, he drilled some wells near Battle Creek and also one at Bay City, Michigan, but he got nothing for his labors. Later, when tools for deeper drilling became available there would be major oil fields where he had pioneered those wells.

He was in Michigan when he heard that oil had been discovered in the Oklahoma and Indian Territories. He decided to go there.

Opal Clark

3

Tulsa in 1903

CHARLES PAGE LEARNED THAT GUTHRIE, THE SEAT OF INDIAN AFFAIRS, and Oklahoma City were two of the largest cities in the Indian Territory. He decided to go to Oklahoma City.

Lucy's son Will, now a dentist, decided to go along with the family to the Indian Territory. Aunt Fannie also went, as she was housekeeper and nurse for Lucy.

It hadn't been long since the run for land on the Cherokee Strip, and the roads into the territories were few with only wagon trails. However, several railroads criss-crossed the land and Mr. Page took his family by train.

As soon as the family was settled into an apartment Mr. Page went about the business of securing oil leases. He drilled a well at McCloud, not far from Oklahoma City, but got no oil. All the while he kept hearing about the aggressive little town of Tulsa.

Tulsa had started making headlines on May 10th, 1901. The population of the little cow town, was 1,390. It was a mere flag stop for the Katy and Frisco railroads and not even on the map. But the Tulsa residents intended it to be.

Having no income from federal pay rolls, as did cities with Federal Administration of Indian Affairs, Tulsa needed industry to grow. Having already maneuvered to get the Katy Railroad six miles off its intended course to bring the cattle business to Tulsa, the people now saw the opportunity to enlarge their borders with the new interest — Black gold.

Although no oil had been found in Tulsa, a mere trickle had been seen in Red Fork, a little hamlet across the Arkansas river, south of Tulsa. A few chosen words in a Kansas newspaper did the trick. Other newspapers picked it up, and Tulsa was on its way. Within forty-eight hours, twenty-five hundred people swarmed into the astonished little town of Red Fork. There were no accommodations to take care of them. Tulsa had been preparing for an influx of people and was on hand to direct the flow of traffic across the river. But they were as astonished as the residents of Red Fork were, as the great numbers of people descended upon them.

The Arkansas River was known to have many quick sand spots, but there were a few shallow rock bottom places where ferrying and fording the river was possible. One ferrying place with a rock bottom strip, ran almost parallel to the shallow creek in the revine at Third Street and Nogalas Avenue. The ferry was attached to a cable tied from tree to tree at either side of the river and was pushed along by a long pole.

There was a larger ferry near Twenty-First Street, called the Ackley crossing. John McLaughlin was the operator of this cable operated ferry, which would accommodate four wagons and teams. The charge for wagons or a man on horse back was twenty-five cents round trip, or fifty cents if the river was high and dangerous.

Two years had passed since the first big influx of people had come to Tulsa, but things were pretty much the same when Charles Page came to look things over. He talked to a realtor who said there didn't seem to be any vacancies anywhere.

As Mr. Page walked along the streets of Tulsa, still called Tulsey-Town by some, he talked to builders who told him that they had kept saws and hammers flying from sun up to sun down and were still unable to provide enough housing for the people who had continued to come to Tulsa. Tents and wagon camps dotted the horizon. There were even restaurants in large tents. Some tents housed as many as eighty men. A revolver, still a part of man's equipment, was tucked under his pillow of personal belongings.

Restaurants were always a good place to go if you wanted to learn about a town. Tulsa restaurants served family style meals for twenty-five cents a meal. Bowls and platters were kept filled and you could eat all you wanted.

Lingering over a cigar, Mr. Page visited with the men who sat at the same long table. They were all enthusiastic boosters of the city. He liked the spirit of the exciting little town. Its citizenry was as varied as any town he had ever been in. He learned that this was Creek Indian country, although the border line to the Osage section of the Territories was just north of Tulsa. The land was owned by the Creeks and the "freed men," who had been slaves to the more progressive Creek Indians. The Negro freed men, had been allotted lands equal to that of an Indian child. The Negro could sell his land, but the Indian could not.

The Frisco Railroad had brought the cattle business to Tulsa, and although the oil business now seemed to dominate, it was still a cow town too. Cowboys wore big hats and boots with spurs that clanked to the hollow sound of each step as they made their way down the board walks.

Mr. Page learned that there were several coal mines around Tulsa, and although people were beginning to use gas for fuel, it was not yet greatly accepted. People were afraid of it. With coal mines so close, coal was cheap and the people were satisfied using it.

As the men talked, one man offered Mr. Page a drink from a bottle he pulled from his boot. "Don't let anyone see you pour it into your glass," he cautioned. "It's against the law to have liquor in the Indian Territory. But we smuggle it in in our boots. See, a bottle fits undetected inside a boot. We call it 'bootlegged' whiskey here in Tulsa. The chock joints at the edge of town have picked up the expression of bootlegging, and the expression is spreading. But it started right here in Tulsa."

Mr. Page smiled at the dubious pride in starting such an expression right in Tulsa, but he accepted the friendly jesture and poured himself a drink.

Upon stating that he had come to stay, providing he could find a place for his family to live in, he was instructed to talk to J. M. Hall, who owned the store across the street, which he did.

"What I need is a three-bedroom apartment, or a house," said Mr. Page.

"These upstairs apartments are only two and three rooms," said Mr. Hall, but I have a story-and-a-half house on Eighth and Detroit that I have just decided to rent. It's furnished and ready to move into."

Mr. Page got his family settled in. Will found a place for his dental practice, and Mr. Page started talking with the oil men about oil leases.

Mr. Page soon joined the newly organized Commercial Club, a forerunner to the Chamber of Commerce and became tremendously interested in helping to build the city to greater heights.

By 1904, Tulsa had its own newspaper, *The Daily Democrat*. The headliner of October 10th, revealed that Tulsa was getting its third railroad, but that it was also a town which practiced the so called "blue laws." *The Daily Democrat* stated:

> "The Midland Valley Railroad reached the city limits on Sunday morning at 8:00. Mayor Cline and his officer met the workmen and explained that performance of labor was forbidden within city limits on the Sabbath. Sunday was supposed to be a day of rest."

The Frisco Railroad had crossed Tulsa about twenty years earlier, catering to the cattle business and other freight. The Missouri Kansas and Texas Railroad called "The Katy, or "M. K. and T," had come through Tulsa about 1898. The three railroads criss-crossed each other going in different directions. Making Tulsa a rail-hub.

On October 18, 1904, Mr. Page got his name in the oil news of *The Daily Democrat*. The paper stated:

> "Charles Page, drilling well #1, for the Chandler Oil and Gas Company, has suspended work at about thirteen hundred feet, on account of the lack of tools for drawing casing, which is somewhat misplaced deep down in the hold."

Having a sense of humor, Charles Page drew bantering from his friends, right from the start. But on October 25th, the news was better.

> "Well #1, of the Chandler Oil and Gas Company on the Fannie Taylor Allotment, was down over thirteen hundred feet, and Mr. Page hopes to complete it by Tuesday."

Having no luck in Chandler, Mr. Page went to the south side of Red Fork Pool, (near where Oakhurst is now,) but he still had no luck. He had drilled these wells for a share in the well, following hunches as to where oil might be found. Strangely enough almost every place he had drilled so far would become major pools when tools were made for drilling deeper than 1,700 feet, but as for now, Charles Page had used up all his money. All he had was the income from a hotel he owned on 1320 Stout Street, in Denver, Colorado. He had to keep that for his family to live on.

However, the oil business had gripped him harder than any other of his ventures. He couldn't give up. Farmers, mechanics, clerks, and even waitresses were pooling their money, forming hastily organized companies, and getting rich. He scouted around for partners. Since he could do the drilling for his share in the operation, he was able to find partners who would finance the project.

He went to the north side of the Red Fork Pool, and set up his cable drilling rig. This method could be used without the use of a derrick. He stationed his "bull wheel" around which the cable was wound and secured the large beam, balanced on top of a post called "a sampson post." As the walking beam alternately was raised and lowered, it lifted and dropped the cable holding the drill bit in the hole. As the hole was dug, casing was supposed to be inserted into the hole. But the casing was expensive. He would wait to see if he got oil before he went to the expense of casing the well. This was called "wildcatting a well."

It took weeks to drill a well, and it was very disappointing when the well turned out to be a dry hole. But he had to keep trying. He drilled a well on the Emarthla allotment, and at last there was oil. It was only a small producer, but it was a start. Feeling victorious, he and his partners named their company the Victory Oil & Gas Company.

As he was feeling good over at last being in the oil business, the news that reached his ears made his discovery seem very insignificant.

Robert Galbreath who had also been at Red Fork, pumping two small wells with so little profit, had just about decided to quit when a farmer, Robert Glenn, came to see him.

In November of 1905, Galbreath went to examine some seepage along a limestone ledge on Robert Glenn's wife's allotment near Mounds. Galbreath examined the rocks, discovering that some of the hollows in the stone were actually being filled with translucent green oil. He got excited. He didn't have money to finance drilling a well, so he talked Frank Chelsey, a business man of Keystone, to join him in a wildcat operation. The oil came in, shooting over the top of the derrick.

It was ten miles from the nearest producing well, but remembering the rush at Red Fork, Galbreath and Chelsey decided to keep it a secret until they could obtain leases on the surrounding areas. They placed armed guards around to keep people away.

On December 27th, *The Daily Democrat* had a small item in the paper mentioning the well, but no one had any idea as to what Galbreath and Chelsey were guarding. However Billy Roesser went to investigate. He grabbed leases left and right before major oil companies swooped in to buy up all the leases. John D. Rockefeller's Standerd Oil Company had run a pipeline across the state on October 28, 1904 and was grabbing all the leases it could buy.

Billy Roesser sold eighty acres of his holdings for $350,000 and still had other leases appraised at one million dollars.

Charles Page went into what was known as the north extension to the Glenn Pool district. He drilled a well for an interest in the lease on the Ispogee allotment. It turned out to be only a gas well. He sold his share in the Victory Oil & Gas Company and bought a lease from Billy Roesser. He brought in a well called "The Taneha," which produced 2,000 barrels of oil a day. The estimated value of the well was approximately one million dollars. He was among the first independents to profit before the major oil companies swooped in to grab all the leases. Charles Page was not as rich as some, but he was now a very rich man.

He drilled another well west of Red Fork, for an interest in the lease and brought in another gas well.

"Let it blow, Charley," said his partners. "Why bother to cap a worthless gas well? If it is allowed to blow, it might bring up a little oil with it." But being a frugal man, Charles bought their share of the well and capped it. He also bought up many of the gas wells that others deemed worthless, and capped them. The plans for the city of his dreams was once more formulating in his mind. At any rate, wasting was sheer folly, and letting the gas go into the air was dangerous.

Occasionally a match was thrown into an escaping gas well to make a torch to light up surrounding areas. Glennpool had so many torches it looked like "Dante's Inferno." But accidents were beginning to happen through such carelessness. Even Mr. Page had thoughtlessly struck a match on the casing of one of his wells. His speed in retreating saved him from injury, but he didn't forget that sudden burst of flames that made him jump and run for safety.

Creeks that oil had spilled into also caught fire. One creek burned for days as the black smoke obscured the sun, causing accidents, and forcing campers to move back from the banks of the creek.

Meanwhile, things were not going well at home for Charles Page. His wife had not known him for three years, and she had become gravely ill. Tulsa had no regular hospitals. Surgery was done in the offices of doctors, mostly set up in their homes. Mr. Page took Lucy to a sanitorium in Colorado hoping doctors there could help her but was told instead that Lucy had cancer in its last stages.

Aunt Fanny, no longer needed, went back to her hometown of Wisconsin. Will had already moved into an apartment near his dental office, so Mr. Page moved into a two room apartment over J. M. Hall's store on the northwest corner of First and Main streets.

After the Glenn Pool excitement the Commercial Club decided that Tulsa should be advertised again. Oklahoma City occupied first place population-wise and Tulsa's ambition was aimed toward supremacy. A mere advertisement in the paper would no longer suffice. They were in "big-time" now, and it would be done with style and finesse. The Commercial Club chartered a train and hired a young man from Oologah, by the name of Will Rogers, who had been doing some pretty fancy rope handling at the fair and in rodeos. He was to do rope tricks to draw the crowds around the train depots along the route of the campaign. The dedicated speakers of the Commercial Club would then take over, promoting their town.

Being a member of the club, Mr. Page went along, planning to stop over to see Lucy.

Will Rogers was rather shy and sometimes got nervous, making mistakes. When he did he remarked about it to cover his embarrassment.

"It's kind'a silly to stand around and watch a guy twittlin' with a rope, anyway," was one remark, and it brought lots of laughter. Will soon realized that the people enjoyed his humor as much as they did his "ropin'."

While the booster train was in Chicago, some of the boosters were given a ride in a two-cylinder motor car named the American. U. M. Burcham, one of the boosters, plunked down $600., and ordered one delivered to Tulsa.

When the car arrived it set off a series of runaway horses frightened by the noise.

Before long, Frank Winters, D. W. Martindale, H. P. Anderson and Paul Clinton had automobiles, but Billy Roesser topped them all. He bought two cars. One was a daring red. Before long the Indians, becoming rich on the oil, were driving cars painted pink and lavender.

Charles Page, being a practical man, was not interested in owning a car. There was no place to drive it. The highways in the Territories were mere wagon trails. You could drive on the unpaved streets of Tulsa, if it hadn't rained lately. When it rained, only a team of horses could keep from getting stuck in the slippery red clay. When the clay was wet it was as slippery as ice. It was a common thing for pedestrians to slide down in the muck. Getting stuck in it was almost like getting into quicksand. It clung to the spokes of the wheels of wagons and buggies unlike ordinary mud that dried and fell off. Clay had to be scraped off. Tulsa was talking of paving the streets.

Tulsa was talking of many things, and also doing many things to improve and enlarge their borders. The town was fast becoming headquarters for the oil business. Workmen worked from sun up to sun down trying to take care of the problem of office space. To encourage those who could afford to build, it was pointed out that building an office building would not only be a good investment, but would also be a monument to the name of the person who built it, if they gave the building their name.

Hotels were going up everywhere too. Tate Brady was constructing the spacious Tate Brady Hotel on the corner of Main and Archer. W. M. Robinson who had remodeled a livery stable into a hotel, outdid himself by building the ever-so-modern Robinson's Hotel. It was a five-story cream-colored brick, on the southwest corner of Third and Main streets. Built with an eye toward catering to the wealthy, it even boasted of a pooltable for ladies and was immediately accepted by the town's elite. Not even the new First National Bank had indoor plumbing, but the Robinson Hotel had full plumbing and running water. However there were no sewer lines in Tulsa as yet, and the waste ran into the back yards of neighbors, who complained bitterly.

In January of 1906, the *Daily Democrat* announced that W. N. Robinson had put the forces into action to construct an outlet sewer to the river. When the sewer was finished, Robinson celebrated by giving the protesting citizens a "sewer banquet."

Although Mr. Page was content to remain in his apartment on First and Main streets, he favored the Robinson Hotel lobby as a meeting place where many of the oil men congregated to discuss the oil business.

The frequent discussions were over the constant battles with larger oil companies who continually grabbed leases before independent operators had a chance. In an effort to guard against monopolies such as this, the Interior Department had made a ruling that no oil producer, natural or corporate, could hold more than 4,800 acres of land for gas or oil purposes.

To get around the law, the leading companies established secret sub-agencies. Oil men who owned 4,800 acres of land had to show that they had at least $40,000 in cash to take care of it, and they had to do the drilling within a limited time. Ten dollar a week clerks began making affidavits that they had $40,000 in the bank, at least long enough for the ink to dry. With these credentials, the big oil company could lease two-dollar-an-acre-land at twenty-five cents an acre and fool the government.

This caused much resentment among the smaller independents who saw oil business possibilities and oil profits being snatched from under their noses.

There were 135 producing wells in the Glennpool district alone. Independents were forced to deal with major companies who owned all the pipelines. Unless they did the drilling at the fee of 60 percent of the proceeds, they refused to let the smaller companies use their pipelines. They had a monopoly on the railroad tank cars as well.

The Atchison Topeka and Santa Fe railroad came through Tulsa in 1905, making a total of four railroads that traversed the town. Even if you had oil, it did you no good unless you could sell it, so in fact, major oil companies even controlled the price of oil.

However, Mr. Page had concern for more than getting his oil to the market. His wife died in 1906.

4

The Salvation Army Comes to Town

THE SUN WAS SHINING THROUGH HAZY CLOUDS AS THE SANTE FE TRAIN pulled into the Lawrence, Kansas, depot. The air was crisp and gave a promise of rain. A playful breeze scattered the drifts of leaves, causing them to whirl and dance across the depot landing. Salvation Army Captain Brinton Flint Breeding looked at his tickets stamped 10 o'clock, a.m. October 18, 1907. Then he looked at his watch. The train was ten minutes late.

"Go kiss your grandparents good bye," said Captain Breeding pushing the children toward Mr. and Mrs. Smith. He turned to supervise the family's trunks and boxes being loaded onto the train. This done, he once more shook hands with his wife's parents and her sister Elsie. He lifted the children to the top step of the train and tossed the hand-carried valises after them.

"Come, Ethel," he called to his wife. Elsie handed Ethel a basket lunch they had prepared for the long journey, and gave her sister a final hug.

Harold held his hands over his ears at the sound of the loud train whistle, as Eva waved from the train window to her grandparents.

Captain Breeding and Ethel settled back to ponder their new assignment as the train rumbled on its way.

"I certainly hope we will do well in Tulsa," said Ethel. "Since the Salvation Army has been in existence for only twenty years, it is sometimes difficult for people to understand its purpose. We need their help to implement our program."

"Well that's true," said Captain Breeding, "The Salvation Army program has only been in Tulsa one year, but I'm sure that everything is going to be all right." He patted his wife's hand reassuringly. "We served in Guthrie, Indian Territory last year and I don't imagine Tulsa will be much different."

"Brinton," said Ethel, "Do you realize that in our six years of marriage we have already served in six different places? We're just getting acquainted with the people when it's time to move on and start all over again."

"We're going to do all right," said Captain Breeding, patting his wife's hand. "God will be with us wherever we go. That is assurance enough."

The Breedings arrived at the Tulsa station at eight o'clock that evening. They had expected to be met by someone from their church, but no one was there.

"It's probably because the train was late," Ethel said, as she herded the two sleepy children into the depot. "It wouldn't have been late if the engineer hadn't stopped to shoot quail along the way. I wonder if they do that often?"

"I don't know," said Captain Breeding, a very meticulous and punctual man. "But it doesn't seem like the way to run a railway."

He left his family in the depot, and went to ask a police officer the directions to the address the former Salvation Army Captain had given him.

The officer directed him with a wave of his hand. "It's on the northeast corner of Fourth and Main streets," he said.

With valises in hand the Breedings made their way up Main Street. They were jostled by a crowd of people, noisily enjoying the evening after a hard day's work.

Red brick covered First Street's intersection from Boulder to Boston Avenue and a strip along the east side of Main Street was being asphalted. It lay like a black velvet ribbon in the moonlight. The moon cast lumpy shadows of deep ruts in the muddy red clay of the unpaved west side of the street.

The family went one block past a little store with the name Younger's Grocery painted across the front of it and stopped in front of a small house on the corner of Fourth and Main. The number was plainly visible in the moonlight. The new pavement had left the house below street level. Captain Breeding tried the doorknob. The door opened and he went inside.

Streaks of light filtered dimly through the windows. Captain Breeding lit the gas lights in each room and returned to help the family down into the house.

"At least it looks as though we were expected," said Ethel. "Everything is clean and as neat as a pin."

"What's a neat pin, Mamma?" asked Eva.

"That's just an expression, dear," said Ethel, as she continued to survey the three-room cottage.

The Salvation Army slogan was, "Soup, Soap, and Salvation," and the Army took it literally. The odor of lye soap hung heavily in the room from the recent scrubbing of the pine floors, the kitchen table and cupboards. A bucket of water with a dipper in it sat on the wash stand.

There was one full-sized bed in the bedroom. "The children will have to sleep with us tonight and we'll see about another bed right away," said Ethel, as she began to strip the coats off the children.

"Do we have to go to bed now?" asked Eva.

"You must get your rest," said Ethel, as she tucked the two children in at the foot of the bed. "Tomorrow we will go exploring, but for tonight we must all go to bed."

There was little rest for any of them that night. Rats ran back and forth across the bed. The frightened children crawled from the foot of the bed to safety between their parents.

They were awakened at daylight the next morning by the shouts of workmen unloading brick for a new building going up on the corner of Fourth and Boston Avenue directly behind their house.

The rats had made off with or spoiled the rest of the food from their lunch basket, so Captain Breeding walked to the little grocery store down the street to get a few things they would need. When he returned he told Ethel that Scott Younger who owned the grocery store was a cousin to the Younger brothers who, with the Daltons, had been bank and train robbers. All except Emmit Dalton had been killed in a shootout with the police.

"Emmit's in jail," said Captain Breeding, "but he is to be released in a few days. He said he was going straight, and they've made him some kind of hero. He's going to work in Younger's store when he gets out."

Eva interrupted. Her thoughts were on the rats. "Daddy, we found some holes where the rats got into the house and Mamma said you'd fix them so the rats can't get in. Will you fix them before tonight?"

"I hate rats," said Harold, wrinkling his nose. "And I don't like'um neither. Will you fix the holes, Daddy?"

"You bet," said Captain Breeding. "I'll have them fixed before bed time, so don't you worry." He dipped some water from the bucket on the cabinet into the wash pan and washed his face and hands. Then he sat down in one of the kitchen chairs.

"That building going up behind us belongs to Dr. Kennedy," said Ethel. "We'll have a grocery store just down the street and a doctor's office right behind us. Isn't that nice?"

Captain Breeding looked at the ceiling. The wall paper hung in pockets. One was right over the front door. "I told the men at the store that this house leaked. They said that with the housing shortage, we were lucky to have any kind of roof over our heads. So I'll just have to put a new roof on." He took a paper from his pocket and went to the telephone on the wall. He asked the operator to ring the City Lumber company.

Ethel called the family to breakfast. "Brinton," said Ethel, "when you return thanks, ask the Lord what we are to do for water. While you were gone to the store, we went exploring. There's an outhouse and a buggy shed, but no well or cistern."

As soon as breakfast was over, Captain Breeding went out to inquire of neighbors as to his prospects in obtaining water. He crossed the street to a white frame house bearing the sign, "Cullins's Boarding house."

Mrs. Cullins was a friendly woman. She informed him that Tulsa's water situation was very bad, because of all the construction. "Only three wells in Tulsa," she said. "One is in my backyard. You are welcome to use it."

"Thank you kindly," said Captain Breeding. Thanking God silently. "That's one worry off my mind. I saw a few hydrants in front yards as we passed last night. We'll have a hydrant put in so that we won't have to bother you for long."

"That water comes from the river," said Mrs. Cullins. "It is supposed to be filtered by the Newblock Water Works, named after Police Chief Newblock. But I wouldn't want it named after me. It's only used for bathing and washing clothes, but you smell worse after a bath than before. Slaughter houses throw their waste into the river in spite of all the warnings from the police." Mrs. Cullins held her nose. "The carcasses lodge on sandbars, and filtering doesn't get the stink out."

"Where do people get drinking water?" asked Captain Breeding.

"There are two springs north of the Arkansas river, at Twelfth and Boulder, called Noah's Springs," said Mrs. Cullins. "Some people haul their water from there to drink. Mark Carr hauls water from springs up in Osage county. He bottles it in five gallon bottles and sells it for 25 cents a bottle. Most people keep rain barrels under their eaves to catch the rain water for washing and bathing. A few drops of kerosene keeps the mosquitoes out of it."

With the water problem solved, Captain Breeding was able to turn to other crucial matters. He hired a drayman to deliver the family's household goods from the freight depot, and as soon as they were unpacked he and Ethel located the holes where the rats came in and patched them.

This done, Captain Breeding went in search of the few Salvation Army members and the tent used for headquarters. Two men of the church took him to where the tent had been, but it was gone. Khaki colored tents were everywhere. They all looked alike except for varied sizes. All were occupied.

Captain Breeding sighed. "Well, we have no tent and no money to buy one. I've been told that we won't find anything for rent, so what are we going to do without a headquarters?" He looked at the two men. Noting the troubled look on their faces, he smiled reassuringly. "Don't worry," he told them. "We are not defeated yet. We'll just trust God to help us through this situation." The three man held hands and bowed their heads. Captain Breeding said a prayer, and they all went home.

East side of Main Street. This was Tulsa as Mr. Page saw it in 1903.

5

The Big Scotsman

CAPTAIN BREEDING KNEW HE HAD TO FIND A PLACE FOR HEADQUARTERS before he could get things started. The list of names of those who donated regularly had been given to him along with his orders to go to Tulsa. The name of Charles Page was among those who gave two dollars each month. This was average.

"The Big Scotsman's office is in his apartment up over J. M. Hall's General Merchandise Store," said Mr. Younger. "Everybody knows Charley Page."

As Captain Breeding walked up the stairs, he noticed that the first door to the left was wide open. He couldn't see the number on the door. However, he felt sure he was at the right place. Two men were hunched over a kitchen table, studying some papers that lay before them. The man facing the door was a big husky man. A battered old hat was slanted at an angle over his eyes as a shield against the glare of the morning sun that streamed in at the east window. The cigar in his mouth was tip tilted toward his hat brim. A stiff mustache nearly covered his upper lip. When he saw Captain Breeding, his brown eyes beneath heavy eyebrows twinkled in a friendly way.

"Sir," said Captain Breeding, as he paused before the door. The big man smiled and straightened, spilling cigar ashes on his wrinkled suit. He didn't seem to notice the ashes. "I'm Captain Breeding, of the Salvation Army, and I'm looking for Mr. Charles Page. Could you tell me which apartment he lives in?"

"Yer-a-lookin' at him," said the big man. "Come on in, Cap," He stood to offer Captain Breeding a chair. Captain Breeding, five feet and eight inches tall, felt dwarfed standing before Mr. Page, who stood at least six feet and two inches, and weighed about 240 pounds.

"This here's Josie," said Mr. Page, motioning to his partner. "Me and Josie have a religion of our own. It's THINK RIGHT." He sat down and leaned his chair back against the wall. "I guess it's more like a motto than a religion. But we try to think right in all our dealings. Right now, we're working on a project that we think will benefit others, as well as ourselves. If it's good for all, it's good business."

"I'd say so," said Captain Breeding. He liked this friendly sincere man.

Mr. Page straightened up, crossed his legs, and began to explain. "You see, we've got these gas wells that me and my partners brought in, and we're trying to figure what it will cost to pipe the gas for customer consumption here in town."

As Captain Breeding, a meticulous dresser, listened to what Mr. Page was saying, he turned his gaze away from Mr. Page's scuffed oil field shoes. They showed no evidence of ever having been polished with a blackening brush.

Mr. Page gestured with his cigar held between his fingers. "You see, Cap, so many of these fellows in the oil business consider a well that produces only gas as worthless, so they don't bother to cap it. They let it blow, hoping that it will eventually bring up a little oil with it. We don't waste anything that can be used. The people need the convenience of gas. And we need to get back some of the money we spent bringing these wells in. This way we all benefit."

"We were mighty glad to find that there was gas in the house we were assigned to," said Captain Breeding. "I won't have to buy coal or chop wood. Gas is cleaner, too. Do you own the utilities on Fourth and Main streets?"

Mr. Page shook his head. "There are others doing the same thing, but not many. Some stick a match to gas wells, making a torch to light the rest of the field. It costs a little to cap a well, and they'd rather put all their money into oil."

The fire from the end of Mr. Page's cigar fell to the red checked oilcloth covering of the table. Mr. Page gingerly swiped it into a little glass dish that was already full of ashes and cigar butts, then he addressed Captain Breeding.

"Cap, I'm sure you didn't look me up to hear about my business, so what can I do for you?"

Captain Breeding told him his problem and added, "So I thought I'd better make my rounds to see if I can collect enough money to be able to rent a place for headquarters. I was given a list of names of those who usually gave to the Salvation Army, and your name was on the list."

Mr. Page took a worn checkbook from his pocket and with the stub of a pencil he wrote Captain Breeding a check for two dollars, and rising from his chair, handed it to him.

"The Salvation Army does a lot of good," he said, as he stuck the checkbook back into his hip pocket. "They feed hungry people. Ma would like that. She couldn't turn a hungry man away from her door. I was afraid for her, being a widow and letting strangers into her house. She kept one of Dad's old hats hanging in full sight, on a nail on the kitchen door, so that they would think a man was in the house."

"That was very clever of her," said Captain Breeding. He rose to go. "Thank you very much for your time and your donation. My wife and children are out selling the War Cry, to raise money, and I must get to work too. The house we fell heir to leaks terribly and I've got to shingle it before more fall rains wash us away. The headquarters tent is missing and if I don't find a place

to use as headquarters, I won't be able to get organized. I'll be out of a job."
He thanked Mr. Page again for the check, told Mr. Josie that it was a pleasure
meeting him, nodded to Mr. Page, and started to leave.

"The next time you come around I'll be on the second floor of the new
National Bank Of Tulsa building." said Mr. Page. "It's on the corner of Second
and Main."

"Yes I know where the building is," said Captain Breeding. "The bank is a
busy place. The post office is in the back."

"There's a pool room   in the basement," said Mr. Page, with a chuckle.
"Have you been there, cap?"

"No," said Captain Breeding, "but I'll go there with my tambourine and
magazines to sell."

"My door is always open, so don't bother to knock, just come on in," said
Mr. Page with a wave of his hand.

"Thank you kindly," said Captain Breeding and went on his way.

Captain Breeding went to every real estate office in town hoping to find a
better place to live and a place for his church. The realtors all shook their
heads as they showed him columns of names on waiting lists. People had
signed up for rooms in buildings not yet built.

Later that afternoon, Captain Breeding heard someone call, "Hey, Cap."
He turned around, and saw Mr. Page hurrying across the street toward him.
He waited.

"Cap," said Mr. Page, in a contrite voice, "I should have given you more
this morning." He took a five dollar bill out of his pocket and handed it to
Captain Breeding.

Captain Breeding set out early the next morning, determined to find a
place for the Salvation Army headquarters. As he walked past Hunt's
Clothing Store on the Southwest corner of Second and Main streets, he
noticed the store had two entrances. One led down into a basement. He went
into the store and talked to Mr. Hunt.

"I'm using the basement for storage," said Mr. Hunt, but I suppose I could
do without it. Could you pay $25 a month?"

Twenty-five dollars seemed like a lot of money, but without the talent nor
inclination to dicker over prices, Captain Breeding thanked him kindly and
told him he would take it. As he left the building he met Mr. Page coming
down the street. "I found a place for my headquarters," he said. "It's in the
basement of Hunt's Clothing store, across the street from the First National
Bank building.

"You'll be right down there where I can watch you from my office window,"
said Mr. Page. "So behave yourself, Cap." He gave Captain Breeding a slap
on the shoulder. Then reaching into his pocket he pulled out a five dollar bill.
"That's to go on your first month's rent," he said.

Captain Breeding thanked him and hurried home to tell Ethel that he had
found a place for headquarters.

When he got there he found that the shingles he had ordered had been delivered. He put on some old clothes and went to work tearing the old shingles from the roof.

He was just getting started when his wife called to him. Someone had telephoned, asking him to conduct a funeral for a family who lived at Crosby Heights. With no church affiliation, the family had no one else to turn to.

Captain Breeding cleaned up and put on his uniform. He walked the two miles to Crosby Heights. When he saw the circumstances of the family it grieved him. There were four small children. Their father had been sick for a long time. The mother looked exhausted and the children looked half starved. What was the poor woman going to do? She couldn't work, with a baby and three other small children.

When the funeral was over and Captain Breeding started to go, he handed the woman the five dollars Mr. Page had given him.

"I'll see what help I can get for you," he told her.

When he went back to town he inquired of Chief Newblock as to what help the town had for such needy people. He was told that charity around Tulsa was a casual thing, done on the spur of the moment. There were agencies to take care of the needs of the Indians, churches gave temporary aid to their members, but for the rest of the people, there were no operating charitable organizations except for a childrens' home north of Tulsa.

"Widows sometimes put their children in the CROSS AND ANCHOR HOME until they can take care of them," said Chief Newblock.

The CROSS AND ANCHOR children's home had been established after a coal mine disaster that had left a number of children orphaned or half orphaned, with mothers unable to support or care for them. The lumber and labor had been donated by the citizens of Tulsa and was dependent upon pledged donations for its continued support.

Captain Breeding felt frustrated that he didn't have the means to help the woman. The next day he walked back to see her, and told her of the children's home where she could put the children for awhile until she could find work. She thanked him and agreed that was the best thing to do. He offered to help her, but she said she had a horse and a light spring wagon. She could take them when she was ready for them to go. Captain Breeding gave her another five dollars and left.

Back home, he worked feverishly on the roof, fearful of a rain before he got through.

Each morning, as he worked on the roof, Ethel and the children went out with an arm load of THE WAR CRY. She went into every place of business, and stopped people on the street trying to sell the Salvation Army, and their magazine, to the people. She explained their cause, and asked for their help. There was a lot of good reading for a nickel in THE WAR CRY. It was a good seller, but many people considered the Salvation Army just another church and felt no obligation to give to any church other than their own.

Each evening Captain Breeding, with his little band of soldiers, met at the headquarters for a brief instrumental practice session. Then with Captain Breeding leading the band, they marched through the streets single file, playing their various instruments until a crowd had gathered. Captain Breeding and his wife both played the cornet. She played the soprano cornet and he played the alto. Swinging from Mrs. Breeding's shoulder was a guitar, which she would play later.

The two Breeding children followed close behind their parents, drawing smiles from onlookers as they passed. Waving small flags and stepping high, more out of step than in, they pranced as the band played, "Onward Christian Soldiers, Marching As To War."

When a crowd had gathered, the band stopped at the corner of First and Main streets, where the street had been paved with red brick. The drummer gave a final drum-roll and the service began.

Pulling a chair up to the window of his upstairs apartment, Mr. Page listened to the service. Later he told Captain Breeding that he was a good preacher and that he had a good band.

"Training musicians is part of the Salvation Army's program," said Captain Breeding. "I'm glad you enjoyed it."

Each night the Breedings played a duet on their cornets. Then Ethel played her guitar and sang a solo. For the congregational singing, she recited the words from her song book line by line, urging the crowd to sing. Many did. When she was through with the singing, Captain Breeding brought the message. Following the message, two members of the group went through the crowd with tambourines to collect an offering, while Captain Breeding urged them to give to the sick and needy people of Tulsa.

Mr. Page could see into the tambourines, and knew they were getting mostly nickels and dimes for their excellent program.

It didn't take long for the little band to earn the respect of the city, however. Chief of Police Newblock posted a sign at the corner where they always stopped to hold services. The sign stated that anybody tying a horse or a horse drawn vehicle and messing up the street on that corner would be prosecuted.

Late one night, Captain Breeding got a call from the ticket agent at the Frisco depot. "There's a man here that they took off the train because he is very sick," he said. "I hear that you are helping such people. Would you come down and see what you can do for him?"

Captain Breeding went down to the depot. "I believe," said the agent, "that your most dependable source of help in emergencies such as this would come from the big hearted Scotsman, Charley Page." He started to tell him where Mr. Page lived, but Captain Breeding told him that they had already met.

Captain Breeding bent over to the man, laying his hand on the man's forehead. The man looked up, helplessly. "Can you walk if I help you?" asked

Captain Breeding. The man nodded. He helped the man down the street to the first hotel he came to. He got him a room and helped him into bed. Then he brought him a large bowl of soup from the restaurant downstairs.

"Do you think you will be all right until morning?" he asked, and the man nodded. "Do you have relatives or friends here that I should get in touch with?" asked Captain Breeding. The man shook his head, unable to speak for coughing. He had a dirty rag he was spitting into. Mr. Breeding took a clean white handkerchief from his pocket and handed it to the man. He bathed the man's face and hands and left.

Early the next morning Captain Breeding went to see Mr. Page in his office in the bank building. By the time Captain Breeding had told him of the plight of the man, Mr. Page already had a plan of action. He lifted the telephone receiver.

"Operator," he said, "This is Charley Page. I want you to get Dean Peck in Denver, Colorado." He gave her the number.

"Dean, this is Charley Page. I want you to do something for me," he said. "We've got a man here who is suffering from tuberculosis. I believe the Colorado climate will help him if anything will. He needs someone to look after him." Mr. Page went on to make full arrangements for the man's care. He placed the receiver back on the hook and turned to Captain Breeding.

"Cap," he said, "I want you to check into the expense of sending this man to Denver. Make a list of everything he'll need and bring it to me."

When Captain Breeding returned with the information, Mr. Page instructed his secretary to write a check to cover the amount needed. Then he dictated a letter to Dean Peck, stating that he would take care of all the man's expenses.

While Captain Breeding waited for the secretary to type the letter, two friends, Ben Rice, an attorney, and William Striker, editor of the *Tulsa Daily Democrat,* paused at the door of Mr. Page's office.

"Come in," yelled Mr. Page, waving his cigar as he did so. "Don't you know that an open door means you're welcome? Come on in." Then jokingly he added, "Hey, Ben, give Cap a dollar to help a poor sick man. You give him one too, Bill."

"Give him one yourself," said Bill.

"He already has," said Captain Breeding. He told them the story and showed them the check. Each of them dug into their pockets and drew out a fifty cent piece and handed it to Captain Breeding.

A day or two later Captain Breeding saw Mr. Page on the street. Mr. Page snapped out the first words as though they were part of an unfinished conversation.

"Cap," he said, "We got a dollar mighty slick didn't we?"

Later as Captain Breeding told his wife about it, he said, "The fifty cents received from each of the other two men seemed more important to Mr. Page than the large amount he had given."

Captain Breeding was about half through with shingling his house when he got a notice that the house had been condemned. It was to be torn down to make way for buildings along Main Street.

ca. 1902. *The First National Bank of Tulsa was only one of several oil-related banks in Tulsa that provided much of the capital needed to develop the surrounding oil fields.*

Tulsa as Mr. Breeding saw it in 1907. The First National Bank is to the left.

6

A Girl Named Lucille

CAPTAIN BREEDING TALKED TO THE MAN WHO OWNED THE HOUSE AND was told that the Commercial Club had condemned the house but with a new roof and some other repairs it would pass inspection. Captain Breeding made the necessary repairs and was allowed to live in the house until July when he would be transferred to another post.

This done, he was able to concentrate on seeing to the needs of the people. He discovered that there were a lot of families in distress due to fathers being injured in the coal mines or oil business.

Since the oil business was new, workers were inexperienced and accidents occurred frequently. There was neither workers' compensation nor insurance. A man was glad to have a job, and worked at his own risk.

One woman, grateful for the help the Salvation Army was giving her, said to Captain Breeding, "There was no one to turn to when my husband was injured. I couldn't look for work with a a crippled husband and three small children to care for. Our neighbors helped us all they could, but they have problems too."

Word soon got around that families were being helped, and others started coming to the Salvation Army headquarters.

From the vantage point of his office window, Mr. Page saw the frantic efforts of the hard working sincere young Salvation Army Captain, trying to take care of those who came to him. He also saw how little help he was getting in the way of offerings.

"Cap," he said, "I see that you need help in taking care of these poor unfortunate people and I'm going to help you. Get what you can from others then come to me."

Captain Breeding went to Mr. Page every morning for help for this one or that, and it didn't take long for the amount of help he was getting from him to amount to hundreds of dollars. It didn't seem right for one person to shoulder so much of the burden, but as Police Chief Newblock had said, "With no operating charitable organizations, you couldn't depend on more than a spur of the moment kind of giving." He worked hard trying to spare Mr. Page, but there were so many people with serious needs that he saw no other way. One morning he expressed his regrets.

"Cap," said Mr. Page, "I believe in shooting square with the Big Fellow. I promised God that I'd give ten percent of all my income to helping those in need. I've kept my promise, and He gave it back a hundred fold. I've never gone to bed hungry since I became partners with the Big Fellow. In fact, He has made me richer than I ever dreamed I'd be. So what can I say if He decides He needs more than the ten percent? Furthermore, I like to sleep well. I couldn't rest knowing that my neighbor was starving while I hoarded my wealth. I have a dream just as everybody else has, but if God wants me to see my dream come true He'll see that it happens. Right now I feel like He wants me to feed his people. So don't you worry, Cap. Everything is going to be all right."

"You're a good man, Mr. Page," said Captain Breeding.

"Naw, I'm not good, Cap. The Big Fellow is just using me. He uses you in your way and me in my way. I'm not good at all, but I try to be fair."

"In other words, you see yourself as steward of God's finances?"

"Well, something like that."

"All the same, I hate to take so much money from one person." He hesitated. "I'm curious, you mentioned your dream. Do you want to talk about it?"

Mr. Page smiled. He didn't often have someone to share his dream with. He talked at length. He told Captain Breeding that it began with his childish boast when the big boys knocked down his houses and trampled his sand village.

"Of course I didn't know what I was talking about when I said I'd someday build a real town, but the more I thought about it the more intrigued I became with the idea. I didn't doubt for one minute that I could do it. All I needed was money. A lot of money. Then when I found it necessary to leave Ma in order to find a decent paying job, the dream took on a different meaning. It was no longer just a challenge to prove man's possibilities to achieve what he sets out to do. It was something I wanted to do for other mothers and their sons. A town owes it to its people to see that there are jobs for both men and women. A widow should be able to find work to support her children. A mother shouldn't have to worry whether a son or daughter is sick or hungry or into trouble as they wander from place to place in search of work. Their home-town should see that there are jobs so that families could stay together. They should be able to invest and see their investment grow. I want an industrial town that will provide plenty of jobs for all for generations to come."

"So you want for other boys what you couldn't have for yourself?"

Mr. Page shifted his cigar to the other side of his mouth.

"Time goes so fast. It seems I didn't get to be with Ma hardly at all. Ma was a good woman. I sent her money, but I should have been there to help her more. I worried about her a lot, wondering if she was sick, wishing I could see her. She worried about me too, but I didn't let her know I was ever broke or hungry. I've been that a lot."

"I can see why this industrial city is so important to you."

Mr. Page nodded. "Before I came to Tulsa, I had the idea that I'd build my town in Denver, Colorado, if I ever got rich. I still own a hotel there. But I like Tulsa. I'd like to buy some land around here. It'll take a lot of land to do what I have in mind. I want to buy all I'll need as soon as I can. Prices go up with demand, and I intend to buy before prices go up."

"Well, I'd say that's 'Thinking Right,'" said Captain Breeding. "The Indians are not allowed to sell their lands yet, but the Negroes who were slaves to the Indians got allotments too. These 'Freed men' have no restrictions against selling their lands. Maybe you can buy from them."

"If you hear of any land for sale, let me know, Cap," said Mr. Page. He leaned forward, shoving the papers on his desk back. He tapped the desk with the eraser end of a pencil.

"Cap, you see, it works like this. You buy your land, and you build some houses. When you get a few people moved into the houses, you build a general store for their convenience, and a few more people will get interested. When you get enough people, you start working toward getting industry interested. Industry draws more people, and people do the rest. All you have to do is give the town a start and turn it over to the people."

"You make it sound so simple," said Captain Breeding. "But then I've noticed, you have a talent for making complicated things sound simple."

"It *is* simple, Cap. People need jobs but they need other services too. Merchants will come, providing goods and services and the downtown business area develops. Farmers will provide produce for the market and before you know it you have everything your residents need, right in their own town. Now that's the way a town ought to be."

He leaned back, took a big draw on his cigar and blew a smoke ring. Then he winked at Captain Breeding who sat fascinated.

"Yes sir," said Mr. Page. "You give the town a start, but it's the people who build the town. It belongs to them and they know it. They take pride in it because it belongs to them . . . and to their future generations."

As Captain Breeding listened, he caught the vision. A quietness fell between them as the two men dreamed.

"I can almost see it happening now," said Captain Breeding.

"Land," said Mr. Page, "It's the surest investment. Land and utilities. Everybody needs them. The oil business is a gamble. But if you take care of land, it will take care of you."

Captain Breeding thought about their conversation all day as he went about his business. He couldn't get Mr. Page out of his mind. The man had many sides to his personality. Captain Breeding had learned from others, that in spite of the crude way Mr. Page sometimes presented himself, he was a shrewd, far sighted and keen-minded business man — not "just the old codger" he often called himself. There was certainly nothing pretentious about this unassuming man. You couldn't help but like him. He was unlike anyone Captain Breeding had ever known. Who else left his door wide open to the public or stopped to talk to bums on the street? Who else, upon becoming a rich man, would leave the floors uncarpeted, furnish his office with merely desks and chairs for himself and for his secretary, a row of kitchen chairs, a drinking fountain and a rack to hang coats and hats on? Who else wore an old hat to shield his eyes from the hanging light bulbs? No other of Captain Breeding's acquaintances kept a Bible on his desk. In fact Cap occasionally caught Mr. Page reading the Bible. Who else took upon themselves the problems of people they didn't know, or would ever see?

Charles Page called it "horse-trading," but his partners knew that he knew when to buy and when to sell. He usually wound up buying everybody's share in partnership deals, then selling at a profit when the time was right. His memory for facts, figures, faces, and names was like a neat filing cabinet. He liked people and was interested in their well being. Charles Page was different all right, and he did things differently. Being optimistic, he believed in about everything, and every body, but Captain Breeding was surprised to learn that he also believed in signs.

One Saturday morning Captain Breeding went into the Robinson Hotel dining room where Mr. Page usually ate. He found him playing solitaire while waiting for his breakfast to be served.

"Cap, I know you think playing cards is sinful," said Mr. Page, "but I don't play for money. I just play for fun. Right now, I'm trying to make a decision, and I want to know if this is a lucky day for me." He finished shuffling the cards and gave them a flip before spreading them on the table before him.

"You know how people tease Arthur Antle and me because we're single? They're always at the business of matchmaking."

Captain Breeding had seen Mr. Page with Arthur, who owned the livery stables behind the bank building. The two men were often seen going places with young ladies.

Mr. Breeding nodded. "Yes, people do tend to play matchmaker."

"Well," said Mr. Page, "being teased doesn't bother me. I don't pay any attention. But one lady who was brought to my attention interests me. Her name is Lucile Rayburn. One of the guys told me that he had found just the girl for me. He said that she was a nice intelligent young woman who had gone to work in a restaurant to earn money for a business education. This guy, Bill, remarked that I ought to loan the girl the money so that she could get on with her education."

Mr. Page spread the cards again before him on the table. then continued. "I told Bill that I always check things out before I invested my money into it. I was just teasing of course, but when he said he was sure I would like what I saw, I got curious. I decided to have a look at this new girl. I ate supper at the restaurant where she worked. She's very pretty. I got cold feet about asking her if she wanted to borrow money. I was afraid she'd misunderstand and slap my face." He grinned like a boy after his first kiss.

Mr. Page started doing all kinds of slight of the hand card tricks as he talked, and Captain Breeding was so intrigued from watching that it was hard to give attention to what Mr. Page was saying.

"So what does your game of cards have to do with the situation?" asked Captain Breeding at last.

"I won three games, Cap, I'm on a lucky streak. I'll ask Lucile if she wants to borrow the money while my luck is holding. Maybe she won't take me wrong."

The next morning when Captain Breeding went to Mr. Page's office, he asked, "Well, did you get your face slapped?"

"No, I didn't. She was very nice . . . thanked me for my offer, but said she would rather not go in debt."

"She sounds like a nice lady," said Captain Breeding.

A few days later, Mr. Page told Cap that Lucy had come to the Robinson Hotel to work, and that she was very attentive to him. "I'm taking her to a lecture tonight," he said.

Mr. Page didn't mention Lucile anymore, but Captain Breeding saw them together now and then in the evenings.

One day Captain Breeding was in Mr. Page's office when four of Mr. Page's friends stopped by to invite him to lunch. Mr. Page was looking over the bills Captain Breeding had brought to him.

"Sit down fellows," said Mr. Page. "I'll be through here in a minute." He took a pencil out of his pocket and wrote a check for Captain Breeding. The men mentioned that they had been talking about building some office buildings.

"Charley," said one of the group, "Why don't you build a building? It's a good business investment, and if you put your name on it, you have a monument to your name."

"What does an old codger like me need with a monument to my name?" asked Mr. Page. "I haven't done anything monumental. Neither have you. But I'll tell you what I intend to do with my money. I'm going to start an industrial town."

The men burst into laughter. "He doesn't want a monument, he wants an empire of his own," they said.

"Actually, Mr. Page's dream is very unselfish," said Captain Breeding, in defense of his friend. "He wants for others what he couldn't have for himself."

"It's all right, Cap," said Mr. Page. "Don't bother to explain to these guys. They wouldn't understand."

7

Oklahoma Becomes a State

ONE DAY CAPTAIN BREEDING AND MR. PAGE WERE WALKING DOWN THE board walk, when a group of men, surrounding Charles M. Haskell, came up Main Street. Haskell's campaign for Governor had been a vigorous one, and he was favored to win. Haskell stood on the fender of Billy Roesser's red automobile to make his speech. He pledged support to the little man in the fight against major oil companies as the crowd cheered.

The latest fight was with the Kansas Natural Gas Company. It had attempted to lay an eighteen-inch pipeline to draw gas from Oklahoma wells through to their Kansas wells where the gas would be sold at a higher price than Oklahoma could get for the same gas. It was also going to use the gas for building industry in Kansas rather than in Oklahoma. The eighteen-inch pipeline was stopped at the border by irate officials.

Haskell won the governor's race and was to take the oath of office on November 17, 1907. President Theodore Roosevelt would sign the proclamation making Oklahoma the forty-sixth state of the Union, at exactly 9:00 a.m. and Haskell would be sworn into office immediately after the proclamation was signed. Plans for a big celebration were made.

But these were not the only plans being made for that eventful day. The Kansas Natural Gas Company had come up with an ingenious plan to sneak the eighteen-inch gas line across the Oklahoma border just six miles from the place where they had been stopped before. By shrewd observance they noticed that Haskell had overlooked the fact that there was an hour's difference in the time from that of the eastern states. In fact there would be an hour after the proclamation was signed that nobody would be in charge of the new state. They intended to take advantage of the oversight. They worked in secret, laying their eighteen-inch gas lines from both sides of the border. At the appropriate moment when no one was in charge, they would connect the two ends of the pipe and it would be done.

November 16, 1907, the long awaited day of statehood finally came. It was a holiday and Tulsa's streets were crowded with people waiting for the final hour. The air was charged with excitement.

The Daily Democrat carried such headlines as:

"ROOSEVELT WILL SHOVE THE QUILL."

President Theodore Roosevelt would use a quill pen to sign the proclamation that would join the Oklahoma and Indian Territories into one state. The pen used would be given to the Oklahoma historical society. Guthrie, the seat of Indian affairs, was to be the state's temporary capital.

Workers, given a holiday, roamed the streets awaiting the final hour. The air was charged with excitement.

Flags were conspicuously displayed, some old, with a new star sewn on the field of forty-five. Some were new with forty-six stars.

Captain Breeding saw Mr. Page standing on the corner of Second and Main streets and he made his way through the surging crowd to join him.

All Tulsans had set their watches to the time of the big clock in the fire station. Mr. Page, Captain Breeding, and others held their watches in their hands, waiting with breathless anticipation, counting off the minutes until the appointed hour. Some counted out loud, and in unison, the last few seconds of that historic moment.

With the first deafening clang of the fire-wagon bell, there arose a bedlam of noises such as Tulsans had never heard before. Next to the fire bell, the train whistles were said to make the most noise. But everyone did his best, with church bells, school bells, sleigh bells, and cow bells. Some beat on tin pans.

The town band played its loudest, blaring their horns and beating their drums, trying to be heard; booming guns added to the din. It lasted for fifteen minutes without ceasing.

Throughout the morning, spontaneous parades and celebrations continued until the enthusiasm had spent itself. The celebrating crowds began to disperse shortly after noon.

A carnival had come to town to help in the celebration. Tents and equipment stretched from First and Main streets to Second and Boulder. Some of the crowd wandered through the carnival, some went home, and others moved on to their favorite places to talk. Mr. Page invited Captain Breeding to have dinner with him at the Robinson Hotel.

"I want you to meet Lucile," said Mr. Page, "and tell me if you think I'm too old for her."

"Who am I to tell you a thing like that?" asked Captain Breeding. "I am eight years older than my wife." However, at Mr. Page's insistence he did accept the dinner invitation, and called to let his wife know that he would not be home for dinner.

Captain Breeding liked the refined young woman who served them at dinner time. She was tall, possessing an unconscious charm and grace. She had light brown hair and a lovely complexion. The way she looked at Mr. Page revealed that she was in love.

"She's a lovely lady," said Captain Breeding, and it pleased Mr. Page a lot.

After their meal the two men went into the elegant hotel lobby where several other oil men had gathered.

"You all know Cap," said Mr. Page "But in case he doesn't know all of you, I'll introduce him." He called each man by name and motioned Captain Breeding to take a chair next to his. As Captain Breeding sank down into the plush upholstery he wondered how many important transactions had taken place in this lobby. Perhaps while sitting in this very chair.

Today's discussion was on the usual concern of the monopolizing tactics and devious practices of the major oil companies. The latest fight with the Kansas Natural Gas Company was discussed with a feeling of jubilation that they had been stopped from drawing gas from Oklahoma.

But there were other problems. The larger oil companies, controlling the pipelines and the railroads refused either to transport or buy the vast quantities of oil, hoping to force other operators out of business — 117,400 barrels of oil a day from the Glenn pool alone.

Independent producers, financially unable to construct proper storage tanks, ran their oil into hastily dug earth reservoirs where both quantity and quality deteriorated rapidly. Much oil was lost as it ran into ravines, over the ground, even into streams of water.

Fires were a daily occurrence throughout the oil fields because the small companies couldn't take proper care of the oil. Recently, one creek had burned for three weeks with a mile long wall of fire and huge billows of black smoke that obscured the sun.

The talk in the Robinson hotel was that these things wouldn't have happened if the oil could have been sold and transported promptly. It was even suggested that the fire might have been set by the "big boys", to further discourage independents.

Eastern oil syndicates had deliberately cut the price of oil to add still more pressure, hoping they could buy out small operators. But Carl Burgess Glasscock and others vowed that they would go broke before they bowed to the pressures of the greedy Eastern oil syndicates. As they talked, they were interrupted by a cry heard on the streets that caused them all to get quiet and listen.

8

The Depression Versus the Dream

"EXTRA! EXTRA! READ ALL ABOUT IT. 'GOVERNOR HASKELL'S QUICK ACTION THWARTS PLANS OF KANSAS NATIONAL GAS COMPANY.' The paper boy came into the Robinson Hotel, and the men had their nickels ready by the time he reached them.

Kansas National Gas Company's scheme had leaked. Governor Haskell got word of it and thwarted the plans. By daylight he had guards stationed along the border with orders to shoot to kill if any attempt was made to continue the construction of the gas line. Then keeping the long distance telephone line open to Washington D.C., the governor took his oath of office at the moment the proclamation was signed. This put him immediately in charge of things, with legal authority to stop the Kansas National Gas Company from connecting the gas line.

The men in the Robinson Hotel lobby cheered. As the news of Haskell's quick action spread around town, a new burst of enthusiasm spread with it. Governor Haskell had proven that he was indeed for the small oil operators and the man for the job.

The day of Statehood had hardly come and gone when the depression that had been plaguing the rest of the country hit Oklahoma.

The first news of the Wall Street panic came on October 22, 1907. The headlines of the Tulsa Daily Democrat stated that The Knickerbocker Trust Co. in New York had failed.

The significance of the event was at first lost upon the great masses of people, especially the people of Tulsa. *The Daily Democrat* backed by the optimistic Commercial Club, declared that Tulsa, "THE OIL CAPITAL OF THE WORLD," had nothing to worry about. One issue stated that various banking institutions would have statements as evidence of the local banking strength. The article read:

"Deposits all along have been normal, and the cash reserve is considerably greater than the law required. The banks of Tulsa are sound to the core, and have remained unshaken during the financial unpleasantness that has afflicted the country in general."

But by late November the optimistic leaders of the city had to admit that Tulsa, too, was in the throes of the depression. The nine Tulsa banks and trust companies announced that they would have to put a limit of $50 per day and $100 per week on all cash withdrawals. This limit proved too high and most of them closed. The Tulsa Central Bank introduced a script into their banking system for the convenience of its patrons. The script was made of heavy paper, oval in shape and about the size of currency. It was issued in various denominations and was accepted as a medium of exchange in the community while the banks were closed.

With banks closed, the oil business came to a virtual stand-still. Before long, businesses built on the strength of the oil went broke or had to close their doors.

In panic, the people roamed the streets or filled their favorite gathering places to discuss the matter. The depression had come quickly, and they were ill-prepared. Many, including Charles Page, had lost their money in the panic of 1892-93 and were very discouraged.

President Theodore Roosevelt assured the people that the depression should be short, and that they would not lose their money. Despite the welcome assurance, people were skeptical. It didn't take long to use up the cash they had on hand. Those who had someplace to go, went. But many had sold their homes elsewhere to come to Tulsa and had no place to go.

The Salvation Army was unable to provide help for so many people. Captain Breeding went to Lou North, the newly elected County Welfare Commissioner, but Lou didn't know how to solve the problem. The wheels of the city's new organizations had not been sufficiently set into motion before the crash, and there were no funds with which to operate.

"Cap, I don't even know how to run such an organization," Lou confessed. "Give me some pointers." Captain Breeding helped him get organized, but with no funds to operate, it still fell to the Salvation Army to do what they could to help the people.

Collecting funds became almost impossible. Still feeding those who had become regular dependents, the Tulsa resident victims were added to the list of families helped by Charles Page. But Mr. Page didn't complain.

"Cap, get what groceries you need at Andy Stoke's Grocery at 112 Second Street," said Mr. Page. "Andy has a family and needs the business. His store delivers groceries. Bring the bills for the day before to me each morning. Then you can pay Andy as you order for the day."

"Why must we pay each morning?" asked Captain Breeding. "It is so time consuming. Why not pay them by the week?"

"We have to think of Andy, Cap. He needs the money to keep his store stocked."

So each morning Captain Breeding went to his headquarters, added up all the bills, took the figures to Mr. Page, who wrote a check for them, then he went to the grocery store. He paid Andy, and with his list of names and their needs he gave Andy his order. It took a good part of the morning. The rest of the day was spent reorganizing as new ones came to him for help. He had certain days for one group of families to be checked on, and other days for other families when he thought they would be getting low on groceries. His Salvation Army soldiers visited some of the families and gave report as to their needs. He, his wife and children and all the members of the troup walked the streets trying to collect nickels and dimes, and to sell the War Cry magazine, but they got very little help from anyone except Charles Page. This didn't seem right to Captain Breeding, but he didn't know what else to do.

Fearing it would take all the money that Mr. Page had, he made no attempt to feed those who were passing through the town in search of work.

With four trains criss-crossing in different directions Tulsa had become a rail hub. Daily, trains came in, laden with passengers seeking jobs in the much-advertised "Oil Capital." Finding Tulsa with the same depressing situation as where they came from, they got back on the train and went on their way. People in buggies and wagons, with all their belongings, made a steady trail through town and out to the open road, passing other hopefuls coming in.

It was a hard, cold, winter, and as the days dragged on, train depots were filled with men who had come looking for work. Men walked the streets or hovered around the big coal heaters in the backs of stores until the crowd got so great the store owners ran them out. With no where to go as they waited to catch the next train out, Captain Breeding offered the Salvation Army headquarters to them as a "reading room," (Tulsa's first library, you might say,) where they could come in out of the cold, with something to do while they waited. He furnished them with books from his own collection, but had the *War Cry* and the *Bible* prominently displayed for their use.

Wayne Kingsberry, one of Mr. Page's nephews had come from Wisconsin, and was now working for Mr. Page. He was secretary, bookkeeper, driller, or what ever his uncle wanted him to do. One day Captain Breeding was in Mr. Page's office, waiting for Wayne to write his daily check, and Mr. Page started talking about his dream.

"I'll be glad when the sale of Indian lands will be legal," he said. "July 27, 1908 seems a long way off. I can't wait to get started on building that town I've always dreamed of."

Captain Breeding looked down at his hands. He felt guilty for taking advantage of this big hearted man's generosity. But he could no more turn his back on the needy than Mr. Page could.

Mr. Page noticed Captain Breeding looking downcast with worry. He slapped the Captain on the shoulder, and said, "Don't worry so much Cap, I'm gon'a have that town yet, you wait and see." But Captain Breeding wasn't so sure.

One cold dismal day Mr. Page made his way down to the Frisco Depot. An early rain had turned to a penetrating sleet that stung his face and stuck to his mustache and eye lashes. He heard the train whistle and stopped to watch it pull into the depot. What he saw made him heart sick. Men without the price of a ticket clung to the sides, on top, and anywhere they found something to cling to. Their wind whipped clothes had frozen around them. Mr. Page's big heart swelled within him when he saw the desperation in their faces. He knew the feeling. Fifty or more half-starved, half-frozen men pulled their stiff fingers loose from the train. Others hurried out of the depot, pushing to get into the empty box cars until they were filled, then hanging onto the top and sides. Train authorities made no attempt to dislodge them.

Mr. Page knew the desperation he saw in the grim faced men. He had experienced the same. He directed them to the Salvation Army headquarters. Then seeing Captain Breeding going down the board walk, he hurried to catch up with him.

"Cap," Mr. Page's voice broke with emotion. He tried to control the tears in his voice. "Cap, these men coming in...are we feeding them?" he asked.

"No, I pass them off as transient because they aren't residents of the town," said Mr. Breeding. "I can't raise enough money to feed the residents of the town, and I hated to. . . ."

Mr. Page interrupted him. "Let's feed them, Cap." He said.

"You're already feeding so many! Mr. Page — you won't have any money left!"

"I know, Cap, I know." His jaw muscles jerked, and he swallowed hard trying to control his voice, and in a low guttural tone, he repeated, "Cap, let's feed them. I can't stand to see a man hungry. I've been hungry many times, and it's an awful feeling."

He drew his watch from his pocket. "Do you see this watch? It's been in the pawn shop so many times it doesn't know who it belongs to." He was trying to joke, to lighten things a bit, but it didn't work. He put the watch back into his pocket. Tears were still in his voice.

"These poor men . . ." he said, and swallowed hard. "People take pity on women and children, but men get just as hungry. These men are fathers. They leave families behind with what little money there is and strike out, they themselves starving as they look for work. We've got to feed them, Cap. I've been hungry a good many times, and the feeling is awful. If you've never been hungry, you can't know how awful it is. But I've never been hungry a day since I started giving ten percent to the Big Fellow."

"You've got to be giving ninety percent of your income by now," said Captain Breeding, but Mr. Page wasn't listening.

"Cap, I'll tell you what I want you to do. Fix some slips of paper and put your name on them and hand them out to these men. Give each man three. We'll give them a hot meal as they come into town, a good night's rest and a hot meal before they leave the next morning. Send them to any restaurant that serves family style meals so they can eat all they want. Let all the family style restaurants know what the slips of paper are for, so the men won't run into trouble."

Bill Warner had a rooming house on First Street, between Main and Boulder, up over a restaurant. With a wave of his hand, Mr. Page said, "Send them up to Bill Warner's rooming house for a nights lodging. He's got cots for fifty cents a night and I owe him a favor. Bill's a friend of mine. He used to work for me in the lumber camps." He grinned, remembering.

"I used to play pranks on old Bill." He gave a jerk of his head for emphasis. "I locked him in the root cellar one night so he couldn't go to town. He had a habit of getting drunk and not making it back in time to get breakfast for the men the next morning. I had a big work day planned and I wanted him on the job." He stopped talking, conscious of the fact that men were hungry, and he was delaying Captain Breeding.

"Cap, you go fix those tickets, and I'll go up to talk to Bill."

Bill had an eye for business. He immediately rented the building next door and filled it with cots. Both buildings were full every night. In addition, Mr. Page paid for cots to be put into the Salvation Army Headquarters. When they were filled he bought mattresses that could be squeezed between the cots, and all of them were filled every night.

Even with meals at twenty-five cents each and beds fifty cents a night, the bill was over $3,000 in two months time, and Captain knew that at that rate even a million dollars couldn't last long at the rate it was being spent. He prayed that the depression would be a very short one. Mr. Page sometimes looked a little worried, but he kept saying "Feed them Cap, I'll think of something to do before I go broke."

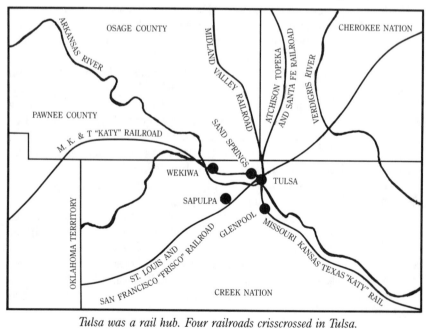

Tulsa was a rail hub. Four railroads crisscrossed in Tulsa.

The Dream Takes Shape

9

A Fool's Enterprise

MANY INDIANS HAD INHERITED EXTRA LAND FROM RELATIVES WHICH they were interested in selling. They preferred cash to land they didn't need and began to look for buyers.

One day in January 1908 Captain Breeding entered Mr. Page's office and Mr. Page introduced him to a group of Indians seated around his desk. "Cap," he said, "these folks are the heirs of Lieutenant Thomas Adams. They want to sell the 160 acre allotment he left them. I'm going to buy it. I'll use it for the good of humanity."

"But the sale of Indian lands is not legal until July 22," Captain Breeding reminded him.

"I know. I can't file the deed until then, but to make sure I get it I'm paying a down payment for them to hold it for me. I'll pay the rest in July when I file the deed."

That night Captain Breeding told Ethel about the land Mr. Page had purchased. "If he spends all his money feeding the hungry, he'll at least have himself a farm, and I feel good about that."

He and Ethel talked long into the night of Mr. Page's dream of an industrial town where a family could put roots down and plan for the future of their children. They caught the vision of the dream, and a longing settled down upon them for a chance to be a part of that dream.

"Brinton," said Ethel "Do you realize that we've been sent to five different places in the six years that we've been married? Our children are going to grow up without belonging anywhere in particular. They need a sense of security and stability. They need a place to call home."

"I agree," said Captain Breeding. He had found in Mr. Page a quality that seemed to have bound him to the man. They understood each other. There was a bond between the two men that he couldn't explain, except that they both had a genuine love for people and wanted to help those in need. He had dreaded leaving Tulsa to go to the next assignment because he hated to leave Mr. Page. He tried to explain to his wife how he felt about the man.

"We don't have the kind of friendship one feels for a buddy — the way he and Arthur Antle are friends. With me, it's more he's my big brother, looking after me, the way I looked after my younger brothers. I don't know what I could have done for the people of Tulsa without his help. I respect him. One day, Tulsa is going to realize what a great man he is. Right now they see him as a little bit touched in the head to bother with all these . . . 'bums and beggers,' was what one man called them."

"How cruel," said Ethel.

"I'll ask Mr. Page to give me a job farming his land," said Captain Breeding. "He's no farmer. Of course he knows about farming, but he doesn't have time. He's in the oil business now. He will need someone to manage his farm. I like planting and watching things grow."

"Well you're certainly trained for that," said Ethel. "You've been a farmer practically all your life and learned more working in that nursery."

The next day when Captain Breeding went to the office with the grocery bills Mr. Page mentioned the land he had purchased. "Cap, what do you think? At least I'll have me a farm," he snapped his fingers. A broad smile was on his face and his eyes twinkled.

"I'd like to work that farm for you," said Captain Breeding. Mr. Page looked surprised, but gave no answer. A few days later Captain Breeding brought the subject up again.

"Mr. Page you are going to need someone to work that farm. I'd sure like to be the one. I'd work without a salary, except that you provide for the needs of my family, if you'll just let me work that farm for you," said Captain Breeding.

"What's your idea of a good piece of land?" asked Mr. Page, testing him.

"There should be at least one hundred acres of valley land and forty to sixty acres on the hill. The land should be timbered so that building material would be available, and it should be near an abundant supply of stone for building foundations and wells..."

Mr. Page interrupted. "This land has springs which give plenty of pure water. It is covered with oak, walnut, hickory, pecan, and about every other kind of tree. There's plenty of building stone less than a mile away."

Both men were enthusiastic as Mr. Page outlined his plans. "Please, Mr. Page, I'd like to be a part of that dream," Captain Breeding entreated.

There was a short silence, then Mr. Page spoke. "Cap are you sure you want to do this?"

"Yes sir, very sure."

"What about your wife? Would she agree to such a thing?"

"Yes sir. We've talked it over. Ethel is as eager to do this as I am. We're to be transferred again in July, but we'd rather stay here and work for you."

"Well, all right," said Mr. Page. He stood up, walked around his desk and offered his hand to seal the gentleman's contract. He went back to his desk chair, leaned back and with a puff from his cigar, blew a smoke ring. As it sailed upward he put his finger into the ring, then blew another one.

"I sure hope you get to realize your dream," said Captain Breeding, as he accepted a check from Wayne Kingsberry for the grocery bills at Stokes' grocery store.

"I don't intend to go broke," said Mr. Page. "I'll have that town, you bet, but to be on the safe side, don't resign your job until July, when the sale of Indian lands becomes legal."

"All right," said Captain Breeding and he hurried on. When he went home for dinner he told his wife Ethel the good news.

Some mornings later Captain Breeding went to Mr. Page's office. Mr. Page looked up from his work when he heard a light knock on the door. By now he had accepted the fact that Captain Breeding would not enter without an invitation. Giving a sweep of his arm, he signaled for his friend to come in.

"Cap," he said, "I've thought of something that will allow me to continue helping these men and still enable me to have my industrial town."

"That's good to hear," said Captain Breeding. "Tell me about it."

"It's simple." Mr. Page leaned back in his chair as he often did when discussing something. "You see, Cap, what a man really wants is a job. Nobody likes a hand out. It robs them of their dignity and self respect. Sometimes that's about all a person has left, and he wants to hang on to it. Being a practical man, I have an idea that will help these fellows and myself. I'll hire some of them to clear my land. We'll plant crops and stock it with herds of livestock. I'll need workers to tend the stock, plant crops, build barns and as I buy additional land it will give more jobs for more men and we'll all benefit, don't you see?"

"Good Idea," said Captain Breeding.

Mr. Page struck a match on the bottom of his shoe, puffed at his cigar and stuck the match in a dish already filled with an assortment of cigar butts and burned matches, then continued.

"I plan to start my project on my forty-eighth birthday, June second."

"The land won't be yours until the 27th day of July," Captain Breeding reminded him. "You can't even file the deed until then."

"I know, but it won't hurt to start clearing the land. It will give us a head start." Mr. Page shoved a small box of matches back and forth on his desk as he talked.

"You see, Cap, as I figure it, a day of birth is a day of beginnings. I want to begin my new year by doing something worthwhile to show God I'm grateful that He brought me through to a new year."

"That's a good thought," said Captain Breeding.

Mr. Page continued. "This property is seven or eight miles northwest of Tulsa. The Katy railroad runs through it. There are three or four springs on the land that bubble up through sand. Sand filters out impurities, you know, so it's very clear and pure water. The Indians call these springs OKTAHU UEKIWA, which means, sand water. One of the springs is a very large one, known for its abundant supply of pure water."

"Could it be the spring that is the stopping place for travelers and freighters along the trail from Muskogee to the mouth of the Cimarron River?" asked Captain Breeding.

"That's the one," said Mr. Page. "Freight wagons, and caravans of people stop at the spring to rest and to refill their water barrels. Long ago, somebody built a low wall of cedar logs around the big spring, evidently to keep animals out of it. The logs are now badly decayed."

"These are probably the springs I heard some fellows talking about the other day. They were complaining at the water situation and one said it was too bad that big spring wasn't in Tulsa."

"Well, since I bought it, I'd just as soon it stayed there," joshed Mr. Page, and continued describing the place.

"It is mostly a wilderness out there, and when it rains, a swampy wilderness at that. The water drains from the hills flooding the valley with no place to drain. The river sometimes overflows during a heavy rainy season too. I've been told that I bought a worthless piece of land, except for the big spring."

"That's too bad."

"Oh it's all right, Cap. We can drain the excess water off. It will cost us a lot of money, but it can be done. The spring is worth what the piece of land cost me." Mr. Page continued.

"There is a ten- or twelve-acre section of open prairie where very tall grass grows."

"Probably buffalo grass. It grows ten feet tall sometimes."

"Well, I didn't walk through it, but it looks as though you could get lost in the middle of it," said Mr. Page. "I talked to Sam Adams who lives down the road a piece, south of the springs. He said the Indians valued this tall grass as pasture for their cattle. During the winter months the dead grass lays like a thick carpet protecting the tender young shoots that grow beneath it all winter."

"That's good. Since it is a little late to plant crops this year, we can stanchion our stock in the grassy meadow," said Captain Breeding. "Are there many people living near your land? I'm just wondering about neighbors."

"There are six or seven Indian families living in log houses scattered about." Mr. Page smiled broadly. "Cap, guess who your nearest neighbor will be?"

"I've no idea."

"Siah Buttons."

Everybody knew Siah Buttons. He was the religious leader among his people and greatly respected. Theirs was a secret society among the Creek Indians. Siah had been given the name Buttons, because he wore the finest collection of buttons on his clothes, especially at their tribal dances.

The Indians held their council meetings and tribal dances under the spreading branches of the giant oak known as the COUNCIL TREE at 1730 Cheyenne Avenue in Tulsa. It was under this giant oak, that they had emptied the fire (or ashes), brought from their homeland. This was where they stopped in 1826, ending their trail of tears. They had camped around about the giant oak, which was sacred to them, until 1899-1900 when they all received allotments.

The Tulsa merchants were generous to donate food for their tribal celebrations held under the old Council Tree. The merchants were made welcome to join the festivities. Many of them did, with gusto, and in full costume. Onlookers enjoyed watching them clown around trying to follow the Indian dance.

"Siah is married to Sallie Salmer, a step daughter to Fus Thulocco, who is mentioned in books of Indian history," said Mr. Page. "Thulocco is buried in a little Indian cemetery on the land. Siah's land joins my land to the west side. His wife's allotment joins his land, and so does her mother's. I'd like to buy all the land that surrounds mine. Siah lives in a two-room log cabin with a porch between the two rooms."

"They call that a "Saddle House," said Captain Breeding. "The two rooms joined by a long roof with the porch between reminds them of a saddle with two side pockets. Having the kitchen separate from the rest of the house keeps the heat and cooking odors out of the rest of the house."

"Not a bad idea," said Mr. Page.

"The rooms at either side provide shade to the porch, and some protection from the elements. Indians traveling at night, upon seeing one of these saddle houses, know that he was welcome to curl up in his blanket on the porch until morning."

"That's very nice," said Mr. Page. "I like that."

On June 1st Captain Breeding went into Mr. Page's office and was greeted warmly. "Well, Cap, tomorrow is June 2."

"June 2, 1908," said Captain Breeding, with a grin. "We must remember that date. You'll be forty-eight years old, and that is the day you started your project."

Mr. Page nodded. "I'm not likely to forget. I've already hired Joe Lord, and told him to choose his own crew to clear the land."

"Mr. Page," Captain Breeding said, reluctantly, "I don't know if you know it or not, but Joe Lord was a drunk until just recently. He claimed to have been saved at one of our meetings, but it's possible he was attracted to the drum and flag, or was broke and hungry and knew he would be fed. I gave him the benefit of the doubt, but I'd hate for him to let you down."

Mr. Page was always a patient listener. When Captain Breeding finished, he grinned. "Cap, I'm not a sin fighter like you are. I take a drink now and then, myself. And I even cuss if I feel like it. You gave Joe the benefit of the doubt and so will I. Anyway, he says he's quit drinking, forever. I believe him. Either way, the guy needs a job and a chance to prove himself. How many jobs are there for a one arm, peg legged man with a disfigured face?"

Several years earlier, Joe had fallen under the wheels of a box car. He had lost one foot, one arm and received a deep cut in the side of his face that disfigured him badly.

Joe found three men to go along with him. Charles Higgins was sixty years old and a drinking buddy of Joe's. He too had sworn off the bottle. Charley was a good worker when he wasn't drinking. He was to do the cooking. Frank Owens was a young physical giant of a man with only one eye. He needed a job and Joe hired him. To him would fall most of the physical labor.

Mr. Gorman of whom very little was known wanted to go along for adventure and Joe took him.

When Joe returned with his motley crew, Mr. Page told him to go to Arthur Antle's Stables on the northeast corner of Second and Boulder. "Tell Arthur I sent you," said Mr. Page. "Get yourselves a wagon and a team of horses. Then go get a tent, camping gear and what ever supplies you'll need and head out there." He gave a sweep of his arm.

The joke around the Robinsons' Hotel, was that Charley Page had bought himself a swampy wilderness and had hired three handicapped men and a gentleman to carve himself an empire out of the worthless dead land. They teased him and dubbed his project a "Fool's Enterprise." They told him it was only visionary and foolish.

But Mr. Page was never shaken by other people's comments. "The trouble with you is lack of vision," he countered. "You would all do well to buy land for yourselves."

"Charley," said one man, "If you think being out there away from liquor joints is going to keep Joe and Charley sober, then you've got another thought a comin'. Don't you know about the liquor-boats? Liquor is brought in by train from Kansas to an Indian trading post at a place called Sennet. They bring the liquor in as cargo, along with a car load of other merchandise. At night boatmen load the elixir into boats and paddle silently down the Arkansas river to the bootleg shacks at the outskirts of Tulsa."

Another man added, "To let the joint owner know that a shipment has arrived, the boat runner fires his gun a given number of shots, and the owners of the joints hurry down to the water's edge to purchase their supply."

"Charley," said another, "If you paid them a surprise visit I'll wager you'd find Joe and Charley drunk."

"Well what a man does on his own time is his business," said Mr. Page, "but if he drinks on the job he's fired. But I'm gonna trust them until they prove I'm wrong."

10

A Tour on the Prairie

A WEEK LATER CAPTAIN BREEDING, CURIOUS AS TO THE PLACE HE WOULD be working, decided to pay the men a visit. Dr. C.W. Kerr of the Tulsa Presbyterian Church, a missionary pastor for the Indian Nation, had also preached at the little Pleasant View Indian school in the community. He told Captain Breeding about the railway service.

"The Katy Railroad runs right by the springs," he said, "but the cantankerous engineer won't stop there unless it's pecan season and he wants to gather pecans from the nearby pecan grove. The Katy's first stop is four miles beyond the springs at Wekiwa. The Indians haul water from the train's water stop and, in hearing the Indians say 'UEKIWA,' which means water, the train men named the place Wekiwa. That's what they thought the Indians were saying."

"Then your advice is to go to Wekiwa if I have to and walk back the four miles, rather than walk seven or eight miles from Tulsa to the springs?"

"No," said Dr. Kerr, "I wouldn't advise that. Those four miles from Wekiwa are the worst four miles of terrain imaginable. Even walking the tracks is treacherous. There are long trestles over canyons. The area is rocks and boulders and a tangled mass of impenetrable brambles. The woods are full of wolves, coyotes, panthers, bobcats and other such animals. You must also watch out for rattlesnakes. The area is full of them." Dr. Kerr shook his head. "There's a wagon trail from Tulsa to the springs, sometimes called Adam's Place, because it was on Adam's allotment, but I hear the wagon trail is washed out."

"Yes, Joe Lord and his crew had to come back and take the north Osage road out there," said Mr. Breeding. "I'm a good walker, I'll just walk down the tracks until I get there."

"I'll worry about you until you return," said Mrs. Breeding. "So time yourself so that you can make it back before dark."

It was nine o'clock the next morning, when Mr. Breeding started out. The river was still out of its banks in places, but not above the tracks. Water stood in small lakes along the right-of-way. Now and then he saw a snake or mountain boomer sunning themselves on piles of debris where the brush had been chopped back from the tracks. An occasional lizard scurried out of sight as he passed and squirrels seemed to be in abundance chattering noisily at his intrusion. All was wilderness except for one field of cultivated land along the whole seven miles. Not a person was in sight.

He couldn't see the camp for the trees, but he smelled coffee brewing as he drew near. He hastened his steps as the smell of salt pork, skillet cornbread, beans and fried potatoes wafted through the breeze.

Checking his watch he saw that it was eleven o'clock. He had made the treck in two hours. That meant he would have to head for home by three o'clock that afternoon.

Nothing ever tasted better, as he ate a leisurely meal with the men.

The men had cleared the brush from the Katy right-of-way, down through the little valley around a series of small springs and part way up the hill was an occasional cleared spot. The decayed cedar logs that had been stacked around the big spring were strewn about where they had thrown them as they cleaned the debris from the spring.

"We killed twenty copperhead and water moccasins from the spring,"said Frank. "But some got away."

"But the water from these springs is the best water we ever ever tasted," said Charley, and the others agreed.

"There seems to be one man missing," said Captain Breeding.

"Gorman came for adventure," said Joe, "and it just took a couple of nights of fighting the battalions of mosquitoes and shivering through the sounds of the night to fill him with all the adventure he wanted. He skidaddled."

"The mosquitoes from all this backed up water," said Charley, "are so big, I believe they must roost in trees. We put kerosene in the pools to kill the wiggletails and to keep the mosquitoes' eggs from hatching."

Frank Owens told of the evening they heard such a frightful sound that it kept them awake all night. "There are panthers in these woods," said Frank, "and we were sure that sound was one of them. We figured the panther was stalking us. We kept the fire going to keep him scared off. The sound continued all night and throughout the next morning. We decided to hunt him down. We couldn't take another sleepless night. We followed the sound to discover that it was nothing more than a mule colt, lost from its mother."

Captain Breeding observed two Negro fellows who were at a house that set back about fifty feet from Adam's road, directly west of the big spring. "Who are they?" he asked.

"They are section hands who maintained the Katy railroad tracks," said Frank. Then pointing to about one hundred feet north of the section house, he said, "that log house belongs to Siah Buttons. The road here is called Adams road because it runs along the Adams families allotments."

When the men were through eating, Captain Breeding asked where the little Indian cemetery was. Mr. Page had given orders not to disturb it. Frank led the way across the Katy tracks to where there were about one hundred graves.

"I asked Siah Buttons why they put those little roofs over the graves?" said Frank, "and he said they were to mark the grave and keep the animals off. Each tribe has their customs. Osage Indians pile rocks on their graves to keep animals from digging in the grave."

Captain Breeding had just conducted a funeral for a Creek Indian. He explained to Frank. "When a Creek Indian dies, even though he may not have died at home, the room in which he slept is vacated. The walls, the floor and the bedstead are thoroughly scrubbed. The mattress, bedding and all his personal belongings not buried with him are burned. A shovel full of burning cedar chips is placed in the center of the room on a large stone, so as not to burn the floor, then the door is closed and not even the wife may enter, until two months of mourning is completed."

"How can they afford to burn belongings?" asked Frank.

"They can't. It keeps the missionaries and community friends busy replacing bedding. Some complain about it. But that's the Creek custom, and they do it."

"That's very interesting," said Frank.

Joe whistled for Frank to come back and get to work. Captain Breeding, left to explore on his own, wandering over the hills and valleys. As he viewed the small lakes where the water drained from the hills, he knew that it would take a lot of tiles to carry the water into the river. As he looked at the shining pools of water he thought of Washington Irving's book, 'A *Tour of the Prairie.*' He had mentioned glassy pools such as these. Going through the timbered area, he also noted that wild grape vines hung like huge ropes. This too was mentioned in Irving's book. Suddenly it dawned on him that this must have been the place where, in the fall of 1832, Washington Irving and his party camped and rested through the winter. It was probably his men who had put the cedar logs around the spring to keep their horses and other animals from walking in it, thought Captain Breeding. He was standing in the timbered area that was so dense that it shut out the sun. Vines of wild grape and ivy were intertwined hanging in tangled masses from century old oaks to the underbrush making ghostly patterns in deeper shadows. An eerie feeling swept over him. Turning, he hurried out of the forest and into the sunlight.

A week later, Mr. Page asked Captain Breeding to ride his horse, Buster, and take some things out to the men, he took Irving's book along. Before he rode into the springs he got his book out and read as he looked about.

"Some times we had to break our way through alluvial bottoms, matted with redundant vegetation where the gigantic oaks were entangled with grape vines hanging like cordage from their branches," wrote Irving.

"Sometimes we coasted along sluggish brooks, whose feeble trickling current just served to link together a succession of glassy pools, embedded like mirrors in the quiet bosom of the forest, reflecting its autumnal foliage, and patches of the clear blue sky."

A picture, identical to the one described by Irving, came into view. Captain Breeding stood transfixed, as he looked long at the sluggish brooks and glassy pools. There was no doubting now, that on October 14, 1832, Washington Irving's party had made camp beside these very springs. Captain Breeding closed the book and hurried on to tell the men in the camp of his discovery.

It was five o'clock in the evening when Captain Breeding got home, but he was so excited that he had to stop by the Robinson Hotel to tell Mr. Page that the piece of land he had purchased had already gone down in history. They were both excited.

The Breedings got a notice in the second week of July that they were to be transferred to another Salvation Army Post. He told Mr. Page about it and Mr. Page told him to go ahead and resign from the Salvation Army and be prepared to move out to the farm in a few days.

Mrs. Breeding took a suitcase from the closet. As Captain Breeding watched, she folded each Salvation Army uniform neatly and laid them in the suitcase. She put her bonnet on one last time and smiled a little sadly.

"I worked ten years for this," she said. Captain Breeding put his arms around her.

"Do you have regrets?" he asked. She shook her head. Then she buried her face on his shoulder and wept.

"It's not too late to reconsider," said Captain Breeding.

She took her handkerchief from her sleeve. "I think we're doing the right thing," she cried. "It's just that . . . Oh I don't know, Brinton, it's just that I have these feelings . . ."

Captain Breeding held her close. "I know, I know," he said, "Go ahead and cry if you want to. Women have to cry. It makes them feel better. Men sometimes want to cry too."

Ethel wiped her eyes and blew her nose. She removed her bonnet and put it into a hat box along with her husband's cap. Then, looking at her husband, she smiled brightly. "Brinton you close the lid of the suitcase and I will close the hat box."

As the lids closed, Captain Breeding said, ceremoniously, "Although we lay aside our titles and the uniforms we so proudly wore, may we always be found faithfully doing our duty toward God and all mankind." They and their children bowed their heads and holding hands, Captain Breeding said a short prayer for God to guide them.

"I've grown accustomed to being called Captain, and it's going to take a little getting used to being called Mr. Breeding again," he said.

"Brinton, I never called you Captain, anyway." Ethel smiled impertinently at him. He kissed her and picked up the suitcase.

"Well, I will no longer introduce myself as Captain Breeding," he said.
"Do we still call you daddy?" asked Eva.

Mr. Breeding kissed her on the top of her head. "You sure do," he said.

On July 21, Mr. Breeding went into Mr. Page's office. "Well tomorrow is the day when I can file the deed to my land," said Mr. Page. "You and your family can move out tomorrow. Your tent is ready. I gave Joe a job in the oil fields. So, Cap, you will have full charge of the workmen. I have an old horse, Bill, whom I had retired to Arthur Antle's ranch across the river. Bill is so gentle, a baby could play under his feet and he wouldn't step on it. He's old, but he can do light chores like pulling a buggy. Arthur brought him over to his stable, and he will find you a buggy. You get what ever else you need and charge it to me."

Wednesday, July 22, 1908, Bill was hitched to a rickety one-horse buggy, and into the buggy were placed a week's supply of groceries, the family and their belongings. They went westward to the Bruner Crossing where the road crossed the Katy railway tracks and followed the left bank of Black Boy Creek. A few hundred yards farther they had to ford a creek. Following the trail that led southwest toward the river, they came to a slough, sixty feet across with a green scum on it. There were tracks leading in and out the other side.

"I assume it's safe to cross," Mr. Breeding said, after looking the situation over. Then he discovered that the whiffle-tree from which the traces of the harness were fastened was near the breaking point.

"I'll have to mend it," Mr. Breeding told the restless children. "If it breaks, the horse won't be hooked to the buggy."

With a jack knife he cut a green oak stick and with wire from a nearby fence, he lashed the green stick onto the whiffle-tree to give it strength and started across the slough. The slime was deeper than he had anticipated, and everything in the buggy was soggy with the mud and green slime. But they were thankful they hadn't been stuck in the mud.

They arrived at the springs at five o'clock in the evening. Their belongings and a few pieces of furniture and lumber had been delivered the day before. Workmen had put a tent up for them on the side of the hill. The tent was stretched over a framework of two by fours and nailed to a plank floor. Rocks were under one side to make the floor level. The kitchen table had one leg tied to a tree and the other three legs tied to stakes driven into the ground to make it level. A smooth place was made into the hill, to set the little wood cook stove on. Wagon sheets were tied to limbs of trees to provide shelter over the dining area. Mosquito netting was pinned to the wagon sheets with clothes pins. They were not as bad as they had been before the men put kerosene into the pools of water.

"It will be nice to have a woman cook for us," said the men, teasing Charley Higgins about his cooking.

Their first Sunday there, July 26, was Mr. Breeding's thirty-third birthday. He and his wife decided that they should have a Sunday worship service, although there would be no one there but themselves and their two children. It was the eight workmen's day off, and they had scattered about — fishing, hunting, or visiting the two Negro fellows Lumus and Orchester, who worked for the Katy railroad.

"What was that!" said Orchester, when the sound of the two cornets split the air. Lumus looked wild-eyed and startled.

"That's Gabriel blowing his horn," said Frank. Then he asked, "Haven't you ever heard music like that?"

"Does they call that music?" asked Lumus.

The Breedings were amused when Frank told them what the section hands had said. Later that afternoon Lumus and Orchester broke into song, and in the spirit of fun, Mr. Breeding asked, "Do they call that music?"

Mr. Breeding learned that on the following Tuesday, July 28th, the District School Board was holding a meeting at the little Indian schoolhouse called "Pleasant View."[1]

The people began to assemble about two o'clock in the afternoon. At the meeting, Mr. Breeding asked if he could make an announcement. Permission was granted, and he announced that he would hold preaching services at the spring the following Sunday.

A bond was voted on to build a new District school. The district was bonded for $1,200.00, and the members of the school board were elected. They were J.W. Clemens, Charles Casper and Mr. J.H. Huddlestone, who was chairman of the board.

Mr. Huddlestone then announced that he had purchased the land with the big spring on it for the new school.

"You must be mistaken," said Mr. Breeding. "That property belongs to Mr. Page. He has a contract with the heirs of Lt. Adams."

"So do I," said Mr. Huddelston. "Mr. Page's contract is void because he made the agreement before the sale of land was legal. We intend to put the schoolhouse right on top of that hill."

---

[1] The little school was located where the box factory now sits, along highway 51 and 64. Mr. Breeding decided to go and get acquainted with the people. The school was a building sixteen-by-eighteen feet, built of native lumber.

11

A Shadow Over Christmas

MR. PAGE LOOKED UP FROM HIS WORK. SAM ADAMS, THE SPOKESMAN for the Indian family who had sold their father's land to Mr. Page, walked through the open door. Captain Breeding was just getting off the elevator when he saw Sam go into the office. He followed, this time without knocking.

"What can I do for you Sam?" said Mr. Page. "Have a chair. You too, Cap."

"I guess Mr. Adams and I came for the same purpose," said Mr. Breeding. Then he told him about what Huddelston had said.

"Is this true, Sam?"

"Huddleston pay more," said Mr. Adams. "I sell to Huddleston."

"Sam, you can't do that," said Mr. Page. "It's dishonest. You sold that land to me. I've already filed the deed."

"Huddleston say your deed no good. He filed deed."

"We had a gentleman's agreement. We shook hands on it."

"Huddleston give me more money. I sell to Huddleston."

Mr. Page knew that the Indian agencies made sure that Indians were protected. As to accountability for their actions, they were excused as innocent children. Mr. Page protested.

"Sam I dealt with you in good faith, assuming that all Indians were honest."

"Sam honest. Sam let you know. Huddelston pay more."

"Yes, you let me know all right. It's more like blackmail. Huddleston SHOULD pay more. It's now improved land. I've had men out there for weeks. I've got a lot of wage hours sunk in that property." Mr. Page saw that it was useless to talk to Sam. He was only interested in getting more money. Then the thought came to him.

"Has Huddleston paid you yet?"

"He say school pay me."

"Sam, it could take a long time for you to get your money if the school is to pay you. I'll pay you whatever Huddleston has offered and get you the money right now."

"You pay all today? Okay," said Sam.

"Come with me," Mr. Page took Sam by the arm, and led him to the elevator. Mr. Breeding followed. Mr. Page took Sam to the registration office and had him to verify that his deed was legal.

"Sam, you can't keep changing your mind," said the clerk. "You declare Mr. Page's claim illegal, then you say it's legal. Make your mind up, Sam. This is your last chance. Who are you selling this land to?"

"Mr. Page," said Mr. Adams.

"Then sign here." Sam Adams signed the document.

"Now Sam, this property isn't yours anymore. Do you understand?" said the clerk. Sam nodded. "You can't sell it anymore."

"Huddleston say he pay me more. Now Page pay same. I sell to Page. He pay me now."

"That's blackmail, Sam. You could go to jail for that."

The smile left Sam's face as the clerk continued.

"Mr. Page doesn't really have to pay you a higher price."

"It's all right," said Mr. Page. "The only thing I'm interested in is getting this deed filed."

Mr. Page took Sam to the bank to get the money. He withdrew the money and paid Sam what he owed him.

"Now go tell Huddleston that his deal is off," said Mr. Page.

Mr. Huddleston was very angry when he heard what had happened. Still determined to put his school at the top of Mr. Page's hill, he sent surveyors out to measure for the foundation of the school. When notified, Mr. Page went to Charles Grimes, the newly elected superintendent of schools.

"I've had men clearing this land for weeks," said Mr. Page.

Mr. Grimes chuckled. "I suspect that is why he wants it. But it's not right. We don't do business that way."

"Siah Buttons owns the land just across the road on the same hill," said Mr. Page. "I feel sure that he would sell enough land to put the school on. I have other plans for my land."

Mr. Grimes talked to Siah, and he agreed to sell the school a parcel of land. Mr. Grimes talked to Mr. Huddleston and put an end to the dispute, but not the hard feelings Mr. Huddleston had.

At the next school board meeting it was suggested that Sand Springs be the name of the new school because it was near the well-known sandy springs.

"Absolutely not," said Mr. Huddleston. "The present school is called Pleasant View and we'll keep that name." He was supported by the majority of the board.

Meanwhile, there was much to be done on the farm. Clean whiskey barrels were sent out to be used as water barrels. A sled was made, and the old horse, Bill, was relegated to the task of hauling barrels of spring water up the hill to the camp.

Mr. Breeding also found another use for one of the barrels. He had announced that there would be a three o'clock service the coming Sunday and in preparing for the meeting, he stood one of the whiskey barrels on end to serve as a pulpit.

The cedar logs that had been cleaned out of the big spring were placed in rows on the side of the hill as seats for the congregation to sit on.

"I sure hope somebody comes," said Ethel, "after all our work preparing for them."

"Oh, I'm sure there will be a few," said Mr. Breeding. "People are always hungry to hear from the word of God."

By 2:00 p.m. people began to arrive — by buggy, wagon and on horseback. By three o'clock, fifty people had gathered.

The Breedings played their cornets. Mrs. Breeding sang a solo, accompanying herself on her guitar and later playing for the congregational singing. There were no extra song books, so Mrs. Breeding quoted line by line, as the people sang.

Mr. Breeding's message was taken from Ecclesiastes 9:11-12 and the title of his sermon was, "Man Knoweth Not His Time."

At the close of the service, Mr. Breeding announced that there would be services each Sunday, thereafter.

By now a crew of eight men were working at clearing the land. A carpenter by the name of Ayers was sent out to build a house for the Breedings to live in.

Hauling lumber was a difficult task because of the sometimes impassable wagon trail. But Frank Owens was a strong and dependable young man. He left the farm at seven o'clock each morning. It was evening before he got back with the lumber. Mr. Breeding also went in for a load when he could.

But things were going slow. Mr. Ayers built an outhouse and shower house while waiting for a stone mason to lay the foundation for the Breeding's cottage.

Earlier, the men had driven a pipe into a small spring that flowed from the hillside. They made some holes in a syrup bucket and hung it on the end of the pipe, making themselves a shower. Thick underbrush had provided privacy for the men, but now a wrap-around wall with a roof was added, high enough off the ground for the water to drain under.

Growing weary of waiting for the mason, Mr. Breeding gathered stones and laid the foundation for his house so the carpenter could get started building.

Work began on the little Pleasant View schoolhouse on the same day the Breeding house was started. A wager among the men was that the Breeding cottage would be completed first.

One day when Mr. Breeding was in town helping to load lumber into the wagon, Mr. Grimes came to the lumber yard. He ask Mr. Breeding if Earl McCormack, a young teacher friend, could ride out with him to see Mr. Huddleston about a teaching job.

"Indeed," said Mr. Breeding. "Mr. Huddleston lives right on my way." Earl climbed on top of the load of lumber. When they came to where Mr. Huddleston lived, Earl got off and Mr. Breeding went on to the farm. A short time later Earl came walking up the hill toward Mr. Breeding. He told him that Mr. Huddleston had refused him a teaching job because he had seen him with Mr. Breeding, who worked for Charles Page.

"I can get another teaching job," said Earl, "but I need a summer job right now. Could you use another hand here on the farm?" Mr. Breeding hired him.

Mr. Huddleston remained so disgruntled and unhappy that after a few months he packed up his things and left town.

Mr. Page and Lucile came out every Sunday evening and had dinner with the Breedings and the men. After dinner, as the women cleared the table, Mr. Page and Mr. Breeding would walk about the place, checking on the progress and discussing business. One Sunday evening Mr. Page seemed very preoccupied. After dinner, he took out a cigar and sat down in a chair in the yard. He lit the cigar and turned to Mr. Breeding.

"Cap, I have a favor I'd like to ask of you and your wife," he said. Mrs. Breeding paused to listen.

"Do you remember Leonard Nolen, the little paper boy?" he asked. Mr. Breeding nodded. "Leonard missed a couple of days bringing me my paper," said Mr. Page. "I inquired about it. I found that Leonard's mother is very ill with tuberculosis. Her husband is in the hospital and Luther, her thirteen-year-old boy is gone somewhere. That leaves Leonard the eleven-year-old trying to take care of his mother and sell newspapers. The Nolen boys are from a former marriage. Their father is dead. Mrs. Nolen's husband, Bill Jones, has four children of his own who are staying with relatives. It's a sad situation, and I think we ought to help them. I thought if we could get the family out here where they could all be together, Mr. Jones could see to his wife's needs until I can find a nurse to take care of her. The air out here among the trees would be good for Mrs. Jones and she could rest easier knowing the family was together and being cared for. What do you say?"

"We'll do whatever we can," said Mr. Breeding, looking at his wife. She gave a nod of approval.

Mr. Page seem relieved. "I'll find Luther, and whenever Mr. Jones gets out of the hospital I'll send him out. He needs a job anyway. Give the boys something to do so they can earn a little money. It will make them feel good."

The next day Mr. and Mrs. Breeding and their two children took the wagon to town. When they got to the Jones home, there was no one there except Mrs. Jones. While Mrs. Breeding prepared her for the journey, Mr. Breeding went shopping for needed supplies and a tent for the woman.

When Mr. Breeding returned, he and Mrs. Breeding put the woman's mattress in the wagon, then Mr. Breeding carried her out. Fearful that night would overtake them before they got home, Ethel wrote a note telling the boys how to get to the farm.

Mr. Breeding pulled a bottle from a paper sack, and reached for a glass in Mrs. Jones' cabinet.

"Mr. Page gave me this medicine for Mrs. Jones," he said. "It's to relieve the pain. We're supposed to give her half a cup before taking her on the long journey." Mrs. Breeding took it to the woman. When she returned with the empty glass, Mr. Breeding stood looking stunned.

Ethel asked, "What's the matter, Brinton?"

Mr. Breeding turned the bottle for her to read the label. "It's wine," he said. "I just gave an alcoholic drink to someone." He sighed and put the bottle back into the sack. "It's for medicinal purposes," he rationalized. "If it eases a dying woman's pain, can we let her suffer? Laudanum is what my father gave for such cases and that's opium."

Ethel took the sack, and kissed her husband on the cheek. "It's all right, Brinton," she said, "but if we don't get started we'll have to give her another dose."

The journey was long and painful for the woman, but she tried to endure, greatful for what was being done for the family. Mr. Breeding drove slow, trying to make the ride easier, but it was so late by the time they got home, that there was no time to get a tent up for the woman. The Breedings took the mattress off their bed and placed it under the trees. Mrs. Jones' mattress was placed on the bed inside the Breeding's tent.

The children were bedded down under the wagon near by. That night about midnight a slow drizzling rain began to fall. Thankful that it was they and not the sick woman being rained on, the Breedings picked up their mattress, and crowded under the wagon with the children.

The sun was shining the next day and a tent with a wooden floor was fixed for Mrs. Jones.

Work on the Breeding's cottage was delayed while they worked on a house for Mrs. Jones.

One hot, blustery day, it seemed the wind was bent on playing havoc with Mrs. Breeding's cooking pots. The lids blew off and before she could retrieve them a gust of wind blew sand into the food that she had cooking on the stove. She yelled for Mr. Breeding, who was working nearby, to come and help her. He helped her collect the lids, and weighted them down with fist size stones.

As he started to return to his work he noticed a small boy coming down the railroad tracks from the direction of Wekiwa.

"Here comes Mrs. Jones' son, Leonard," he said. "The Katy men have evidently refused to let him off at the springs, and he has had to walk back that treacherous four miles in this heat."

Leonard turned in at the springs. Hot and exhausted, he fell down on his stomach and began to drink from the spring. He splashed water on his face and drank again. He lay so long drinking that it seemed he would burst.

"That's the best water I ever tasted," he said, as Mr. Breeding walked down the hill to meet him. Running back, he took another drink from the spring.

When Mr. Page heard that the conductor had made such a little boy walk four miles through almost impassable terrain, he was furious.

"If I ever get a chance, I'll make them pay for the way they treat my people," he said. "I've talked to them about making a flag stop at the springs, but they won't do it."

Luther arrived two days later, and about two weeks after that, Mr. Jones came, bringing his three little boys. Howard was eleven years old. France, whom they called Bud, was nine and Cuba was seven. Relatives keeping Mr. Jones' little girl asked him to let her stay with them a little longer.

One half of the crew was rushing to get the Jones' house finished while the other half worked on the Breeding house. As soon as Mr. Ayers got the roof on the Breeding cottage the Sunday services were held under the shade of the roof.

The Pleasant View District School was completed first, and after its completion it was used for community affairs, including church services, with Mr. Breeding as pastor.

Mr. Jones, appreciative of what Mr. Page was doing for him and his family, was a very good worker. He was especially good at building fences. When a fence to hold hogs was finished, hogs and milk cows were purchased to share the pen until separate pens could be built.

Upon hearing that Mr. Page was buying animals as well as land, people came to him. One man came with a team of blind horses. One was blind and the other had only one eye. "But they are very good workers," the man explained.

"That appeals to me," said Mr. Page, recalling that his father was a good worker although he had lost an eye while cleaning his gun. Mr. Page bought the team and sent them to the farm.

Various needy people were sent out to the farm after that, some needing a job, some sick or old and unwanted by their children. They were all bivouacked in tents with wood floors. They were not bad to live in. Mr. Page continued to send people out, and the place soon looked like tent city.

Additional carpenters were hired to build a house to be used as a kitchen and dining room. The crew continued to work fast, hoping to get finished before cold weather.

The lowland south of the Katy tracks was covered with timbers and undergrowth. It flooded every time it rained. A sixteen-inch concrete drain pipe was laid from the lowest part of the land to the river to drain the water off. When the land dried it was cleared of trees and underbrush.

A large creek fed by a spring had added to the flooding. A dam, placed across the south end of the creek turned it to the east allowing it to run its course until it formed a large lake.

The first five acres were finally cleared, except for the gigantic tree stumps. Earl McCormack, the school teacher, was given the job of pulling the stumps up, using the team of blind horses. However they were not strong enough to budge the huge stumps. Someone told Mr. Page about a man who worked with six yoke of oxen. He charged $7.50 an acre to plow and break up the soil. The man was called a "shaker." When the eighteen inch plow struck a tree stump the oxen simply leaned in the yoke until the plow went into the root. The man held the plow and when it went into a stump the man would shake the plow to loosen the stump. He kept shaking, and the oxen kept pulling until the root was pulled out of the ground. It was interesting to watch — and everybody did.

At last the ground was plowed and five acres of peach trees were planted.

One Sunday Mr. Page told the Breedings that he had purchased the 160 acres adjoining the Adams allotment along the north side from Sam Williams, a black "freed man."

Mr. Page had realtors Legas Perryman and Sam Davis looking for land for him. Others hearing that he was paying cash, began to come to him. He bought all they had for sale, some sight unseen.

Things were going nicely. The Breeding house and the house for Mrs. Jones and a practical nurse was finished. Mr. Jones and the five boys remained in the tent.

As September drew near, school was often the topic of discussion. Leonard decided he wasn't going to school.

"Mr. Page quit school when he was eleven and he did all right," he argued. Mr. Breeding asked Mr. Page to talk to him.

Mr. Page called Leonard to him. "My boy, you have to go to school if you want to work for me," he said. "You have no idea of the difficulties I have had because of my lack of an education. I've had to hire things done for me that I could have done for myself if I had had a better education."

"I want to work on the railroad like my dad did," said Leonard. "You don't have to have an education to do that."

"Well, if the Katy doesn't become more accommodating, I just might build my own railroad out here, and if I do, I'll keep you in mind. But right now, you have to go to school."

School started with about thirty-five students in the one room school house. When Mr. Breeding saw all the school children, he knew there should be a Sunday School for them. He went to Tulsa and talked to the various ministers about sponsoring a Sunday School and decided upon Reverend A. F. Romeg, a Presbyterian home missionary. He told Mr. Page about his decision.

"Well that's fine," said Mr. Page, "but why Presbyterian?"

Mr. Breeding grinned. "Because they offered to supply us with literature for the first three months, free of charge."

"Cap," said Mr. Page, "I suspect that you're a maverick."

"It will be called a Community Church anyway," Mr. Breeding hastened to explain. "There will be people of different faiths worshiping together, and it really doesn't matter. It's what is in the heart that counts." Mr. Page agreed.

Throughout the winter, land clearing continued. Farmers living about the country were also given jobs to help with the clearing. The going price for clearing land, was seventy-five cents an acre. They were also paid seventy-five cents for a cord of stove wood measuring two feet long. A cord was a stack that measured four feet by four feet by eight feet long.

Much valuable wood was cut into firewood because there was no way to transport it to a sawmill. All tents had wood stoves in them and it took a lot of wood to supply the needs of the camp.

The men clearing land decided to burn the dry underbrush in the pecan grove, so they could find the pecans when they fell. The fire got out of hand. The tall grass caught fire and spread rapidly into the Indian graveyard. The men tried vainly to beat it out with wet burlap bags but the little houses that marked the graves were burned. Mr. Page told the men to fence the graveyard while they still knew where it was.

As Christmas drew near everybody was excited, decorating a Christmas tree in the little one room Pleasant View school. There were a few of the local residents, including one twenty-one-year-old young man who had never seen a decorated tree.

There would be a program and fruit and candy for all. But the excitement of the coming of Christmas was not confined to the children. The Breedings were excited because Ethel's parents, Mr. and Mrs. Milton Smith, and her sister Elsie were coming from Lawrence, Kansas, to spend Christmas with them.

On Christmas Eve, Ethel's sister, Elsie, took all the children to the Christmas program. The Breedings and Smiths stayed with Mr. Jones. His wife had grown steadily worse. She died on Christmas day.

There was no graveyard for white people in the vicinity, so she was laid to rest on a grassy knoll beside the lake. Mr. Breeding conducted the funeral. Lucy, Charles Page and all the farm folks attended.

The Creek Indians put little houses over their graves to keep the animals off.

12

Between the Horns
of a Cow

ETHEL BREEDING'S PARENTS HAD NOT BEEN FAVORABLY IMPRESSED when she wrote that she and her husband had given up all they had worked for to work on a farm for someone. The Smiths had come to see what was going on.

Mr. Breeding explained to them that he and Ethel were still dedicated to helping humanity. "We knew that Mr. Page had a compassionate heart that compelled him to help those in need," said Mr. Breeding, as he told of Mr. Page's dream of an industrial city and of his vow to help widows and orphans.

"But he doesn't only help widows and orphans," said Ethel. "Look at these needy old folks that he has sent out here. Their family couldn't or wouldn't be bothered with them, so Mr. Page took them." Ethel gestured with a nod toward two old men getting sticks of wood from the wood pile. Mrs. Webb was making her way back from the outhouse to her tent. "With no mother, we will also have the care of these five boys while Mr. Jones works on the farm," Mrs. Breeding added, "so you see we are still helping others."

"We liked the thought that Mr. Page had about giving families a chance to stay together from one generation to the other," said Mr. Breeding. "We feel that our children need a place to call home, where they can make lasting friends, and not have to leave and start all over every year or two."

"We like it here," said Eva, "but I wish there were some girls to play with. They're all boys." She wrinkled her nose.

"We found wild grapes and wild strawberries," said Harold. "Mamma made us some pies." Mr. Smith tossed the four-year-old into the air making him giggle. They had been taking a tour of the place as they talked.

"There is an atmosphere out here that I like too," said Mr. Smith. "I can't explain it, but I like it. I like Mr. Page too."

"I get the same feeling," Mrs. Smith admitted. "Elsie what do you think?"

"I like it." Elsie agreed. "It seems exciting to pioneer."

"Mr. Page thinks this place is paradise," said Mr. Breeding. "He thinks it's a cure-all for everything."

Ethel was enthusiastic. "He pays cash for land and the Indians who want to sell are flocking to him. He now owns hundreds of acres of land, sometimes buying sight unseen."

"If he buys land with a house on it," Mr. Breeding interposed, "he lets the family living in the house pay their rent in crops or livestock to feed his children and animals."

As the Smiths and the Breedings tramped through the woods, Mr. Breeding told them of Washington Irving's book *Tour On The Prairie*. The lofty trees that Irving had mentioned were now bare, with the exception of an occasional evergreen dispersed throughout the forest. The century-old grapevines that hung like cordage from the trees were draped with poison oak and ivy in lovely leafy patterns of rust, crimson and gold. Sumac, down below, peeked through the tangled mass of underbrush, displaying leaves in deeper duller shades of red. Crisp green mistletoe, with berries sparkling white, clung for sustenance to the uppermost branches of stately oak and blackjack trees. A light blanket of snow sparkled in the shafts of sunlight, filtering through the mass of tangled branches.

Elsie got poetic. "I can just see the moccasined Indians stealing silently through the trembling ferns and mosses in search of game to feed their hungry children," she said, with a far away look in her eyes.

"I got a spooky feeling when I first walked through these woods," said Mr. Breeding. "But things were green then and like a canopy overhead, with hardly a shaft of light filtering through the matted branches."

That afternoon the Smiths visited with Mrs. Webb, whose nose was half eaten away with cancer. She was a sprightly tart little old lady, with a sense of humor, and a quick wit. They spoke with others who were, as Mr. Breeding put it privately, "candidates for the poor farm."

Sunday evening the Smiths were impressed as they watched Mr. Page romp with the children. He got into a snowball fight with the boys, and got one to the side of his head. Later, they noted his genuine concern as he inquired of the elderly as to their health.

A workman came to report that he had found a hollow tree filled with honey. Mr. Page raised his eyebrows in surprise. A smile spread from under his shaggy mustache as he turned to Mr. Breeding.

"See, Cap, what we have here is a land of milk and honey. Who could beat that?" Then he turned to the man who had reported finding the honey. "Don't cut the tree now," he said. "The bees would die of starvation. Mark the tree and wait until spring when the fruit trees blossom. We'll then swap nectar to the bees for honey. That way we'll both benefit."

"I hear you buy some lands sight unseen," said Mr. Smith, when the man had gone.

"I bought a farm yesterday, and I need to go see what I've got," said Mr. Page. "While the women fix dinner, why don't you and Cap go with me? There's a family living there."

The three men got into the buck board and drove to the farm. As they pulled into the yard a man came out on the porch.

"Do you know who owns this land?" asked Mr. Page.

"I reckon old man Page bought it," said the man. "The son-of-a-bitch is buying up everything around here."

"I'm Charley Page," said Mr. Page, offering his hand. The man laughed and apologized.

On the way back Mr. Page asked Mr. Smith what line of business he was in.

"I'm a rough carpenter," said Mr. Smith.

"We could use you out here," said Mr. Page. "Why not stay?"

The women folk were excited when Mr. Smith told them that he had decided to stay. "Elsie and I could cook for the workmen," said Mrs. Smith. "Ethel has about all she can handle with her own family the five Jones boys and the old folks to care for."

"That sounds like a good idea," said Mr. Page.

The Smiths went home, sold their property and returned to the farm in early 1909.

Mr. Smith and Mr. Jones worked well together, building barns and fences.

The clearing of land had continued throughout winter. By spring about seventy-five acres had been cleared of trees and underbrush and was ready to be plowed.

But the new ground was more than a team of horses could handle. The teams of oxen were again called upon to do the job. Crops were planted. Then the spring rains came. The lowlands were flooded where no tiles had been lain to carry off the water. This made travelling back and forth with a wagon load of lumber even more difficult. With so much building going on, Mr. Breeding often drove one of the wagons. One day right after a hard rain, Mr. Breeding went after lumber and a few groceries.

He left the wagon, as always, at Arthur Antle's livery stable and then went by Mr. Page's office to report on the farm's progress. Mr. Page said that he had found another carpenter. Mr. Green was to ride out with Mr. Breeding.

"I hope we make it home before dark," said Mr. Breeding as Mr. Green climbed atop the load of lumber beside him. "There was a mudhole down the road that I barely got through this morning. With this load of lumber it will be even more difficult."

They made it through many mudholes, but one held them fast. It wasn't very wide, so the two men got out and, wading through the mud, carried all the lumber and groceries to the other side. The horses were then able to pull the lightened wagon out of the mud. They proceeded to reload everything and went on their way. Near a place called Bruner the road led over a sandbar for about one half mile down the center of the river bed. At the end of the sandbar was a portion of shallow river about twenty-five feet wide. The wagon bogged down in the mud and they were unable to get it out. Mr. Breeding unhooked the team and led them out of the water and tied them to a tree on dry land.

"Mr. Morgan lives about a mile straight down the road from here," said Mr. Breeding. You go and ask him to get his team and pull us out. I'll stay with the wagon." Mr. Breeding gave the lantern to Mr. Green.

When the light from the lantern was gone it was so dark that Mr. Breeding couldn't see anything around him. There wasn't a star in the sky. Not being able to see anything was so scary that even the distant hoot of a night owl brought tingles up his spine. He could hear the water lapping against the side of the wagon but he couldn't see whether the water was rising or not. Sitting atop the lumber, he couldn't reach far enough to feel how high the water was rising. He didn't think he was in one of those quick sand traps, but fear began to grip him as he sat rigidly upright on top of the lumber. He had the feeling that water moccasins were crawling into the wagon. He couldn't recall ever being so frightened, as he sat alone in the middle of the river on this   black night, miles away from any human being. All night he sat trembling with fear until he ached all over. It seemed the night would never end.

At last in dim light of the morning he saw a light coming toward him. When it got closer, he saw that it was Mr. Green with one of the farm's wagons.

Mr. Green explained that another man had borrowed Mr Morgan's team and that he had walked all the way to the springs for another wagon and team.

Mr. Green suggested that they carry the lumber to the wagon he had, and then both teams could pull the wagon out.

Mr. Breeding was too exhausted to bother with getting the wagon out of the mud. He had had enough of the whole thing. He took the groceries and waded across the mud, crawled into the waiting wagon and told Mr. Green to head for home. Somebody else could go pull the wagon out of the mud. He was going to bed.

Two farm hands went after the wagon load of lumber. Mr. Green laid down on a cot in the mens' tent and went to sleep.

The farm was finally coming to life with the cleared tracts of land, the school just across the road, the two houses finished, and many other buildings started. The peach orchard looked pretty with its not-too-straight rows of trees. Practically every tree planted had survived the winter. Mr. Page was proud of it all. He dropped by occasionally with a friend or someone he hoped to interest in moving out there.

In anticipation of a bumper crop of corn they built a large corn crib with a full upper floor to be used as a bunkhouse for the workmen who had to stay over night.

A "Spring House," with an upper and lower floor, was built into the side of the hill, covering one of the springs. Being built on the side of the hill gave both floors a ground level entrance. The upper floor would be the residence of the Smith family. The lower floor, with a spring running through it was turned into an ingenious refrigeration system. The cement slab floor had a trough for the spring to flow through that measured four feet wide and one foot deep. The spring flowed diagonally from the mouth of the spring at the northeast corner to the southwest corner, and out through a drain pipe, giving a continuous flow of cool spring water to cool the five gallon cans of milk and other perishable foods.

The porch roof of the Spring House doubled as a handy place to air the cleaned milk vessels.

The cream separator that had been used on the Breeding's front porch was taken to the Spring House. Mrs. Smith and Elsie were put in charge of the milk products.

Mr. Page had had a cement barn built on the north side of the Katy tracks the fall before. The spring rains flooded the barn and the cows had to be taken out of it. When the barn dried out a three inch layer of sand had been deposited on the floor. Mr. Page had carpenters to build a larger barn on higher ground south of the Katy tracks at the edge of the pecan and hazel nut grove.

In the month of April, of year 1909, Mrs. Breeding, who was four months pregnant, decided to go to town. Mr. Page's faithful old horse, Bill, was hitched to the buggy, and with her two children Eva and Harold beside her, Mrs. Breeding went on her way. On the return trip they passed Sias Buttons' son Jimmy. He had one end of a rope tied to his saddle horn and a bawling cow tied to the other end. She didn't like being passed by the buggy.

About a quarter of a mile on down the road, Mrs. Breeding saw a friend, Mrs. James Sanders in her front yard and stopped to talk to her. As they talked, Jimmy passed again with the cow. The cow looked sideways at them and bawled as she passed. Mrs. Breeding said good-bye to Mrs. Sanders and headed for home at a fast trot. They caught up with the boy and as they started to pass, the angry cow decided she'd had enough of this passing game, and made a sudden lunge at the horse. Bill dodged her, and the cow landed with her two front feet inside the front of the buggy. The two back wheels crumbled beneath her weight. Tossing her head in an effort to free herself, she caught Eva between her horns and swung her out of the buggy and into the muddy road. At the same time her horns scratched Harold's neck and jerked his cap from his head, flinging it into the mud.

Ethel scrambled out of the buggy and unfastened the harness from Bill, fearful that he might get excited and drag the buggy making the incident a worse catastrophe. Bill stood still faithful to his trust.

"Are you hurt?" asked Mrs. Breeding as she picked Eva up out of the mud. She was checking her over, when she heard a loud cry from Harold whom she thought had escaped injury. He had climbed out of the buggy and was sitting in the muddy road, scooping mud out of his cap with a small stick. His mother ran toward him. "What's the matter, Harold," she cried.

"That old cow throwed my Sunday cap in the mud," wailed Harold angrily.

Jimmy finally managed to get his cow's feet out of the wrecked buggy and went on his way. Mrs. Breeding led Bill over to a shade tree. She and the children sat down on the grass to wait for Mr. Breeding, who would pass with a load of lumber.

Frank Allspaugh and Clem Brown, a couple of men from the neighborhood came along, and seeing the wrecked buggy stopped. Clem stayed to explain to Mr. Breeding about the wrecked buggy, and Frank took Mrs. Breeding and the children home.

One day Mr. Page brought a goose out to the farm. Old Goose was given the run of the place. It hissed at Mr. Breeding every time he came near. Its persistence so enraged Mr. Breeding, one day he grabbed it by the neck and gave it a sling.

"That goose should be put into a pot," he grumbled.

"Aw Cap, that old goose doesn't mean any harm," said Mr. Page, hating the thoughts of roasting the old fellow.

"He doesn't bother anyone but me," complained Mr. Breeding. "I don't know why he has it in for me."

"Well now, Cap," said Mr. Page, "He's doing that in self defense. Geese are very intelligent creatures. He knows you don't like him and he's reacting to your attitude. I'll wager he'd like to be your friend if you'd just go half way."

Mr. Breeding thought it over. He certainly hadn't been friendly. He was curious to give it a try. He began to speak kindly to Old Goose, and in no time at all they were friends. On Sunday he told Mr. Page about it.

"That a goose is smarter than I," he said. "I learned a lesson from a goose."

About the first of May Mr. Page told Mr. Breeding that he had been made chairman of the Welfare Board.

"I hate to hear that," Mr. Breeding told Ethel. "He is the logical one for such a job, because he's such a caring person, but I'm afraid for him. He's too gullible when faced by human suffering. I don't know what more he could do for people, but likely as not, he will wind up carrying too many burdens."

It happened even sooner than Mr. Breeding expected.

The old goose.

13

Cross and Anchor

MR. BREEDING CAME IN FOR A LOAD OF LUMBER AND AS WAS HIS CUSTOM, left the wagon in Antle's Livery stable yard, behind the bank, and went up to see Mr. Page. He paused at the open door of Mr. Page's office. Mr. Page was studying some kind of ledger. His hat tip tilted to shade his eyes from the hanging light bulb over his desk. Mr. Breeding knocked lightly on the door facing.

Mr. Page sighed wearily and leaned back in his chair. "Come in, Cap," he said. Mr. Breeding sensed that something was wrong as he pulled up a chair.

"You seem worried, Mr. Page."

Mr. Page's brow furrowed. "I've got a problem, Cap." His voice seemed tired. "A very big problem," he added, rubbing the back of his aching neck. "I can't seem to solve it."

Mr. Breeding waited. He figured that if there was anything too big for Mr. Page to handle, it was certainly too big for him.

"It's the Cross and Anchor home for orphaned children. It seems the anchor didn't hold, and the poor little kids are bearing the cross. They are in deep trouble. Everything is mortgaged, even the beds the kids sleep in. The home is about to go into the hands of the receivers and I don't know what to do. There's little money in the welfare treasury and it will take a lot of it to bail them out."

"I don't know much about the children's home," said Mr. Breeding. "That was not within my jurisdiction. I know that Reverend Long was in charge and I didn't interfere with his business."

"Well, I suppose it started out all right, but it was a hit-and-miss proposition. They depended on donations for support. That's too risky. The lives of children are too precious to be left to chance. But I guess they did the only thing they knew to do at the time."

"I understand the land was given to them and the local carpenters and other workmen donated their services.

"But furniture and building materials were bought on credit. Then someone got the idea to build the kids a school, rather than bring them into town. They mortgaged the home to build the school and that on top of all their other debts did it. I am one of the regular monthly contributors and I guess I'm as guilty as the rest for assuming that everything was going well. I guess we should have checked it out."

"Checking things out is sometimes resented. Some feel that you are doubting their ability to do their job. I don't think you should feel guilty about that," said Mr. Breeding. "I'm sure your donations helped a lot."

Mr. Page looked down at the book. "The freewill donations are few, and dropping. As for monthly pledges, it seems I'm the only one still giving. I've decided that since I'm not too busy today, I ought to go out and talk to Mr. Long. I'd ask you to go with me but I know you have to get that lumber loaded and get home before night."

"I'll be on my way then," said Mr. Breeding. "I hope things can be worked out for the children." He started toward the door.

"Well, don't worry, Cap, I'll think of something to do."

As soon as Mr. Breeding had gone, Mr. Page told his secretary to tell Wayne where he had gone. He now left the drilling and tending to the wells to Wayne, and had a secretary to do the secretarial work. Mr. Page straightened his hat on his head, brushed the ashes from his suit, and left.

In the distance the home looked lonely and desolate. One lone tree was silhouetted against the sky behind the children's home, which sat in the center of a vast sea of prairie grass.

Mr. Page turned into the long lane that led down to the home. He could see children begin to gather in the front yard. As he reined his horses to a stop and got out, they rushed over and began to cluster around him as though there was excitement in just seeing another human.

"We saw you coming from away back there," said one child.

"What's your name?" asked another.

Mr. Page picked up a pretty little sad-eyed girl and turned to the girl who had asked the question.

"My name is Charles Page," he said. "Now you tell me what your name is."

Her blue eyes sparkled. "My name is Sarah Davis and that's my sister you're holding. Her name is Harriet." Sarah pointed to three other little girls. "She's my sister and she's my sister and she's my sister, and Asa is our brother." She tapped the head of a small boy standing beside her.

"That makes six of you," said Mr. Page.

Sarah, smiling, shook her head. "You made a mistake. There are eight of us. Joe didn't come. He didn't want grandpa to send us here. He's sixteen. We don't know where Jess is."

As she was talking, Harriet squirmed to get out of Mr. Page's arms. He set her down on the front porch and she ran into the arms of her older sister.

"She just got back from being adopted, and she's afraid you might take her away," the big sister explained, stroking the child's hair.

Mr. Page was shocked. "What do you mean? Are children adopted from this home?"

"Yes," said the girl. "Some people adopted Harriet, but she wouldn't stop crying so they brought her back. She just got back this morning."

"She cried because she wanted to be with us," said Sarah.

Mr. Page didn't know what to say. He had no idea that such things went on here. Another child spoke.

"She cried for three days and so did we. We're glad she's back." She hugged Harriet.

"That's Nancy." Sarah motioned toward the little girl who had just spoken. "Nancy's eight years old, but I'm ten." Sarah began pointing to her sisters according to their ages.

"Martha is twelve, I'm ten, Nancy is eight, Clarissa is six, Harriet is five, and Asa is four years old."

Mr. Page's thoughts were still on the subject of adoption. "You mentioned a brother Jess. You said you didn't know where he was. Did someone adopt him?"

"No," said Sarah. "When Mr. Long was taking us out here to the home, he had to stop in town for something and Jess got out of the wagon. He said he wasn't going to no home. When Mr. Long came back to the wagon and asked where Jess was, we told him. But he just went on. We haven't seen Jess since. He's fourteen."

"My little brother was adopted out," said a little girl in the crowd, "I don't have anybody but me and Pauline, now."

Mr Page's heart was in his throat as others told that they had lost little brothers and sisters through adoption. He hurried in to talk to Mr. Long.

Mr. Long had put another man in charge and Mr. Page was ushered into the man's office.

"I want to know by whose authority you have been tearing families apart?" Mr. Page asked. "All those poor little kids have is each other. This home was not set up as an adoption center. It was supposed to help children, not tear their hearts out."

"We had to do it," came the response. "There's not enough money coming in to feed them. We've borrowed and mortgaged everything just trying to keep food on the table. We thought we should try to find homes for those we could. The place is due to go into receivership right away and I don't know what we will do with the rest of these children. Older ones are harder to place."

Mr. Page wrote out a check and handed it to the man. "Try to hold the creditors off as long as you can. This should feed the children until I can figure out something." His voice was always lower when he was emotionally disturbed. He tried to keep the tears out of his voice. "These poor little helpless kids . . . Don't tear anymore families apart through adoption. I'll see that they are fed and what to do about the debts."

As he turned to go he said once more, "No more adoptions unless it's an only child. Do you understand?" The man nodded, and thanked him for the check. He left the man's office and went back outside.

The children rushed toward him as he stepped off the porch. One little girl took hold of his hand. He lifted her up and swung her around. She squealed with delight. They all began to squeal, "Swing me, swing me."

"Well, line up," he ordered, and even ten-year-old Sarah got into the line. He took them one by one and swung them around until each child had had two turns.

"Kids, I've got to go," he said, "I've got things to do." They clung to him until he got into his buckboard. He waved good-bye and drove down the lane. The good-bye cries followed him for awhile, but the scene of the hauntingly sad faces pressed hard into his mind and lay heavy in his heart.

He worked all week trying to get permanent help for the children. He decided to talk to the oilmen who frequented the lobby of the Robinson Hotel where he now lived.

Mr. Breeding had come in for lumber and when he stopped by Mr. Page's office he was told to go to the Robinson Hotel. Mr. Page had some workers to send to the farm with him. Mr. Breeding could hear Mr. Page's voice when he stepped in the door. He sat down, unnoticed, over to one side from where a group of men sat. Mr. Page was standing near the unlit fireplace. The men had lain aside their newspapers or cards and were listening to what Mr. Page was saying.

"Now if I could get ten good men to sign with me to see that these children are taken care of, we'd be all right. This time we need it in writing. No more dependence upon mere promises. Children need security."

He went on to explain the children's plight and waited for volunteers. All he got was advice.

"Charley, do you realize what you are asking?" said one. "No one wants to get involved in the lives of children. Those twenty-one orphans represent twenty-one sets of problems. I've got enough problems with my own children."

"But these poor little kids have no one to turn to," said Mr. Page. "Something has to be done quickly. I've talked to the man who holds the mortgage on the property and he's willing to give us a month longer. But he says he is going broke from so many loans and has to have the money or the property."

"Charley, this isn't something for individuals to handle," said a big man sitting in the corner. "Turn it over to the welfare, or a church or some such organizations."

"The welfare is new and not well organized. There is no money to help the children," said Mr. Page. "That's why I'm appealing to you."

The man waved his hand. "Don't ask me to do a foolhardy thing like that. I don't want the responsibility. A bunch of kids can give you problems like you never dreamed could happen."

"Think of all the doctor bills, the education, clothes, and food," said another. "Charley, let some organization worry about them. You get too stirred up about such things. There are organizations to take care of things like this. It's bigger than it looks right now. You'd better just get out of it. Don't get involved is my advice. I'm sure these others agree." He looked to the other men for agreement. Some picked up their papers and started to read.

Mr. Page knew the subject was closed as far as they were concerned. His temper flared. "How could anybody be so callous as to the needs of children. *Don't get involved!*" he thundered. "How can you not get involved? If you would drive out there and look into the sad faces of those half-starved children — *you'd get involved!* But you'd rather not be bothered." He threw his hat into the chair. "By God, I intend to save those children some way, if I have to do it by myself."

"Now be sensible, Charley," said one. "No one person can take on the responsibility of an orphanage. There's more to it than footing the bills. There will be disappointments, heartaches and frustrations . . . Think it over. You've never heard of one man taking the responsibility of an orphanage and you won't. It has never been done."

"Well, there's always a first!"

"And you're just fool enough to try it. You're a nice guy, Charley, but don't go doing anything so irrational. Let some organization worry about it."

"I hear this organization stuff. Now just who do you suggest? I've asked around already, and everybody is having hard times and can't handle it. But time is crucial for those kids. If there was something to gain by helping, you'd all chip in. But these kids . . ." His voice caught in his throat. "These kids . . . can't bring you cash dividends."

"Aw, come on, Charley, be fair. We don't mind a donation now and then, but it's this legal document you want us to sign that we object to. We don't want the responsibility of all those children around our necks for the rest of our lives."

"Well, if you don't mind donations, why didn't you pay your pledges? If you had, these children wouldn't be in this mess. Promises aren't good enough. They don't pay grocery bills. If I'm willing to take the risk, by God, some of the rest of you ought to be. These are helpless little half-starved kids that we're talking about!" He grabbed his hat and stalked across the lobby. "Well keep your damn money. I don't need it. I'll see that those kids get fed if I have to do it alone."

As he went out the door, Mr. Breeding heard one of them say, "He'll do it if it kills him. And it probably will."

Mr. Breeding quietly got up out of his chair and left. Mr. Page was walking rapidly down the street. A couple of wagons rounded the corner in front of Mr. Breeding. By the time they had gone, Mr. Page was nowhere in sight. Mr. Breeding hadn't yet loaded the lumber he had come for, so he went on about his business so he would be home in time for supper.

When he got home he was surprised to see Mr. Page's buckboard on the road beside his house. Mr. Page sat on the porch steps, deep in thought. When Mr. Breeding rode up, two of the workmen took over the unloading of the wagon.

Mrs. Breeding came out on the porch and called the two men to supper, when she heard Mr. Breeding's voice. Eva and Harold were playing in the yard. "Go wash your face and hands," said Mrs. Breeding as the two children brushed past her in the doorway.

"Cap," said Mr. Page, "I saw you in the lobby, but I was angry when I left and didn't want to talk to anybody. I've worked all day trying to get somebody to help with those poor little kids but I haven't been able to get anybody to help me. How people can be so calloused I don't know." The two men waited until the children finished with the wash pans, then they washed their faces and hands.

The children waited with hands folded at the table until the men were seated, and their father returned thanks.

Mrs. Breeding passed the bowls and platters to Mr. Page first, then waited on Harold's plate. Eva liked doing things for herself.

"I've decided," said Mr. Page, "to take over the responsibility of those kids myself."

This didn't surprise Mr. Breeding. It just made him feel bad that so much always fell into the lap of this man, just because he cared about people. So now he was going to take the whole responsibility of an orphanage. This would surely be goodbye to his dream. Mr. Page was telling of his experience with the children, as he picked at his food.

"I have to do something about the mortgage before the month is out."

"Do you plan to pay the mortgages?" asked Mr. Breeding.

"No. I'll pay for the furniture, but I don't want the rest. On the way out here I thought it all out, Cap. I thought of all those trees we cut down and that those little kids have only one measly shade tree. There is nothing for them to look at for miles around, but grass, grass, grass. It must be hot there in the summer, and desolate in winter. Kids need trees to play under, to climb and to hang swings from. What do you think about me bringing them out here?"

Mr. and Mrs. Breeding looked at each other in shock.

Where would we put twenty-one children out here? thought Mr. Breeding. He knew that Mr. Page loved the land and thought it was some sort of paradise. But not for children. Most of the water had been drained from the low land, but much of it still flooded when it rained. When it was dry and windy, the sand blew into everything, and practically the whole camp was on the side of a hill. Tables and cook stoves had to be propped up on one side to make them level. But Mr. Page's description of the place was quite different.

"They would love it out here. Look at the trees."

And we're cutting them down as fast as we can, thought Mr. Breeding.

"They'll be next door to a school. They can swim in the pools, fish in the lake, hike over the hills. They can breathe God's good country air . . ."

Mr. Page noticed the shocked look on the Breedings' faces. He swallowed hard. "Cap, wait until you see those kids. I've got to do what I can for them . . . but I'll need you folks to help me. I don't know anything else to do. I can't just turn my back and pretend they don't exist."

"Nor can I," said Mr. Breeding, "and I'm sure my wife feels the same." Mr. Page looked at Mrs. Breeding. She smiled.

Mr. Page looked as though a heavy load had just slid from his shoulders. He held out his hand. Mr. and Mrs. Breeding shook his hand on it and it was agreed.

"Get those carpenters busy," said Mr. Page, getting excited. "We only have a month to get things ready for them. They can use the dining cottage we were building. All they'll need is a place to sleep. They have the whole outdoors to play in. It shouldn't take long to build four or five three-room sleeping cottages. When we get a proper home for them built, the cottages will come in handy for other uses."

Mr. Page was smiling happily as he got into his buckboard. He put up his hand as a good-bye wave and called to Mr. Breeding. "It's going to be all right, Cap. You'll love those kids."

Arthur Antle's stables — Arthur kept Mr. Page's horses.

14

Buttermilk Bribe

"Cap, I'll try again to see if I can't get the Katy to stop here to give you transportation," said Mr. Page.

A few days later Mr. Breeding got word that Mr. Page had fixed it with the railroad, and that they agreed to make a flag stop at the springs, beginning immediately.

Mr. Breeding needed to go to town for some supplies so he decided to go by train to test it. When the train was due he straddled the rails, held out his left arm and waved a lantern with his right hand, just as the colored section hands had instructed. It worked! The train came to a screeching halt. Mr. Breeding set the lantern down and got on board.

When the conductor learned he had stopped the train for no big emergency, he upbraided Mr. Breeding. Mr. Breeding explained that he had received notification that trains would make a flag stop at the springs.

"Well I received no such notification!" snapped the conductor. "But since you are on the train we're not stopping again to put you off. But you will pay the full fare from Wekiwa to Tulsa."

When Mr. Page heard about the Katy incident he was angry. He again talked to the officials and they said they would take care of it. But the next time, Mr. Breeding walked to Tulsa rather than to unsettle the conductor. However, his business took him longer than he had anticipated. He was very tired and it had started to rain. He decided to go back by train.

The train was not known for keeping a good schedule. The officials not only stopped to shoot quail and other wild game, when it was pecan picking time, they brazenly stopped the train to gather pecans and hazel nuts from Mr. Page's pecan grove, while still refusing to stop for passengers at the spring.

When the train pulled in, it didn't stop at the pre-determined place it was supposed to. Mr. Breeding had to walk, carry his burlap bag of supplies in the rain, down beside the tracks past a long string of freight cars to the caboose. He was the only passenger. As he sat shivering in his wet clothes, the conductor swung onto the caboose. He stopped and looked at Mr. Breeding.

"Where are you going?" he asked tartly.

"To the springs," said Mr. Breeding. He explained that Mr. Page had made the arrangements with higher officials for a flag stop at the springs. The conductor glared at him.

"I received no such notification," he snapped. "And this train is not stopping until we get to the water stop at Wekiwa!" With that he left Mr. Breeding alone to worry about his predicament.

Mr. Breeding was very discouraged and exhausted. His feet hurt and his bones ached from the chilling walk in the rain. He had been on his feet all day after walking the seven miles to town, and now he must walk the four miles back from Wekiwa which he had never done before. He had no lantern and had heard of the treacherous terrain, the rattle snakes and wild animals. When his pregnant wife saw the last train pass the springs, she was going to worry.

Mr. Breeding straightened his back against the hard bench and looked up. In desperation he said out loud, "Lord, you can take care of this situation. You could break this train in two if you wanted to."

At that moment something snapped. The train rolled to a stop. Mr. Breeding jumped to his feet. Where were they? He looked out into the night. The train had stopped at the springs. He hurried off the train, and started up the hill, thanking God as he went.

"One of these days I'll build my own railroad out here," vowed Mr. Page later. "And if I ever get the chance I'll make them pay for all the trouble they have given my people. But as for now, I'll just have to keep trying to get them to cooperate."

Mr. Page came to the farm to help out, every chance he got. One day as he was eating dinner with the workmen he got the idea that if the train officials knew the fine people on the farm, they might feel a little more accommodating. He invited the conductor and the train engineer to dinner. He introduced them to everyone and dinner was served. They all sat down to a table of plenty. Mr. Breeding returned thanks, and everybody started eating. The conversation was congenial and the men seemed to be enjoying themselves. Mr. Page, who was partial to fresh churned buttermilk, noticed that they were too. They refilled their glasses more than once. He got an idea.

He asked, "Did you ever taste finer buttermilk?"

"Can't say as I ever have," said one, and a nod came from the other man, whose mouth was too full to talk.

"I'll tell you what we'll do," said Mr. Page. "You fellows make a run past here everyday at about eleven o'clock, so why don't you stop and Mrs. Smith will give you a quart of buttermilk for your lunch."

"Oh that would be nice," said the engineer. The conductor smacked his lips and nodded in agreement.

And so each day, rain or shine, busy or not, Mrs. Smith or Elsie stood at the railroad tracks with a quart of buttermilk for the men. After about three weeks of giving them buttermilk they still refused to make a flag stop at the springs. So Mr. Page ordered the buttermilk-bribe to cease.

The little Pleasant View School. Built in 1908.

PHOTO TAKEN BY MRS. BREEDING JUST AFTER COMPLETION.

House built for the Breedings in 1908.

15

A Wagon Load of Orphans

Mr. Page had expressed a desire for the children to be sent out to the farm on his birthday, as his birthday gift to humanity. So, on June 2, 1909, four wagons were sent to the Cross And Anchor home. The children were loaded into one wagon with Mr. Breeding. The furniture and housewares was loaded into the other wagons. Mrs. Coakley, the children's matron, with her own two small children, seated herself in the seat beside Mr. Breeding.

The caravan of happy, squealing children came through Tulsa. Mr. Page had told Mr. Breeding to stop on their way through town, that he had a man that he was sending out to the farm. When they stopped, the men with the wagon loads of furniture went on ahead so that they could get the furniture in place sooner.

Mr. Breeding didn't need to go up to his office to get Mr. Page. He heard their voices through the open window, and was on his way down when Mr. Breeding met him. With him was a heavy-set elderly man whom he introduced as Governor Williams.

"The Governor doesn't want a handout," explained Mr. Page. "He wants a job. He says he's a good gardener, so put him over the gardens and let the boys help him. They'll need something to do until school starts. A little work is good for them. Mrs. Coakley can give the girls chores too. Maybe some can help with the little ones or the sick folks out there."

By the time they got outside where the children were, a crowd had gathered. When the children saw them coming they squealed and yelled hello to him.

"How are my kids?" he asked, and got a squealing response.

"Are we your kids now?" asked one little girl.

"You bet," Mr. Page assured her. "And no one will ever again separate one of you from a little brother or sister. You're gonna like it out on my farm. There are lots of trees for swings, and shade. You'll have a real good time."

Bystanders shook their heads. What was Charley up to now?

"You're crazy, Charley. You can't take those kids out to that God forsaken wilderness of yours. It's seven miles from anywhere and there isn't even a decent road to the place," said one bystander. "What if one of them gets sick?"

"I'd get a doctor out there if they got sick," said Mr. Page. "And as to a road, I'll make a decent road to them."

"Listen to the man. He's going to make seven miles of road at his own expense?" They shook their heads.

"Why are you doing this?" asked another. "Are you laying your ground work for some political office and using the children as an attention getter?"

Mr. Page faced the man squarely. His jaw muscles jerked in anger. "Don't judge us all by yourself," he said. "Doing something for somebody else just because it's the right thing to do makes me sleep better at night. You should have shown concern when they needed you. They don't need you now, and neither do I." He turned on his heel and, waving good-bye to the children, went into the bank building and up to his office.

Governor Williams crawled into the wagon. The children scooted over, making a place for him where he could lean back against the wagon seat. Amid the squeals and laughter, the wagon wound its way through town and headed west.

Mr. Breeding asked Governor Williams what state he had governed. "None," said Mr. P.T. Williams. Then he told Mr. Breeding and the children how he came by the title, 'Governor,' as he pulled his honorable discharge papers from a bag that he was carrying. They were from company K.I.V.S. Cavalry with Indian wars.

"In the early days in Kansas," he said, "There was strong contention between Lecompton and Kansas City regarding the establishment of a territorial capital. A man in Lecompton was demanding recognition for himself as Governor of Lecompton. He was causing quite a stir and disrupting procedures. A party of soldiers was ordered to find him and arrest him. We found him in a dugout, which served as his office and Governor's mansion. He was armed," said Mr. Williams, "But I surprised him. In a quick move I threw my arms around him, pinning his arms to his side. He dropped the gun in the scramble and the men placed him under arrest. As they took him out, I sat down at his desk. The other men saluted me and called me Governor. And that's what they persist in calling me."

Mr. Williams told the children stories of his soldiering days, keeping them captivated all the way to the springs. When they got there the men were putting the beds together and placing them in the houses. There had only been time to build two additional cottages. The Jones house had been scrubbed, fumigated and aired. Mr. Jones was moved into the bunk house with the other workmen, and his boys added to the group of children from the orphanage, along with Calvin Morey, who had come a little earlier. Counting the five Jones boys, Mrs. Coakley's two children, the two Breeding children and Calvin Morey, there were now thirty children on the farm, and it seemed like more, as they ran around exploring.

It was late afternoon when they got there, and the children were starved. While the men set up the furniture in the three houses, the children washed up for dinner.

Mr. Lot, a colored chef, had been sent out earlier to cook for the children, who were to eat in the dining room. He had a bountiful meal cooked and the children ate heartily.

Each house had three rooms. Mrs. Coakley and her two children occupied one room in the house for the under school age children. The children from school age up would occupy the other two cabins, one for the girls and one for the boys. However, there were only nine full-sized beds. The children had been sleeping three and four in a bed at the Cross and Anchor Home, and until more beds could be sent out, they would have to continue to do so.

One room of the house was to be the private bedroom of the matron in charge of the children. Two rooms would hold beds and dressers necessary for the children. The three little Jones boys were moved to the cottage with the children their age, and Mr. Williams and the older boys of the group were put in the Jones familys' tent.

That evening Mr. Page drove out to see the children. They recognized his buckboard and started down the lane to meet him. He stopped to let them hop aboard. As many as could, piled in. The others ran along behind as they made their way to the springs.

The folks at the top of the hill watched as the children clung to Mr. Page. "Are we really yours?" asked one little girl, catching hold of Mr. Page's sleeve and looking up at him.

"You sure are. You can ask Cap, here," said Mr. Page, as they reached the top of the hill.

"Are you our daddy now?" asked another child.

Mr. Page looked surprised. He thought for a moment. "Well, you belong to me and I belong to you, so I suppose you could say that I am."

Squeals of joy arose. "Daddy Page, Daddy Page," they cried. Mr. Page looked at Mr. Breeding and smiled. Mr. Breeding saw something in his eyes that he had never seen before. It was a mixture of embarrassment and joy.

Mr. Page grabbed a child by each hand and started marching up and down the hill singing "Oh The Moon Shines Tonight On Pretty Red Wing." Children took turns with him holding their hands, marching up and down the hill, singing over and over again, the old song, "Pretty Red Wing."

It was a moon-lit night and the people on the hill pulled chairs out of their tents, and sat watching. Even the Breeding children were running back and forth with the crowd, yelling, "Daddy Page, Daddy Page, Daddy Page."

"No father could be prouder of his children," said Mr. Breeding. "I've never seen him so happy."

At nine o'clock Mrs. Coakley called attention to the time, saying that the younger ones should go to bed.

"What time is it?" asked Mr. Page, pulling his watch from his pocket. "I didn't realize it was so late." He got into his buckboard and, waving goodbye to the children, he rode through the trees and out of sight. The sound of his voice could still be heard, singing, "Oh the moon shines tonight on pretty Red Wing."

From that day forward the children all called him Daddy Page, and he referred to them as his kids.

It was a few days later that Jess Davis came out to the farm. Mr. Page had found him working as a dishwasher in one of the restaurants downtown. He had been sleeping on a cot in the kitchen. A short time later Mr. Page also brought Joe, the sixteen-year-old Davis boy, out to the farm to be united with his brothers and sisters.

But Mr. Page was only able to get one or two of the children back from adoptive parents. They had been legally adopted, and no amount of money could pursuade the new parents that the child was better off with brothers and sisters.

Later, Mr. Page told Mr. Breeding that the townspeople had changed the name of his project from a "Fool's Enterprise," to "Charles Page's Folly." They both laughed.

Mr. Page put Mr. Breeding in charge of the older boys. "Give them all chores to do, then offer jobs for pay to those who want to earn a little money," he said. "It's good for kids to have responsibilities."

Grandpa Williams was active despite his age and weight. He was seventy-five years old and weighed two hundred pounds. But he was a very good gardener. The boys were assigned to work in the gardens with him. They liked him a lot and started calling him Grandpa Williams. He had a way with boys and told them many interesting stories.

Mrs. Webb was a fiesty, little old lady, in spite of the cancer on her nose. She was always saying something sassy, or clever, and kept the girls laughing. They thought she was fun, and started calling her Grandma Webb.

Mrs. Coakley had been hired as temporary matron over the girls until Mr. Page found a suitable woman. It had to be somebody special. His mother had always provided a room for the village school teacher, hoping her children might benefit from her presence. He decided that he would find someone who was educated, and one who could teach the girls the social graces that would fit them for any walk in life. He found such a woman through Dr. Seth Gordon, the president of Kendal College.

"Miss Newhouse happens to be a guest in my home at present," said Dr. Gordon. "I don't know whether she would be interested, but she is just the one for the job. She is a sophisticated lady from the east. She doesn't need the money, but perhaps would enjoy the challenge. I'll talk to her."

Miss Newhouse was told of the crude surroundings and of Mr. Page's plans to build the children a proper home. She accepted the position. She considered it her Christian duty to do what she could for the "dear little orphaned girls." She would teach them the social graces they might have received in a "Finishing School."

When Miss Newhouse stepped from the buggy dressed in fine linens, white gloves, large organdy hat, and carrying a small lace parasol, Mrs. Webb stepped back behind a tent flap and started giggling. "Who does Miss "Outhouse" think she is with all that high flutin' get up?" she whispered, making the girls giggle. Unfortunately, it was never explained to the girls what Miss Newhouse had come to do for them.

Twenty-one orphans were hauled to the wilderness swamp.

Charles Page

October 20, 1901 — Mr. and Mrs. Brinton Flint Breeding on their wedding day.

Six yoke of oxen and the shaker man pulling up stumps to plow and plant the first little peach orchard, 1908.

1909. *The under school aged children in the nursery cottage with matrons, Mrs. Slack and Mrs. Coppage. Two older girls stand in the doorway (one is Martha Davis).*

One of the buildings in the park where flood victims stayed.

The Sand Springs Park in 1921. Note the dam spillway and the railroad tracks past the lake.

*Galloway's sand stone lions guard the entrance
to the Sand Springs Park.*

Scenes from the park.

A group of early day Home children.

1912. *Sand Springs first jail.*

Left: *Outdoor cooking. Note the roller towel on the clothesline for the children to dry their hands on and the orange crate table beside the cook stove.* Above: *Jim, Mr. Page's beloved German Shepherd.* Below: *The home is completed and the children move in March 1910. To the right, in the back: Grandpa Williams, Joe Davis, Mr. Jones, and Mr. Breeding.*

Mr. Page's first train. It made its first run May 29, 1911. This picture was taken in 1920 when the train ran on a spur to Shell Creek carrying cement, sand, and crushed rock and steel for building the dam. Pictured here are: Frank Stenson, Leonard Nolan, Harold Fox, George Dale, and Jay Jones.

Mr. Page's electric train. It had a sweet sounding bell.

These trailer cars were hooked to the powered cars during the summer to accommodate the many passengers to the park.

Mr. Houston and Mr. Edgar Stevens are pictured on the left.

Billy Bruner

1912. *Sand Springs' first dairy company.*

1916. Back row: *Charles Page, Miss Maud Darrow and Mrs. Mary McClain.*
Front row L-R: *Some of the older girls: Harriett Davis, Alma Eldridge, Anna Moore, Elizabeth Moore, Myrtle Durham, Ruby Clapper, Effie Clapper, Geneva Rogers, Ruth Johnson and Bertha Casey.*

1911. Mr. Page put in a cotton gin. This picture was taken next year after assuring the farmers that if they planted cotton he would guarantee a market for it. Mr. Page had these wagons photographed to show a buyer that he could furnish all the cotton they wanted. Note Mr. Page in the dark suit standing proudly beside one of the wagons.

A Casual picture of Charles Page.

Sand Springs Hospital built in 1914.

Exterior of the green house before the brick office was added.

Charles Page with his kids —
Joan Edger, Margaret Gosnell, Martha Stone, Raymond Stamps, and Josephine Dobbs.

The original Widows' Colony

Circa 1912. *Inside the Sand Springs greenhouse when it had glass walls and ceiling.*

Galloway and one of his carvings done for the 1915 San Francisco World's Fair. Most of his other pieces were destroyed by fire.

Galloway's manual training shop.

Mr. Page's dog, Jim, poses with children at the Shellcreek Club House. **Left to right front row:** *Elma Endicott, Josephine Dobbs, Mable Raymor, Thelma Hartly, Cecelia Kyler, Winnie Harris, Opal Bennefield, Madge Raymor, Bess Chambers (behind Madge).* **Second row:** *Hattie May Stone, Maudie Chance, unknown, Ellen Mcculla, Alma McGahey, Augusta Dobbs, Othene Endicott, Nancy Nipps, Johnny Huddler, Zelma Garoutte.* **Back row:** *Violet Chambers, Joan Edger, Pauline Ritchey, Frieda Lewis, Irene Nichols, Sarah Harris, Mary Barnett, Martha Stone.*

Coin Harvey's vacation lodge, Monte Ne, Arkansas.

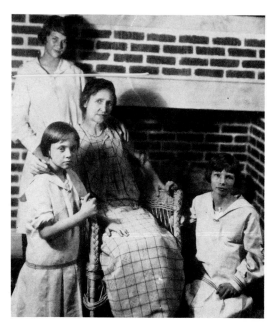

1925 or 1926. L-R: *Ellen McCullah, Winnie Harris, Miss Lindsay and Opal Bennefield Clark.*

111

1921. *Home children, taken on Sunday, while we were all in our Sunday best.*

About 1926. *Charles Page, his daughter Mary on his left and most of his Kids. There were 105 at the time and 110 at the time of his death.*

1918. *Mr. Page thought of everything to make his babies happy in their new penthouse nursery atop the new children's Home.*

16

Getting Organized

MISS NEWHOUSE WAS EFFICIENT IN GETTING THINGS BETTER ORGA-
nized. "Older children should be separated from younger ones," she said,
and immediately started grouping them according to age. All under-school-
age children were considered "babies." The girls from ages six to twelve,
were listed as "little girls." Those thirteen and fourteen were called the older
little girls, the fifteen and sixteen year old girls were dubbed "Middle sized"
girls. Over sixteen were "older girls." This method of separation made it
easier to address an age group as to responsibilities, or privileges.

More furniture was purchased to add to what they already had, so that
there were only two children to each full sized bed.

Everybody who was able was given some chore or responsibility. Having
their own duties gave them a sense of being needed, a pride of accomplish-
ment and feeling of belonging. It also kept children occupied and out of
mischief.

"Give the older boys and girls a job where they can earn a salary," Mr. Page
had said, remembering his own pride in having money to jingle in his pockets;
money that he had earned.

"Girls need spending money too, so let them earn a wage helping with the
canning of our food for the winter," said Mr. Page.

Some of the children in the home had living mothers. Mr. Page gave them
jobs. In that way the women could be near their children and still have a job.

Mrs. Coppage was hired to give the girls piano lessons. A piano was sent
out from Tulsa and placed in the storeroom of the store.

The children only had about three changes of clothing each. A seamstress
was sent out from Tulsa with bolts of material and a sewing machine, to see
that each child had new clothes before school began.

Mr. Lot, a fine looking intelligent black man who was sent out to cook for
the children had a good voice and he liked to sing. The children started
hanging around in the kitchen to hear him sing while he worked. He liked an
audience and began telling them stories and the crowd got bigger. It wasn't
long before he was forgetting that he was a cook, not a story teller. The
children were run out of the kitchen so he could get the meals on time.
However, they hung at the windows to listen to him sing.

Miss Newhouse tried teaching the children to call Mr. Lot "Chef."

"Daddy Page calls him 'Lot,'" said one of the girls. Miss Newhouse raised her eyebrows, and said no more about it. So the children continued calling him Lot. When she heard one of them calling the others "kids," she corrected them.

"Kids are goats," she said. "Don't call each other kids."

"Daddy Page calls us his kids," they quipped.

"So he does," said Miss Newhouse in despair.

Miss Newhouse's attempts to teach her girls the art of social graces were received with much grumbling. She sat at the older girls' table and soon managed a semblance of order, but never without complaints. However, she did manage to get them to line up when the bell rang for dinner, march to the table and stand behind their chairs until "grace" was said. She taught them the short prayer that would still be said, long after she was gone.

"God is great and God is good. And we thank Him for this food. By His hands we all are fed. Give us Lord, our daily bread."

Each girl, in turn, was to take her place at the head of the table. She then carved the meat and served the plates, passing them on to the other girls. No one was to take a bite until all were served. This seemed an unnecessary delay to a bunch of hungry children.

In an attempt to stop some of the chatter and their gobbling down of food, Miss Newhouse made a rule that when the first girl at the table had finished eating, the meal was over for everyone else at the table. The girls caught on, and made sure that the fast eaters slowed down. But Miss Newhouse was never able to quiet their talking at the table.

She also taught the children the bedtime prayer, "Now I lay me down to sleep. I pray the Lord my soul to keep. If I should die before I wake, I pray Thee Lord my soul to take."

One morning, Mr. Breeding was working out on the hill when an Indian woman came to him leading a little white boy, four or five years old. Although she couldn't speak English, she made it plain that she wanted to give him the child.

"Burl, Burl," was all that Mr. Breeding could understand. She turned and left the child. Mr. Breeding went into Tulsa for a load of lumber the next day and took Burl with him, to ask Mr. Page what to do about him.

"Well, the child has been abandoned and we don't know his name, so go get him a birth certificate. Give him a birth date and a name."

Mr. Breeding named the boy Burl Carter, and determined his age to be five years.

Mr. Page continued to send needy people out to the farm. It was cheaper than paying their rent in town. With so many services needed for the children, he hired the able bodied ones in one capacity or another to care for the children. Some were hired to do washing, ironing, sewing, or what ever was needed. Ladies were bivouacked in tents with a wooden floor. Those able to cook for themselves had a little wood cook stove either inside the tent or outside, depending on the weather.

There were now many tents on the hill, with children everywhere, like a hill of ants, and still the people continued to come. They were mostly old folks, and as some of the men remarked, "candidates for the poor farm." Mr. Smith said it looked like a gypsy camp.

"Either name would be appropriate," said Mr. Breeding, "but to Mr. Page, this place is 'Paradise.'"

Mr. Page now had hundreds of acres of land but he wanted his dependents together, to be looked after.

Mr. Page was a bit of a romantic. A young couple by the name of Ruebsan came to him wanting to work. "Cap," said Mr. Page, "the couple seemed so very much in love, that I'm setting up a chicken farm and I'm going to let Ruebsan run it."

1909. Workmen's dining hall and kitchen being painted inside. After the 21 orphans came, the children got the dining hall. Note the slope of the hill.

17

Fifty Seven Head of Goats

Mrs. Mabel Ruebsan worked for a short while as a matron, then started running the store. However, it was a job keeping the store stocked with everything having to be brought in by wagon. All efforts seemed to fail in getting the Katy to make a stop at the springs. One day Mr. Breeding was unloading supplies from the wagon when he saw Mr. Page coming. He paused and waited.

"Cap I finally got it," said Mr. Page waving some papers in his hand. "I finally got a permit for the Katy to stop at the springs. I went to the top man," said Mr. Page. "I explained to the corporation commissioner that the Katy railway stood to make a lot of money, with all the business I could give them. I told them that I was building a children's home as soon as I could get enough materials out here, and that I also intended to build an industrial town. That got him interested. I had the contract already drawn up, and all he had to do was sign it." Mr. Page chuckled. "They don't know it but I fixed the Katy for being so inconsiderate of my folks out here. In the contract I had a clause that if at any time their tracks crossed another track on raised ground onto my land they would have to pay me for every foot they traveled on my land. You see cap, I intend to have my own railroad one of these days, and I'll see that there is raised track where they have to cross my land."

"Did they sign the contract?"

"Oh sure. The commissioner grinned when he saw the clause in the contract. He said what is this in here for. There are no other railroads on your land, and it's all level ground. He figured I was just a stupid bumpkin that didn't know how to draw up a contract and that I had added a lot of nonsense to it. His mind was on all the money he was going to make off me."

Mr. Page got out of the buckboard and walked to the top of the hill. "Cap," he said, "I'll send some men out to run a spur to the top of the hill to where our new children's home is to be built." He showed Mr. Breeding where he wanted it.

"The engineer will run the car loads of building supplies off onto the spur and leave them for us to unload. They will get the empty box car later, as they bring the next load."

Mr. Page stopped and surveyed his surroundings. He spread his arms wide. "Cap, now we can get things done a lot faster," he said, smiling broadly from beneath his shaggy mustache.

But things didn't go faster. He was faced with a man shortage. The depression had been over for a few months and jobs were becoming plentiful.

The 1907-1909 depression was proclaimed the shortest depression in history. President Theodore Roosevelt was proving to be a man of his word. He had predicted a short depression. He had also stated that banks had gone broke because of mismanagement and bad business practices. He urged people who had money to spend it.

"To make money you have to spend money," he declared.

The end of the depression was good news and bad news for Mr. Page. Many of his workers who lived in Tulsa found jobs in town for higher pay than they got for farm labor.

However, the farm was looking good. The five acre orchard had leafed out, with few trees lost over the winter. The crops were in good shape and the garden was supplying fresh vegetables for the table.

Andy Stokes, the grocery store owner whom Mr. Page traded with, also dealt in livestock. He had sold Mr. Page some cows, and one day he came to Mr. Page's office. Andy had fifty-seven head of goats and he wanted to know if Mr. Page was interested in buying some goats for his farm.

"I know very little about goats," said Mr. Page. "What are they good for?"

"Oh," said Andy, "they give richer milk than cows do. It would be good for your sick folks and your kids too, and goats are smart. They can be trained to pull a cart for light loads. They are meat for the table and you don't have to feed them. They'll eat anything. Even paper or rags. Their favorite food is weeds and thistles. They'll clear that underbrush right out for you."

"Well now, that sounds like cheap labor," said Mr. Page with a chuckle. He bought all fifty-seven head of them. Andy got a helper and herded them out to the farm that very evening. There was no place to put them except in the pig pen. A smaller pen for them could be fixed later.

Everyone was awakened early the next morning by the bleating of goats. Goats were everywhere. They had climbed the corner braces of the fence. Some had hung themselves by the horns trying to get over the fence. The five acre orchard that had looked so promising was next to the hog pen. The goats had stripped the bark off many of the trees, chewed the top out of some and trampled others.

Even the children tried to help get the goats back into the pen. A pack of neighboring dogs joined the chase. The dogs caught two of the goats and were tearing the bleating goats to pieces. Mr. Breeding fought in vain to beat the dogs off but there were too many of them. It happened so fast that Mr. Breeding had no time to go for his gun until it was over and the dogs ran away.

The goats continued to be a nuisance. Mr. Page said to get rid of them by eating them, but neither the children or the men like the meat.

"Give them to anybody who will take them," said Mr. Page. They finally wound up paying someone to take them.

The Spring House. Mr. Smith, Mr. Breeding and Mr. Page.
Note the sled used to haul water barrels up the hill.

18

Spare the Rod and Spoil the Child

MR. BREEDING HAD GIVEN THE OLDER BOYS THE JOB OF CLEARING WEEDS and brush from the land, but he wasn't getting much work out of them. As soon as he left to check on other projects, they would stop working to play until they saw him coming. One day he called them together.

"Boys," he said "I know that you need time to play, but you were hired to work. I'll tell you what I'm gonna do. I'm putting you on the honor system. I'll mark off a space that each of you must clear for your day's work if you want to be paid. You can help each other, or do it anyway you want, just so you get it done. When you have cleared your alloted space, you are free to go fishing, swimming, or whatever you want, so long as you don't get into trouble."

This arrangement pleased the boys. Each morning they found their names written on trees where the bark had been skinned off. Within the boundary of four trees bearing their names they were to clear the land and pile the weeds and brush to be burned.

The boys flew into their work and finished it with such amazing speed, that Mr. Breeding thought maybe he wasn't giving them enough to do. Each day he increased the size of the plot, and each day they completed the job quickly, and still found time to play.

One day a man named George Wright came out, riding Mr. Page's horse, Buster. He introduced himself and said he just came to look around. He and Mr. Breeding talked. He told of hunting deer in the woods around the farm in years past. About a week later he came back and moved into a little house on a hill just east of the camp.

On Sunday, when Mr. Page and his wife came out, Mr. Page said, "Cap, I've been getting reports that you aren't watching the boys as closely as you should. They've been seen running a hand-car up and down the tracks."

Mr. Breeding was embarrassed that he had been seen as being derelict in his job. When the Pages had gone home he told his wife that Mr. Page had sent a spy to check on him.

"I was suspicious of George Wright the day he rode Mr. Page's horse out here and started poking around looking everything over," he said. "It doesn't make you feel good when you work for your room and board and not be trusted." Then he told Ethel what had happened.

The colored fellows who work for the Katy railroad had a small four-wheeled hand operated car which they lifted onto the railroad tracks when they needed to do repairs. When not in use they lifted the hand car off and left it beside the tracks. The boys coming along saw the hand car and decided to take a ride up and down the tracks. They had been doing it for days.

Mr. Breeding cut some switches and called the boys into the barn. "Boys," he said, "you've been seen riding up and down the rails for days. You could have been killed. I'm going to have to punish you. The Bible says, 'By your stripes are ye healed,' I'm going to put some stripes on your back to remind you that when you do wrong you have to pay the consequences. It's going to hurt, but not as bad as it would have if you had been hit by a train.

"You didn't tell us we couldn't play with the hand car," said Luther Nolan.

"So we didn't disobey," said Jess Davis. "The hand-car was just layin' there. You told us we could go fishing or whatever we wanted to do, so we decided to take a ride."

"I told you to do whatever you wanted to do so long as you didn't get into trouble," said Mr. Breeding. "Why didn't you ride past the springs?" asked Mr. Breeding.

Burt Evans grinned. "We knew we'd be in trouble if you saw us."

"By that statement you've shown that you knew you were doing wrong," said Mr. Breeding, as he picked up one of the switches, and told Burt to turn around and lean over. "I'd take this whipping for you if I could, but . . ."

"Ok, give me the switch," said Burt, holding out his hand.

Mr. Breeding finished his sentence. "But that wouldn't teach you a thing. When I get through you'll think about the consequences before you do anything like that again."

He made stripes on the boys backs that bled through their shirts, and it made all the women on the hill angry.

A couple of days later, Mr. Page came out and the children made their usual run to see who could get to him first. The boys showed him their backs. He looked displeased, but didn't say anything. When he got inside the Breedings home he spoke to Mr. Breeding.

"Cap, don't you think you were a little hard on the boys?"

"I did what I thought best for the boys," said Mr. Breeding. "The Bible teaches that if you 'spare the rod you spoil the child.' A child needs to know that when he does wrong he has to suffer the consequences. A mere scolding or a tap on the shoulder would have been no deterrent. With so many children to care for, you have to be strict or things would get out of hand. I love these boys too, but I want them to be good boys. Since I am responsible for their behavior I have to handle things as I see best. I would have done the same if it had been my children."

"I know, Cap, but did you have to whip them so hard?"

"The Bible says to train a child in the way it should go and he will not depart from it, but will thank you when he is grown that you put forth the effort to teach him right from wrong. That's all I'm trying to do. You are spoiling them. You're more like a doting grandfather than a father. They know they can go tattling to you, and you'll baby them. That's not good for them. It only makes tattle-tales of them, and impertinent to those in charge of them."

Mr. Page shrugged and tilted his head to one side. "Well, I suspect that we both have to give a little. Maybe I do spoil them, but these kids need lots of love. We're all they have, you know. But I still say the punishment didn't fit the crime. These boys aren't malicious or mean. They were just being boys. Boys don't think of the danger. That's the way boys are. You ought to remember that. You would probably have done the same." He paused at that thought, knowing how religious Mr. Breeding was. "Well, Cap, I don't suppose you ever did anything mischievous, but I did." He chuckled. "I'd have been the ring leader of that episode, and never given one thought to the dangers of my actions."

"But if your dad had given you a sound whipping for your actions you probably wouldn't have done it again, would you?"

"I guess you're right, but he wouldn't have whipped me as hard as you did the boys here. I still think you were a little too hard on them. I suspect that we'll both have to give a little. I know you're doing your best as you see it, but let's not expect perfection from these boys. I want them to grow up to be good, responsible adults, but they don't have to be preachers."

Mr. Page's old horse Bill. Miss North, private school teacher, sitting in the new buggy. Jimmy Buttons' cow broke the first buggy in 1909.

19

A Matter of Life or Death

ONE DAY, ABOUT THE THIRD WEEK OF JULY 1909, MR. PAGE CAME OUT TO tell Mr. Breeding that he was going on vacation. He had several saddles in the buckboard.

"Cap," he said, "these boys need something more to entertain themselves, so I brought some saddles so they can ride horses now and then. But don't let them prowl around the country at night. They might get into mischief."

The boys were elated. They had met other young people in the neighborhood and they hurriedly finished their chores so that they could go riding.

When Mr. Page returned from vacation he announced that he and Lucy had gone to Denver, Colorado, to get married. Dean Peck, a preacher and longtime friend had performed the ceremony on July 22, in the year of 1909.

Because Mr. Breeding was the neighborhood minister, the residents of the vicinity often turned to him when in need. One day a man came to him with a message from a young widow who lived near the old Pleasant View School. She had a four year old son who was very ill and needed help. Mr. Breeding grabbed Mr. Page's horse, Buster, that happened to be at the farm, and rode bare back to the woman's house. Having been the eldest son of a doctor, he had learned a little about caring for people who were ill. When he got there he looked at the child's throat, and knew he had diphtheria. The child was burning with fever. He told the mother to bathe the child's face to bring the fever down, while he pondered what to do. He knew that he couldn't ride into Tulsa and back with the doctor in time to save the child.

"If we only had a telephone," he said, "that would cut the time in half."

"There's a telephone at the stone quarry across the river," said the woman, and Mr. Breeding was gone in a flash.

He had heard of the stone quarry, at a place known as Lost City, where criminals hid in a maze of limestone bluffs during the Judge Parker days. He headed his horse toward the river.

George Wright and his wife had pitched a tent along the river directly south of the springs, and George had put in a ferrying business. Mr. Breeding reined his horse up to the front of the tent and called to George.

"Mr. Wright, can you take me across the river to the stone quarry?" he asked in a loud voice. George was still in bed, but he sensed that it was an emergency and came out putting his pants on.

"What's the emergency?" he asked.

"Get me across. I've got to call a doctor," said Mr. Breeding, as he rode the horse onto the ferry.

With the doctor on his way Mr. Breeding hurried back to the woman who sat tearfully rocking her child.

"Maybe we should bathe his face in cool water again," said Mr. Breeding, feeling the child's forehead.

The mother handed the child to him and went for a pan of water. The boy took a deep breath and died in his arms.

Mr. Breeding conducted the funeral. The four-year-old was buried at the lake beside the grave of Mrs. Jones.

When Mr. Breeding informed Mr. Page of the incident, Mr. Page was very concerned. "We've got to get a telephone out here," he said. "With Mrs. Breeding in the family way, you may need to get a doctor quickly. A telephone would cut the time in half." Then he told Mr. Breeding of his own experience when he made the thirty-five mile dash to get his wife to a doctor.

Mr. Page called the telephone company, but they told him that they couldn't run a line seven miles out in the country for one customer, but if they strung their own line she would give them the service.

Mr. Page thought the situation over. Buying the wire was simple, but putting in seven miles of telephone poles and getting the wire strung was something else. Mrs. Breeding's baby was due in about a month, and he didn't have as many workers as he had had. He knew they couldn't get it done in time. He was driving out to tell Mr. Breeding the bad news when the poles along the Katy tracks caught his eye. He turned his horses around and rode back to town. He made a deal with the Katy Railway to use their poles to string his wire on. The wire was purchased and the job began with only one man experienced at installing telephone lines.

Meanwhile, there were other things happening at the farm. Mark Carr had found a spring up in Osage County and had launched a business of supplying spring water for the residents of Tulsa. The water was hauled in wooden barrel type water wagons. It was filtered and bottled in five gallon bottles, and sold for twenty-five cents a bottle. Mark was doing a good business until August of 1909, when the Osage spring dried up.

He came out to the big spring for samples of the water to have it tested for purity. The report was that the water was very pure. Mark made a partnership deal with Mr. Page, and started hauling water from the spring to his bottling plant.

"Cap, we've got our first enterprise," said Mr. Page.

However, filling the barrels and driving seven miles over the sometimes impassable road was slow and tedious. One load a day was all the three wagons could make. They were going to have to buy more wagons or build a regular road, if they were to supply enough water for the needs of the people of Tulsa. This would eat up their profits.

"Mark," said Mr. Page, one day, "Why don't we pipe the water to the bottling plant and save all this hauling?"

"It's a good idea," said Mark, "if I could afford it."

"Well why don't I just buy you out, and you can work for me, bottling the water?" said Mr. Page. "It can still be called the Osage Water Company." Mark agreed.

Mr. Page estimated how much pipe would be needed and ordered it from St. Louis. While he waited for the pipe, he went about securing land necessary to lay his pipe line into Tulsa.

"I need this strip of land anyway," he confided in Mr. Breeding. "I intend to have my own railway as soon as I can manage it. Then I won't have to rely on the Katy Railway."

Mr. Page had to pay a good price for some of the land to make a right-of-way for his railroad and water line, but he was happy to get the land. Among the parcels of land purchased was a forty-acre piece of land with good rich soil, about half way between the spring and Tulsa.

"Here Cap," he said, as he handed Mr. Breeding some papers. It was the deed to the forty acres of prime land. "You're good at growing things and this land has good rich soil. It is also right on the line where I intend to run my railroad. For your convenience I'll have a stop right at your corner, in case you decide to build out there."

Mr. Breeding thanked him graciously and went in to show his wife what Mr. Page had given them.

Mr. Page was always thinking and planning, and had a multitude of projects going at the same time. One project seemed to develop out of another. The building supplies had started coming by freight, and he was excited. He was always pushing for things to move faster.

"Cap," he said, "That outdoor shower can't be used much longer. We've got to get a bathtub for these kids before winter sets in. I believe in utilizing wasted space, and there is a lot of room in the spring house where the cooling system is. We could close off one end of it for a bath house. I've already ordered a tub and a hot water tank. Get Mr. Smith busy partitioning the spring house so we'll be ready when the tub gets here."

The room was partitioned off and the tub arrived. Bill was hitched to the sled to take the tub down to the spring house. The hot water tank came days later when there were no men around to see that it got down to the spring house. Mr. Breeding told them to set it on his back porch out of the weather for the time being.

On the first day of August Mr. Page came by to tell the Breedings that he had to go out of town.

"I've sent a plumber out," he said, "and I've also talked to an engineer about the home for the children. If they come while I'm gone you take care of things, Cap. You know where I want everything to be."

On that very day after Mr. Page had gone, both the plumber and the engineer rode up. Mr. Breeding was a little flustered, but he tried to take care of both. He showed the plumber where the spring house was and told him that the hot water tank was on his back porch. He would get a man to haul the tank down to the spring house after he got the engineer started on the foundation for the children's home.

"The building is to be forty-two by forty-four feet," Mr. Breeding informed the engineer. He stepped to a point which he considered should be the southwest corner of the building. The engineer measured the rest from this point and put the stakes in.

The digging for the basement began. "Where is the blueprint for the basement?" asked the engineer. "The men have to know where to leave the holes for windows and doors."

"I guess Mr. Page thought you would use your own judgment on that," said Mr. Breeding, "but if you'd rather I get a blueprint for it, I'll go to Tulsa and have one made. Daniel Eichenfeld is the architect Mr. Page likes to use."

It was evening before Mr. Breeding returned with the blueprint.

The plumber had just finished his job and came for his pay.

"It ain't gonna work," said the plumber.

"What do you mean?" asked Mr. Breeding. "What won't work?"

The man took off his hat and scratched his head. "Well, you see, the water will have to run five-hundred yards up the hill to get to the hot water heater on your back porch. By the time it gets back down the hill, the water's gonna be cold."

When Mr. Page got home and heard about the fiasco, he drew his eyebrows together and looked at Mr. Breeding. "Now Cap," he teased, "Are you sure you didn't forget to get the tank down there on purpose so that you would have hot water in your house?" Mr. Breeding insisted that it was an accident.

"Oh well, it's all right, Cap," said Mr. Page. "I'm sure more hot water will be needed at the top of the hill than down. The people and the kitchens are up here. A luke warm bath is good enough during the summer, and we have plenty of those big iron pots to heat water if we need to."

Later, Mr. Smith closed in half of the Breeding's back porch where the water heater was, and a tub was installed to make a bathroom for the Breedings. However, since there were no sewer lines, outhouses were still necessary. The water from the tub ran down the hill and soaked into the sand.

Stone was hauled from the hills and the outside walls of the basement were completed by the time Mr. Page got back from his vacation. The windows were mostly above ground in order to give maximum light.

Late in the month of August, Margaret Lindsay, Mrs. Breeding's best friend, came from Pittsburg, Kansas to be with Mrs. Breeding during the birth of her child. Miss Lindsay, in her mid twenties, was also a member of the Salvation Army.

Mrs. Breeding's child was due any time now and every effort was being made to get the telephone wires on the railroad's poles in time.

A horse was kept saddled so that someone could ride for a doctor, in case the baby came before the line was strung. As a further precaution, Mr. Page told Arthur Antle to keep a buggy ready for Doctor Cunningham. It was not a bright picture to have to ride seven miles over the forest trail in the black of night, and everyone hoped the baby would arrive in the daytime.

Stringing seven miles of telephone line through briars and brambles proved more difficult than had been anticipated. The line had so many crimps and broken places wired together that Mr. Breeding feared it might not work. The job was finally finished by lantern light at nine o'clock on the evening of September the third. Anxiously, the workers waited as Mr. Breeding called to see if he could get the operator on the line.

"The operator's voice is as clear as a bell!" exclaimed Mr. Breeding. "It's just like a modern city phone." Then he told those waiting that the telephone number would be 25.

A short time later that evening Mr. Breeding had to call the doctor. The doctor was there in one hour, which was a record. The baby was born at eleven o'clock that evening and was given the name of Margaret, after Ethel's friend. The doctor, who had spent the night at the Breedings, reminded them of the fact that little Margaret was the first white baby born in the vicinity.

Men at work.

20

The Problem Solver

IT SEEMED THAT THERE WAS A CONTINUOUS FLOW OF PEOPLE BEING SENT out to the farm. Tents were set up for them, and the place was so crowded that people were sometimes irritated and grumbly. It was late September, the children were now in school, and the fall rains had set in, slowing the work down. On one cold rainy day, Mr. Page brought an old man out to share a tent with two other old men. He and Mr. Breeding got the man situated. Then with coat collars pulled up to prevent rain from going down their necks, they hurried through the rain to the Breeding's front porch to wait for the rain to slacken up a bit before Mr. Page started back. As Mr. Page gazed out across the hillside, Mr. Breeding watched the trickle of water from Mr. Page's hat brim make a tiny rivulet down his back.

"Mr. Page," he said, rather hesitantly. "There are too many people out here now and you keep sending more. These old men and women would be better off at the poor farm than bivouacked in tents. I know you love this land of yours, but it isn't a cure-all. Why doesn't the welfare help these people?"

Mr. Page answered without turning around. "Well, Cap, it seems right now that I am the welfare. There aren't enough funds to take care of all these folks and, if I didn't help them, they would be sent off to a poor farm. Have you ever been to a poor farm?" Mr. Breeding said that he hadn't.

"Well I hope you never have to go there. People send their old folks out there just to get rid of them. Then they forget all about them. Everybody else forgets what contributions these good people have made to society. Their children forsake them, and they sit there lonely and just waiting to die. I can't send these good people off to that farm of forsaken people just because they can't work anymore. That's like throwing them away. They would rather live in a tent and know they are loved, I'm sure. Anyway these tents are warm and comfortable, and with a floor in them they aren't too bad."

"I understand," said Mr. Breeding, humbly, thinking, "was there ever a man, other than Jesus, who had more compassion for his fellow man." His admiration for Charles Page grew even stronger.

There was a moment of silence, as the cold drizzle of rain pelted the roof with a staccato rhythm. Mr. Page continued to look out over the water soaked land.

"Cap," he said, "I know there are too many people out here and that they are complaining. I hear them when I come out to give you a hand with things, but let's be patient with them. They're bound to be cranky. Things are crude and uncomfortable for them. I intend to do something as soon as I can, but I can't get enough workmen to do all the things I have planned. I've got to get projects finished that will bring in a little money. There's more money going out than there is coming in. The oil business is so shaky that I'm just holding on. Friends all around me are going broke. I've spent a lot of money on land, but I've got to have land and lots of it and I've got to buy it now, while I can afford it. The price keeps rising. It's the land that I'm depending on to feed my kids."

Mr. Page suddenly seemed embarrassed at showing emotion and concern. He stretched and yawned.

"I wish this rain would slacken. I need to get back to the office."

The rain soaked grounds were void of the usual hustle and bustle, with the children at school and the residents on the hill snug in their tents. Circles of smoke from their wood heaters made a comforting feeling to the cold rainy outdoors. Mr. Breeding was just about to suggest they go inside when Mr. Page spoke.

"Cap," he said, "just look at this place. Can't you get it cleaned up? I'm bringing people out, trying to get them interested in settling here, and what do they see but a bunch of trash? Get somebody to clean this place up."

Mr. Breeding looked at the stacks of debris which were numerous. Cut trees lay where they had been felled along with stumps and logs. Piles of rock, lumber scraps and the usual trash and litter from the camp were strewn about. He admitted that it looked bad, but he was hurt at begin scolded about it. "I'm doing everything I can," he said, "but you can think faster than we can work. We aren't through with one project when you start another. Men have to be pulled off one job to help with another more urgent one and nothing gets finished."

"Well, hire more of the men who live in the vicinity."

"I've hired everyone I can find but there is just too much to do."

"Well, Cap," said Mr. Page. "I'm sure you're doing the best you can. But as I say, we've got to get this thing going so we can get some money coming in. There is so much to do and so little time."

The next Sunday when Mr. Page and Lucy came out, Mr. Breeding watched to see what Mr. Page would say when he saw that the piles of debris had been cleaned up or burned. When Mr. Page didn't say anything, Mr. Breeding called his attention to it.

"I even painted the sled," said Mr. Breeding proudly.

"Yes, I noticed," said Mr. Page. "I also noticed that you painted it with expensive indoor varnish. The weather will take the varnish off in no time."

Mr. Breeding was crestfallen.

Both Lucy and Ethel were the kind of women who walked in their husbands shadows. They never interfered in anything the men did. However, when Lucy saw Mr. Breeding's disappointment she told Ethel that Mr. Page was worrying about a lot of things.

"He prides himself in being able to think his way through anything, but the problems have been weighing him down so lately, that he walks the floor at night trying to think what to do."

The next time Mr. Page and Lucy came, it was Mr. Breeding who was in a state of agitation. He and Lot had just had an argument. Lot's popularity with the children was giving him an air of importance and a feeling of authority. He stirred the feelings of the children, especially the boys, against Mr. Breeding and made them resentful to corrections. When Mr. Breeding confronted him, Lot refused to talk or listen.

"Lot is becoming intolerable," complained Mr. Breeding. "He is belligerent, sarcastic and contemptuous. He thinks he's suppose to run things out here. Either he goes or I do."

Mr. Page walked to the dining cabin. "Lot," he said, "Cap tells me that you are giving him trouble." Lot looked sullenly at the big roast he was putting back into the oven. His jaw was set. But he said nothing.

"Now Lot, I hired you as a cook. I put Cap in charge out here and I'd appreciate your being a little more cooperative."

"The kids out here don't like Mr. Breeding," said Lot, stubbornly. "And I don't like him either. He's too strict."

"Well, he's just trying to do his job and you've got to attend to yours. He is a man I can trust, and although he may not be perfect, neither are we. He has a lot of responsibilities, and he's doing the best he can. Now you do the best you can too." He slapped Lot on the shoulder in a friendly way. "You're a good cook, Lot, so stick to what you're hired to do." With that he left.

When Mr. Page could get a day off from his work in town he went to the farm to help with the storing of the fall crops. It seemed that every day he was out there he heard a woman yelling at her neighbors about one thing or another. She seemed to be an industrious woman who even swept the ground around her tent, but she complained all the time.

"You know what's bothering that woman?" Asked Mr. Page, not waiting for an answer. "She needs a husband to boss around and make a fuss over." Mr. Breeding grinned.

The next Sunday when the Pages came out, Mr. Page seemed in a jovial mood. "Cap." He put his hand on Mr. Breeding's shoulder. "I think I've taken care of one of our problems."

"What do you mean?" Mr. Breeding looked surprised, and so did   Ethel and Lucy, as they paused to listen.

"I have a man in his early thirties who works for me in the oil fields," said Mr. Page. "Jake's a bachelor and a shy kind of guy who said he never got married because he didn't know any women that he had the nerve to ask for a date. I told him that I had just the woman for him and that I'd fix him up with a date. I told him that I had a fine industrious woman out here with three nice little children."

"Charley!" Lucy stared at him. "You aren't playing matchmaker? That's serious business."

Mr. Page laughed. "Lucy, I'm dead serious. There's nothing wrong with matchmaking if both parties are fine people. And that they are. Mrs. Fallacia is a good woman. She's cranky because she needs a man to boss around, that's all. Anyway, it was matchmaking that got us together, wasn't it?" Lucy smiled and blushed. Mr. Page went on with his story.

"I told Jake that he needed a woman to darn his socks, cook his meals, and to warm his bed at night."

"Charley!" Lucy exclaimed, looking at Miss Lindsay, who was blushing. Mr. Page turned to Miss Lindsay. He always called her by her last name.

"Lindsay," he teased, "If you start giving us trouble out here, I'll find a man for you."

Mr. Page gave Jake some theater tickets and told him to go out to the farm and ask for Mrs. Fallacia. "Tell her that you've got an extra ticket and that I suggested that you invite her to go with you."

Mrs. Fallacia was quite flattered that Mr. Page had selected her as the one suitable to accompany the young man, and she boasted about it to the other women. Mr. and Mrs. Breeding were amused, but said nothing. There was a short romance and the couple were married.

It took many weeks to complete the water line. When they laid the last joint of pipe, the line was two miles short of reaching the bottling plant. Weary from waiting and anxious over not being able to supply enough water to all who needed it, Mr. Page ended it there at 25th West Avenue.

"Having to haul water two miles is better than seven," he said. He told the pipe fitter to attach the hydrant to the pipe.

Mr. Page said "I'll telephone Cap. He can signal to the man who is to turn the valve on to let the water flow through the pipe. "I'll hold the phone at this end of the line and when the water comes through, I'll let Cap know."

The signals were relayed from man to man until it reached the man who, in turn, opened the valve. But the water wouldn't flow through the five miles of pipe.

21

Cast the First Stone

WHEN THE WATER REFUSED TO FLOW THROUGH THE FIVE MILES OF pipeline by gravity, Mr. Page knew that the cost in getting it to flow would eat up at least a year or two of profits he might realize. He needed a plant location, a pump installed, a steam boiler and a man capable of maintaining them. Meanwhile the water wagons would have to keep rolling — good weather and bad.

Mr. Page decided to install the equipment in part of the corn crib rather than build a shed for it.

Everything was going so slowly it was making him nervous. He had hoped to get the children settled into their new home before Christmas, but at the rate things were going it would be impossible. Building supplies weren't being delivered on time, and often the most essential things were missing from the order, causing many delays and costing Mr. Page money. It was also hard to find workers who would go so far into the country to work. Skilled workers demanded the same pay as they got in town, which was really not consistent with the times, but only due to the demand for laborors.

"Cap could make things move faster out there if he tried," said Mr. Page. "He doesn't see the need to hurry. I tell him that there is so much to be done, and so little time to do it, and he just grins. The other day he asked me if I thought the world was coming to an end, or something. He doesn't understand that I'm using money faster than it's coming in. It scares me. It's not just you, Lucy, that I have to look out for. Those kids have got to be taken care of and that takes a lot of money. They're growing fast, and I don't have anything out there where they can find jobs. I've got to get this town started so there will be jobs for them."

"I know, Charley, but don't worry so. It isn't good to have to worry about so many things." She put her arms around him. "Everything is going to be all right," she said.

"Lucy, I think I should tell you that I'm not only afraid my money will run out, I'm afraid my time will run out before I have secured the future of those kids. I'll soon be fifty years old. I've only got about fifteen years to get my town going and enough industry to provide jobs for all my kids. Every year that passes means I have one year less to do all the things I need to do to secure the future of these kids."

Lucile kissed him. "Charley, you're the healthiest person I know. You can work circles around everybody else. Now you quit worrying. Everything's going to be just fine. I know it is."

But everything wasn't "just fine." Miss Thornbird, one of the women whom Mr. Breeding thought had the flu, grew steadily worse and Doctor Kennedy was called. Miss Thornbird had a touch of the flu all right, but she also had a venereal disease. Mr. Breeding was very disturbed. He called Mr. Page and told him what the doctor had said.

"I'm greatly concern for the children, especially the older girls," said Mr. Breeding. "They sometimes help care for the sick and elderly, and two of the girls have sore eyes. I'm afraid they may have caught the infection from the woman. Three of the boys have sores on their faces. I hope the infection hasn't spread throughout the camp."

"Well, what did Doc say about that?" asked Mr. Page.

"He didn't think so, but he will look at the girls' eyes, and check the boys. He advised against telling anyone else about Miss Thornbird's illness for fear of causing alarm in the camp."

"A good idea," said Mr. Page. "Tell Doc to come by my office when he gets through examining the children."

The doctor examined the girls' eyes and found that they had trachoma.

"Some of the Indians have trachoma," said Doctor Kennedy, "and the government has sent two eye specialists to Oklahoma to care for them. Dr. Peter Cope White and his brother Dr. Daniel White are in Tulsa now. Perhaps we can get them to come out here. Trachoma can cause blindness. Sometimes surgery is required." He examined the eyes of the other children but five-year-old Burl Carter was the only other child to have trachoma.

"Burl, the little five-year-old, was brought here by an Indian woman," said Mr. Breeding. "He may have had trachoma when he came and the older girls who help with the babies caught it from him."

"That's very probable," said Dr. Kennedy. "Now as to the three boys with sores on their faces. There is nothing to be alarmed about. They evidently had a cut or mosquito bite and scratched it with dirty hands, getting it infected. They need to wash with soap regularly to ward off infections such as these."

"We'll have to give more attention to cleanliness," said Mr. Breeding. "Boys don't always see the necessity of washing, if left to their own discretion."

"Soup, Soap and Salvation" was the motto of the Salvation Army. Miss Lindsay, who was still visiting the Breedings, decided to help with the cleanliness problem. She gave the children a lecture on cleanliness.

"You've got to wash your hands and face before every meal," she said. "If I see a child with a dirty face, I will not only scrub his neck and ears, I will scrub his whole head." And she did. There were a few red necks and blushing faces that day, but she got her message across.

Mr. Page drove out to the farm after work the next evening. After a short romp with the children and a word to the hill residents he excused himself and followed Mr. Breeding into his cottage where they could talk.

"Doc contacted Doctors Peter Cope White and Daniel White to see what can be done for the children who have trachoma," he said, looking very tired and worried. He reached in his pocket and handed Mr. Breeding a box of salve for the sores on the boys' faces and drops for the girls' eyes.

Mrs. Breeding was getting Harold and Eva to bed. Miss Lindsay was ironing on a cloth covered board placed on the backs of two kitchen chairs. Before Mr. Page could speak to the women, the two Breeding children ran to him, calling him Daddy Page, as the other children did. The Breedings smiled, amused at their innocence. Mr. Page winked at Mr. Breeding as he lifted five-year-old Harold to his knee and put an arm around seven-year-old Eva who leaned against his chair. He bounced Harold on his knee, causing peals of laughter as he sang a funny little song.

When the song was ended, Mrs. Breeding hurried the two children off to bed.

"Cap," said Mr. Page, "we've got to see that these boys wash their faces and hands. We don't want them getting sick."

"Miss Lindsay took care of that," said Mr. Breeding. Then he explained Miss Lindsay's actions. "I don't think we'll have much trouble while she's on guard. She's a strict disciplinarian. She tolerates no disobedience to her rules. She scrubbed a few heads today."

"Well good for you, Lindsay," said Mr. Page. "We want to take care of our kids."

Miss Lindsay smiled, but said nothing. She put the iron she was using back on the stove, released the handle, and clipped it onto another iron that had been heating on the stove.

"What will we do about Miss Thornbird?" asked Mr. Breeding. Mr. Page turned uneasily in his chair. A worried look clouded his countenance.

"She is neither old, nor a widow," said Miss Lindsay. "How did she get out here, anyway?" She wet her finger and touched it quickly to the bottom of the iron. The spit sizzled. Satisfied that it was hot enough, she continued to iron the circular skirt of a dress.

"Brinton brought her out," said Mrs. Breeding, with a grin. Shocked, Miss Lindsay turned her gaze on Mr. Breeding.

With a red face, Mr. Breeding explained. "I was in Mr. Page's office one day when a man called and told Mr. Page that there was a woman in the Brandon Hotel who was very sick and had no money and nobody to care for her. The man wouldn't give his name. Mr. Page asked me to go get her and bring her out to the farm." Mr. Breeding raised his hands in an attitude of despair. "I don't know why everybody calls him. He isn't over the welfare. He's only the chairman of the welfare board."

Mr. Breeding looked at Mr. Page who sat with head bowed, deep in thought.

"Well, yes, I do know why they call Mr. Page," he said.

Mr. Page grinned. "They know I'll send the needy ones out to Cap."

Mr. Breeding shook his head. "Soon there won't be anybody left in Tulsa. He'll have them all out here."

"What will you do with the woman?" asked Miss Lindsay.

"Well, I don't know just yet," said Mr. Page. "I've been thinking about it. We'll have to take care of her. We can't just throw her away."

Miss Lindsay stared in shocked silence, as Mr. Page continued. "I feel sorry for her. I've been trying to think how I would feel if she was one of my sisters, friendless, too sick to take care of herself, and nobody to care if she lived or died. The poor woman must be scared to death. The doctor said she had syphilis and that it could cripple. The woman is only in her late twenties. Whatever would she do if she were crippled?"

"Is she a friend of yours?" asked Miss Lindsay.

"I never saw her before she came out here," said Mr. Page.

Miss Lindsay put the irons on the back of the stove. "You shouldn't have to be responsible for her," she said, as she took the board from the chairs. "Let her friends take care of her. She's not your responsibility. You didn't even know her."

"Lindsay," said Mr. Page, "The poor woman has no friends. Only users. She's known about town, but no one feels obligated to her. When women like her get old or something like this happens, they are cast out. Nobody cares whether she lives or dies. But she's a human being with feelings. She deserves a second chance. Everybody does. She has nobody but us. It's up to us to take care of her."

Miss Lindsay stiffened. "Well, I don't think the children should be around that kind of woman."

Mr. Breeding sat silently looking down at his hands. Mrs. Breeding was rocking the baby and looking worried.

"Cap?" Mr. Breeding raised his head and waited to hear what Mr. Page had to say. "When the woman who had been caught in adultery was brought to Jesus the people wanted to throw stones at her. What did Jesus say to them?"

Mr. Breeding smiled. "Jesus said, 'Let he who is without sin cast the first stone.'"

"There. You see? I can't throw stones at this woman. I'll tell you what I've been thinking. I just bought a piece of land not far from here that has a little house on it. I'll move the woman into the house and hire someone to take care of her until she is able to care for herself."

"You're a good man, Mr. Page," said Mr. Breeding. "But this is a long-term illness and it's going to cost a lot of money."

"I know, Cap, I know. But what can I do? I can't just throw her out with no place to go."

Mr. Page got to his feet and put his hat on. "I'm sure the poor woman is scared and worrying about what is going to happen to her. Let's go and ease her mind so she can sleep tonight, Cap."

"Don't you think one of us women should go with you?" asked Miss Lindsay.

Mr. Page grinned. "Come on, Lindsay," he said. "Mrs. Breeding is busy."

When they got to the woman's tent, Miss Lindsay called from the outside of the tent. "Miss Thornbird? Mr. Page and Mr. Breeding want to talk to you. May we come in?"

"Might as well," came the voice from within.

"We're going to see what we can do for you," said Mr. Page, as the two men entered behind Miss Lindsay.

"Why don't you just let me die?" asked the woman as she turned her face to the wall. "Life ain't so wonderful." She cursed and mumbled something else under her breath.

"Life is always worth living," said Mr. Page trying to comfort her. Then he told her his plans to move her to a house and get someone to take care of her until she was well.

"Why would you be doin' this fer me? You don't even know me."

"Sure, I do," said Mr. Page. She turned over and searched his face. He continued. "You are a woman in trouble and we are going to help you. Aren't we, Cap?" Mr. Breeding smiled.

They didn't stay long. On the way back to the Breeding's house Mr. Page said, "She is as hard as nails. The poor woman must have seen some rough times for her to fall into such a trap."

The next evening Mr. Page rode out to the farm again. "I want you to know that I've found a practical nurse to take care of Miss Thornbird for a while. Let's go tell her that she will be moved this week end."

Mr. Breeding wondered why Mr. Page would drive out to tell the woman what he could have had one of them tell her. When they were inside the tent Mr. Page pulled a Bible from his coat pocket and laid it on the woman's bed.

"You were discouraged," he said, "and I thought this might cheer you, Miss Thornbird."

The woman covered her eyes with her arm and began to laugh. "Where do you think that stuff is going to get me?" she sneered.

Mr. Page shoved the Bible closer. "When you're feeling low, just read this Bible. It will give you a lift. Even an old stagger like me gets good out of reading the Bible."

"If there WAS something to religion, I'm too far gone for help," said Miss Thornbird. "I ain't blamin' God. I ain't never done nothin' fer Him, and He ain't never done nothin' fer me and I ain't hollerin' fer Him to help me now."

"God works through others," said Mr. Breeding. "He knew that Mr. Page really cared about people, and He must have seen something very worthwhile about you, for you to wind up out here where you could get help from this good man. Mr. Page sincerely wants to help you."

The woman uncovered her eyes, and looked at Mr. Page, who always felt uncomfortable when any one called him good. The woman mistook the expression of embarrassment as one of shame. She raised herself on her elbow.

"Nobody does nothin' fer nothin'," she said. "So why're you doin' this?"

Mr. Breeding had a hurt look on his face. He started to defend his friend, but Mr. Page just smiled. He was getting accustomed to being accused of having ulterior motives. It didn't bother him anymore.

"I'm just trying to help you," said Mr. Page. "I expect nothing in return. You just read that Bible when you're feeling low. You'll be surprised what a lift it can give you."

"Are you some kind of religious fanatic?" Her brows arched.

Mr. Page chuckled. "No, that's Cap," he said, slapping Mr. Breeding on the shoulder as they started to leave. "But we both believe in God. The BIG FELLOW can help you when nobody else can. Right, Cap?"

"Absolutely. Just go to God with your troubles. He'll never close the door in your face."

As they made their departure, Mr. Breeding went over to the little stove in the corner of the tent and added another couple of sticks of wood to the fire. "I see that you need more wood," he said. "Ethel and I will be back later and I'll bring you some wood. With that flu you don't need to get chilled."

When Mr. Page went home, Mr. and Mrs. Breeding left the children in Miss Lindsay's care and went to take Miss Thornbird some wood. The next evening Miss Thornbird was feeling better and they visited her again. Mr. Breeding brought more wood. His Bible was tucked under his arm.

Mrs. Breeding asked Miss Thornbird if she had taken her medicine and chatted with her while Mr. Breeding stoked the fire. When he was through he sat down in a chair beside his wife.

"I see you've been reading the Bible," he said, noticing the Bible that lay open on the bed beside her.

"Yeah, I ain't never read the Bible before," said Miss Thornbird with a smile. "To tell the truth I ain't never read nothin, much. I ain't had much schoolin'. But when Mr. Page left, I looked at the Bible a layin' there and I seen a piece of paper stickin' out of it. Now that old fox put that paper in there knowin' I'd be curious. I opened the book to see if it was a letter, or what. It wasn't nothin' but a piece of paper." She held the paper up. "I knowed he wanted me to read on them pages. Jest curious, I did. It was jest like God was talkin' t'me. It said I wasn't to let my heart be troubled, but to believe Him. I reckon I do believe in God, but I ain't thought much about it." Her eyes were shining. "I ain't never read the Bible and I didn't know it was so interestin'. I just kept readin'."

"The Bible is very interesting," said Mrs. Breeding. "You can read it over and over again and find something new every time you read it. You never get tired of reading the Bible. You can't say that of any other book."

"The Bible was written by men with the inspiration from God," said Mr. Breeding. "No other book can change your whole life and attitude, if you read it daily, as the Bible can.

Miss Thornbird sat up. "Is that a fact? You're not jest funnin' me, are you?"

"It is a fact. I assure you that if you pray and read the Bible every day, before you realize it you'll start seeing things differently. And you'll start doing things differently.

"God can make such a change in your life and give you an inner peace that is hard to explain," said Mrs. Breeding. "It's just wonderful. He forgives you for all your wrong doing, and gives you a new start."

"No matter what you've done?"

"Absolutely," said Mr. Breeding. "God loves everybody. He can put our broken lives back together and give us a new life. All you have to do is repent of your sins, ask for forgiveness and when He has forgiven you, you'll know it. Peace fills your heart, and nobody needs to tell you that God has forgiven you. You know that He has."

"Will you pray for me? I want this peace. I want this second chance that Mr. Page spoke of."

Mr. and Mrs. Breeding knelt in prayer beside the woman's bed. Miss Thornbird gave her heart to God, and promised to make good on her second chance. When the Breedings rose to go, she was laughing and crying for joy. She knew God had forgiven her.

"Now forget the past," said Mr. Breeding, "move forward and always remain true to God."

"I will, thank God, and want to thank all you good people for caring enough to help a woman like me," said Miss Thornbird, through the tears. "I'll never let you down."

"Don't thank us, thank the Lord," said Mr. Breeding.

He called Mr. Page and told him what had happened. He was glad.

The two girls with trachoma had to have eye surgery. Burl's eyes got well with treatment. The doctor's bill for the woman and the children were staggering. Mr. Page decided there had to be a doctor in the vicinity to serve all the people.

A drug salesman, M. F. Calhoun wrote to his brother, Dr. Charles Edward Calhoun, a widower with a small son, who was practicing medicine in Shawnee, Oklahoma. He told him that Mr. Page was building a home for orphaned children and wanted a physician to locate in the area.

Dr. Calhoun went to talk to Mr. Page.

22

What is God Telling Me?

Mr. Page was generous to a fault, but having learned by perception and parental example the folly of deliberate waste, he found wasting intolerable and often gave lectures on it.

"Cooks are wasters," he said, when he saw whole loaves of bread and whole fruits and vegetables thrown into the pig pen. The hog trough was within reach, but sometimes one of the cooks found it easier to set a pot in the pen than to empty it into the hog trough. This angered Mr. Page. Not only was it unsanitary, but large heavy aluminum pots were expensive. One day he became so irate that he jumped over the fence, picked up a large aluminum cooking vessel and climbed angrily out of the pen.

"Cap!" he stormed, "I put you in charge out here, and you are responsible for all this waste. I'm tired of seeing whole fruits, vegetables and loaves of bread thrown to the hogs. There's enough food wasted out here to feed a lot of hungry people. When are these cooks going to learn how to adjust the amount of food they cook to the number of people they feed? They wouldn't be so wasteful if they were paying the grocery bill. It's easier to throw food out than to bring it in."

"I didn't notice," said Mr. Breeding, apologetically.

"If you wouldn't notice, it's because you're a waster too." He thrust the pan toward Mr. Breeding. "My mother would love to have owned a nice pan like this," he said, "and I don't want to see pots in that pen again. Don't they know what a hog trough is for?"

Mr. Breeding was embarrassed. "I'll talk to the cooks," he said.

Later, Mr. Breeding expressed how he felt to his wife and Miss Lindsay. "I don't understand how a man who gives thousands of dollars away so freely can gets so angry over garbage."

"Well, I see his point," said Miss Lindsay, who was a thrifty Scottish maiden in her mid-twenties. "Small wastes add up to big expenses. You must remember that Mr. Page is feeding a lot of people. With fifty pounds of flour at $1.35 and sugar at $1.00 for just eighteen pounds, to say nothing of all the other needs, the cost must be astronomical."

"Well, of course it is," conceded Mr. Breeding, who ordered the supplies. "And you are right. I admit I'm not a bargain hunter, but neither am I a waster."

"Brinton doesn't like to shop with me because I shop for bargains," said Mrs. Breeding.

"I don't have that kind of time," said Mr. Breeding. "I know what I want when I go to town. I find out who sells it and I buy it. It's women who scour the town in search of bargains and waste a lot of money on things they can do without. But as Mr. Page says, I am responsible for things out here and I'll try to do better. He is my employer and I do want to please him."

Mr. Breeding called all the cooks together in the dining cottage for a conference. The three women cooks promised to do better, but Mr. Lot, whom Mr. Breeding suspected being the one who put the pots in the hog pen, sat belligerently, saying nothing. His dark eyes had a flat, steady defiance in them as Mr. Breeding spoke. His contemptuous stare transferred itself from Mr. Breeding to the kitchen window. When the meeting was over, Mr. Lot's back was to the door. When he heard the door open and close, he thought Mr. Breeding was gone.

"We was hired by Mr. Page," he muttered. "It ain't none of old B.F.'s business what we do."

Mr. Breeding had opened the door again to say something more, and when he heard what Lot had said, he stood, stunned and motionless. Noticing the look on the women's faces, Lot turned around. A momentary look of surprise flickered across his face and quickly faded. The impenetrable, defiant mask slipped back into place. Mr. Breeding looked at him with hopeless exasperation and went on out the door.

The next time Mr. Page came out, Mr. Breeding gave him the ultimatum. "That cook has to go or I do," he said. "I refuse to tolerate his insolence any longer."

"I hate to fire him," said Mr. Page. "He's a good cook and he needs a job. I like to be fair. I gave him a little piece of land in the area of the old Pleasant View school, and he's not going to want to leave his land."

Both Mr. Page and Mr. Breeding were silent all through supper. Soon after, Mr. Page excused himself and went to the dining cottage.

"Lot," he said, "I warned you. You know what I'm talking about. You've forced me to have to fire you. I gave you a second chance. I don't owe you a third." Lot stiffened.

"You said yourself, I'm a good cook. I can find me a job in one of them restaurants."

"Sure you can. You're an intelligent man. How would you like to go into the real estate business on the side? I'll give you a bonus every time you sell a home to one of your friends within the neighborhood of the land I gave you."

"Sho-nuff?"

"Sure enough," said Mr. Page. He mapped out the plan, and the area. Mr. Lot sold two lots right away.

The Jim Crow law had gone into effect in 1907 forbidding Black people and whites to mix. The trains had a place for the Negro and one for the white people and that was the way everything else was. Mr. Page had sold a few people on the idea of building their homes in the vicinity and they were in the process of doing so. When they saw Black people moving into the area, they reminded Mr. Page of the Jim Crow law.

"They are clear on the other side of the Katy railroad tracks," said Mr. Page. "They are fine people, and besides, wouldn't it be nice to have them handy in case you need domestic help or yard work?" The complainers thought about it and decided the Black people could stay.

Some of Mr. Lot's friends were interested in forming a Negro colony in the vicinity, but lacked the funds to buy. Mr. Page loaned them money to build and promised them jobs laying ties for a railroad he intended to build.

"I've discovered clay north of the lake, suitable for making brick," he said. "And I've sent for some Mexican fellows who know how to make brick. When we get it to going some of you can work there too."

Miss Lindsay took Mr. Lot's place as cook after he left. She scrubbed the tables and the floors with a brush and lye soap every evening. Determined to have no more sores from unsanitary conditions she scrubbed everything in sight, still watching for dirty faces, still scrubbing them if she found one. In fact she practically ran things around there. But Mr. Breeding didn't mind. It took some of the work off his shoulders.

Miss Lindsay was an excellent cook. According to Mr. Page, her light bread was light enough to fly. She was strongly against wasting food, insisting that the children eat everything they put on their plates. Her almond flavored pudding made with left over bread was a delicacy that even the children praised. She was quick to learn how much food to cook, but when she did over estimate how much the children would eat, she found a way to use the food that wasn't eaten. She made great stews using leftover roast beef or chicken, using whatever vegetables left over and adding fresh ones. Some said the stew was more flavorful made from meat that had been roasted.

As if that wasn't enough talent for one person, Miss Lindsay was a good bookkeeper and a careful shopper. She shopped by telephone, driving a hard bargain with merchants eager to get the volume of business she could give them. Mr. Breeding smiled at her blunt insistence that she get full measure, good quality and lowest possible price. This pleased Mr. Page very much. He called her an asset to the foundation.

By now, with the farm and community springing up, it was referred to as the sand springs area. Eager to get his town started, Mr. Page asked Mr. Smith and Mr. Jones, who were very good at putting up fences, to help him line out where the town should be. The store, the canning factory and recently a saw mill, were all along Adam's Road, and it was decided just to continue on south with the town. Drainage ditches had been dug, and tiles laid to carry the water off, but when the fall rains came, everything was flooded. Disappointed, they gave up on trying to line the town out without the help of a professional engineer.

Mr. Page was very fond of animals. One evening he wandered into the barn and seeing the holes where the horses had pawed the ground, he called to Mr. Breeding.

"Cap, just look at those holes where the horses have to stand all night. Standing with a foot in a hole throws their hips and shoulders out of line. They're bound to be more tired in the morning than they were from a day's work. We work these horses hard. They deserve better treatment."

"I'm sorry. I didn't notice," said Mr. Breeding.

"There seems to be a lot you don't notice," said Mr. Page. "See that those stalls are cleaned out, the floor leveled, and throw some hay in the stalls. Then keep it that way."

Mr. Breeding was ashamed that he hadn't noticed the condition of the barn stalls. There was just too much to do, and too much to keep in mind. He had tried to consider the hard working horses, refusing to let the boys ride them at night, so the horses could rest. He allowed the boys to ride them on Saturdays and on Sunday after the morning worship service until supper time. Then the horses were to be back in the barns to rest for work the following day. At least that's what he thought was going on.

However, the boys had been slipping out most every night, riding about the neighborhood. Mr. Williams, who slept in the tent with the older boys, worked hard and was a sound sleeper. When he started snoring, the boys who had crawled into bed with their clothes on, sneaked out to the barn, saddled the horses and walked them quietly down the sandy road past the tents and the Breeding's cottage.

One night while the boys were attending a neighborhood party, the saddles were stolen from their horses. This didn't stop the boys. They rode bare back.

A few days later, Mr. Breeding was straightening the barn floor, and happened to notice that the saddles were missing. He assumed someone had stolen them from the barn. Being the secretary of the Anti Horse Thief Association, he called a meeting at the little school and reported the stolen saddles. The association members, having pledged not to steal horses from each other, hadn't seen much action. They got excited. They swore to catch the saddle snatchers.

The day after the meeting, Mr. Page came out. He reined his team to a stop in the road across from where Mr. Breeding was working.

"Cap," said Mr. Page, very calmly, "it seems the boys have been roaming the neighborhood at night. These saddles were taken from the horses while the boys enjoyed a neighborhood party. They were brought to me as evidence of their running around at night. I'll put the saddles back into the barn." He clucked to the horses and drove on. He put the saddles in the barn and left.

Mr. Breeding's shoulders drooped. Discouraged, he left what he was doing, went into the house and slumped dejectedly into a chair.

His wife looked at him in astonishment. "What's the matter Brinton?" she asked. "What did Mr. Page say that made you so despondent?"

Before he could answer, Miss Lindsay opened the back door and called, "Yoo who," as she always did, to let them know she was coming in. "What did Mr. Page want?" she asked.

Mr. Breeding told them about the saddles. "Mr. Page has so little confidence in me that he has someone spying on me again. I just know it was George Wright."

Mr. Breeding leaned forward with his elbows on his knees and his head in his hands.

"Now what am I going to do?" he asked, "It's going to be very embarrassing to tell the ANTI HORSE THIEF ASSOCIATION that the saddles were stolen as evidence of my neglect of the boys. No matter what I do, somebody is going to criticize. If I discipline the boys, everybody on the hill will be angry at me again. If I don't punish them, no telling what they'll be up to next. It seems I'm a failure at anything I do."

"He tries so hard to please," said Mrs. Breeding, "but Mr. Page has been so difficult lately. Now the boys have put Brinton in a bad light again."

"Well," said Miss Lindsay, "I say the boys need a good whipping. You need to teach them a lesson."

"The boys aren't mean," Mr. Breeding said, "They're just getting big enough to notice the girls, I imagine, and so full of excess energy. They don't think about consequences."

"All the same, you have to keep strict discipline with this many children, or they will get control over you." Miss Lindsay's lips were pursed tightly. She continued, "Now if you confront them, they may deny that they have been slipping out at night. What you should do is catch them at it."

"That sounds so sneaky. But I suppose you're right. These boys are very clever. I may have to catch them in the act."

That night, Mr. Breeding seated himself in a chair by the window and waited in the darkness. It wasn't long before he heard hushed whispers, and saw the horses silhouetted in moonlight as the boys led them down the sandy road. He waited for awhile before he put his coat and hat on. He went to the barnyard and put a padlock on the gate and waited in the barn. About ten o'clock he saw them coming back, riding the horses slowly up the road. Mr. Breeding hid behind a bush, curious as to what they would say when they found the gate was locked.

One of the boys dismounted. "Damn!" he said, rattling the gate. "Old Bull Frog Breeding has locked the gate. What'll we do now?"

Mr. Breeding stifled a chuckle as he realized the joke was on him for eavesdropping. He always signed his name B.F. Breeding and was amused to learn that the boys had decided the B.F. stood for bull frog. His anger left him.

Mr. Breeding came out from his hiding place. He opened the gate and followed the boys into the barn. They put the horses in their stalls, and waited for their punishment.

"Where are your saddles?" asked Mr. Breeding.

"Somebody stole them," said Luther Nolen.

Mr. Breeding told them that they had been stolen and taken to Mr. Page to let him know that they were riding at night. Then he sent the boys to bed.

Grumbling because their night prowling had been stopped, they whispered, "I'll bet old Bull Frog is the one who took the saddles to Daddy Page, just to get him mad at us."

It was not long after that when the older girls took matters into their own hands. They resented Miss Newhouse's strict rules. Martha Davis accidently broke three plates while helping to set the table. Miss Newhouse seeing the accident as a rebellious act, sent her to bed with only bread and water for supper. The five older girls staged a sullen, silent protest. That night they slipped out of the house and caught the last train to Tulsa to report to "Daddy Page " that they were being mistreated.

Mrs. Page opened the door and ushered the girls in where Mr. Page sat reading the newspaper. He looked surprised.

"Does Newhouse know you've come here at night?" he asked.

"No, Daddy Page, she doesn't know," said one of the girls. "We came to talk to you about her. We don't like her."

Mrs. Page slipped into the kitchen and made some hot chocolate. With cookies from the cookie jar, she served refreshments to the girls as they voiced their complaints.

"Girls," said Mr. Page, "have you talked to Miss Newhouse about how you feel?"

"Heavens no," said one of the girls. The other girls giggled.

"Well, she is a fine christian woman. I'm sure that if you talk to her, you'll understand what she is trying to do for you."

The girls looked at each other and grinned. "Mrs. Webb calls Miss Newhouse, Old Lady Outhouse. She thinks she's silly with her white gloves and lace parasol," said one of the girls.

Mr. Page shook his head. What else could go wrong? He excused himself and told the girls to enjoy their refreshments. He went to Arthur Antle's stables and got his buckboard. His high hopes for the girls to obtain the cultural advantages that Miss Newhouse could teach them were dashed. It was a matter of communication. With all her knowledge of the social graces, Miss Newhouse lacked the ability to communicate her intentions to the girls. What was he going to do? How was Miss Newhouse going to feel when she learned that the girls didn't appreciate her efforts?

Miss Newhouse had discovered the girls were missing and was at the Breeding's cottage. She was relieved when she saw their safe return.

Mr. Page had a habit of calling people by their last names. "Newhouse," he said, "Here are your girls. They have something they want to talk over with you." He hoped that when the subject was brought up, Miss Newhouse would make the girls understand. But that didn't happen. Miss Newhouse gathered the girls together in their cottage and gave thanks to God that they were home safe and unharmed, but made no mention of what she was trying to do for them.

"Cap," said Mr. Page, as he slumped into a chair, "so many things are going wrong, that I'm wondering if God isn't trying to tell me something. Maybe He had other plans for the kids all along, and I was too quick to take them. I guess it takes more than loving kids to be able to train them right. Maybe an organization knows the best way to do it. Several opinions are bound to be better than one." He sighed heavily.

"You're right, Cap, I am spoiling the kids, and it's making it hard on those who take care of them. It isn't doing the kids any good either. It's just making more problems. I guess I'll have to trust those in charge to use good judgment, or replace them."

Nobody said anything, and Mr. Page added, "Maybe we're trying to give our girls a college education when they aren't out of grade school yet," He gave a big sigh.

"Do you think maybe I'm having so many problems because God is displeased with me?"

Mr. Breeding was reminded that Mr. Page put a lot of stock in signs. "Mr. Page, things happen to everyone," he said. "It rains on the just and the unjust. Everybody has problems. It seems that you have more, because you have more things going than most people do. I can't see why God would be displeased with you. You did the only thing you knew to do. Nobody else wanted the children. You saved families from being separated. You took half-starved children that might have been scattered abroad to whatever fate. For the few who had mothers, you got them back together by hiring mothers to take care of their own children. Could God be displeased with that?"

"Well if God is so pleased, why is everything going wrong? Why can't we get anything done? The oil business isn't doing well and yet it is all I have to depend on until I get something going out here to bring in some money. I've spent about all my money on land and drilling dry holes in the ground. I've got to get things going, or I won't be able to feed my kids. I'm depending on my land to support my kids, but I fear I'll go broke before it starts paying off. Sometimes I think God would rather I turn the kids over to an organization experienced in such matters. Maybe He wanted me to take them for the time being, because whoever he had in mind wasn't ready for them. I don't know." He looked very tired. His air of self-confidence was missing. He looked down at his feet. His voice broke when he said, "Cap, I love these kids . . . I don't see how I could part with them . . . but I've got to think of what is best for them. I'd be mighty careful who I turned them over to. I'd never desert them . . . I'd keep my eye on them all the time. I don't know what I'll do, but God knows that what ever I do it will be because I love them."

"I know you do. So do I."

Mr. Page smiled. He seemed his old optimistic self again. He rose to go. Mr. Breeding followed him to the buckboard. As Mr. Page drove away he called, "Don't worry Cap, I'll think of something to do. I can't give up. I've gone too far to give up now."

"So have I," said Mr. Breeding, as he waved good-bye.

Miss Margaret Lindsay

23

The Broken Contract

ALL THROUGH THE YEAR OF 1909 PROBLEMS CONTINUED BOTH ON THE farm and with the oil business. More and more small independent operators were squeezed out of business.

President Teddy Roosevelt had attempted to relieve some of the pressures on smaller oil firms by enforcing stricter anti-trust laws. The major oil companies found a way to get around these. To settle some of the disputes the President put fixed prices on oil. Still the fights continued.

The Tulsa petroleum development was hindered by not having adequate markets. Three major oil companies had pipelines crossing the state. Governor Haskell had convinced the Oklahoma oil men that the major oil companies would aid them in shipping their oil out too, but what they did was to force those who used their lines to sell their oil to them at such low prices that the small companies couldn't afford to operate.

These major oil companies not only owned the pipelines, but they continued to hold a monopoly on all the railway oil shipping facilities. The majors actually took bids for the use of their pipelines and the rail services. The price of oil was already ruinously low. Independents were forced to sell their oil to the *big boys* for twenty-five cents a barrel and less, or let it waste on the ground. Many ran their oil into feverishly dug earthen pits while they waited for a chance to ship it. Much of the oil stored in this fashion was lost through seepage and evaporation and the quality of the oil deteriorated rapidly.

It was heartbreaking to bring oil up out of its safe storage in the earth, only to have it wasted this way, but no one seemed able to stop drilling and allow his competitors to draw all the oil from the ground.

Glenn Pool field, which had spawned the little town of Glennpool and given Tulsa the title, "Oil Capital of The World," had reached its peak in 1907-1908 and was now declining. But there was still too much oil for the number of pipelines.

Mr. Page told Mr. Breeding that many of his friends had already been forced to sell their wells to the major oil companies. Some held out until they went broke.

"I can't afford to go broke, so I'll take what I can get," said Mr. Page.

The price of oil was down to forty-one cents a barrel at the start of the year and by October it was down to thirty-one cents a barrel.

Most of Mr. Page's wells were gas, but he still had the Tanaha, and several small oil wells. He had earlier consolidated his small wells into one company called the Margaret Oil Company, after Margaret Lindsay and her namesake Margaret Breeding. He sold the Margaret Oil Company to the Central light and Fuel Company for the sum of $38,659.16

On October 15, 1909, Mr. Page made a contract with the Gulf Oil and Gas Company to construct gas lines out to the springs area and into Tulsa for consumer consumption. The line was partly at his expense and partly at the expense of the Gulf Oil Company. Charles Page paid $16,279.10 at the signing of the contract and was to pay the rest in payments. His last payment would fall in July of 1913.

An added stipulation to the agreement, was that Mr. Page would furnish gas to the Gulf Oil and Gas Company at the rate of three cents per thousand cubic feet.

With gas lines extended to the springs area, Mr. Page became very excited. Gas utilities were a good inducement toward getting residents and industry interested. He began to push harder toward finishing projects so that he could turn more attention to getting his town started.

But the difficulty in hiring workers for Mr. Page's projects continued. Tulsa had continued to grow, with plenty of jobs that paid higher wages than farm labor.

"I can't fault a man for wanting to better himself," said Mr. Page, "or to want to work in town where all the excitement is. But I sure wish I could get these projects finished."

With the oil business in the condition that it was, the citizens of Tulsa decided that perhaps their future would be more secure if they turned some of their attention toward real estate and the promotion of industry. They actually organized clubs which planned strategy to deal with the situation.

On May 13, 1909, the Chamber of Commerce of Tulsa was organized to compete with the Commercial Club. November 18, the name Chamber of Commerce was changed to Tulsa Industrial Company, becoming a corporation so the club could buy property for industrial purposes.

With a sudden demand for land, the price of land skyrocketed.

Three local brick plants were kept busy as the skyline of Tulsa changed rapidly. Between 155 and 160 houses were being built each month. Earlier, a twenty-five-foot lot downtown that had been offered for fifteen-cents now sold for $225 for one half share of the lot.

Indian lands had gone from $2 and $3 an acre to $300, which compounded Mr. Page's problems. With the price of land shooting so high, lawyers with devious and unscrupulous practices were hired to find loopholes in contracts. Many Indian lands were reclaimed and resold at triple the price.

Some Indians sold leases on their allotments for cash to every buyer who applied. The money was spent and when the oil men were ready to drill, they discovered they had been duped.

"Cap, these shyster lawyers are stirring things up," said Mr. Page. "They're examining all my contracts to see if they can find any loopholes. They think they've found loopholes in the deeds for some of the lands I have purchased. I'll have to hire lawyers to defend me. Just another expense."

Aside from all the business problems, there were many mundane tasks on the farm that demanded attention. It was time to take the stock to market.

Plans were made to take the hogs to Tulsa. "Cap, get someone to help you load the hogs, then leave them at Arthur Antle's stable. Come up to the office for me," said Mr. Page. "I'll do the talking to the stock buyer".

The next day Frank and Mr. Breeding finally got the squealing hogs into two wagons and drove them to town.

"Mr. Page said to leave the hogs at Arthur's Stables, but it is no more trouble to take them on to the stockyard," said Mr. Breeding. "That will save having to leave the noisy things up town."

Frank stayed with the hogs, and Mr. Breeding went to notify Mr. Page.

"I won't come in," said Mr. Breeding, sticking his head in at the office door. "I smell like a hog. The hogs are down at the stockyard waiting for you."

Mr. Page looked at him. "Cap, I told you to take them to Arthur's Livery Stables."

"It wasn't any more trouble to take them to the stockyard so I thought I'd save you time and take them on down there," said Mr. Breeding.

"Cap, you're a poor business man. Don't you know that when the man saw you bringing those hogs in, he knew that you would take about any price rather than take them back out to the farm. You lost your bargaining power right there. I intended to get the price first and then take them down there."

When they got to the stockyard the man was so sure of his purchase that he had unloaded the hogs into one of the pens. He glibly gave Mr. Page his price.

"Help these boys load them back into the wagons," said Mr. Page, sternly. Both Mr. Breeding and the stock man looked shocked. Mr. Page took the cigar from his mouth. His jaw muscles jerked. He looked angrily at the stock man.

"You can't do that to me," he said. "I know today's price for hogs." He started to go, then turned. "Just load 'em up and take them back to the farm, Cap. Next time do as I tell you." He walked back toward the office.

Mr. Breeding grumbled all the way home. "All this work to be done over again for a few pennies more?" But in his heart he knew that Mr. Page was right. It was more the principle than the price.

One day when Mr. Breeding went into Mr. Page's office he was introduced to a man by the name of George Nye. Mr. Page had discovered George poking around in the alley searching through trash cans for anything he could find to eat, or sell, to buy drugs. He was a raw-boned giant of a man about forty years of age, but looked much older. His back was bent from crippling rheumatism. Mr. Breeding could smell the man before he got close to him. Mr. Page didn't seem to notice.

"George needs our help, Cap," said Mr. Page. "He's a fine man . . . used to be a druggist. He told me that his rheumatism got so bad that he started taking drugs to ease the pain. Before he realized it the drugs got the best of him. He has no job and no place to stay. Andy Stokes told me about him. He said George had been sleeping in a piano box behind Andy's grocery store with only rags from the garbage to cover him. I went down and got him. He needs our help, Cap."

George sat with head bowed as Mr. Page spoke. Tears fell to the uncarpeted floor. He raised his head slightly. The tears had made streaks through the crust of dirt on his face.

"Mr. Page," he said, trying to steady his voice. "I've been praying for help. The pain in my back is so severe that I know I won't last the winter in that piano box. If I could just get a job and a place to stay," he wiped his eyes on his sleeve. "But who would hire me in my condition?" He paused, trying to gain composure. Mr. Page pulled a white handkerchief from his pocket and gave it to George.

George thanked him. He wiped his eyes and blew his nose before he continued.

"I went to the pastor of the Christian church, but he couldn't help me. I listen to the Salvation Army when they have their street meetings, and the other day I asked them to pray for me. When you found me this morning it was God's answer to my prayers. I believe God wants to help me. If I can just get a job, and a place to stay."

Mr. Page removed the cigar from his mouth. "George," he said, "I need someone to get my mail and run errands for me. But first we've got to get you well enough to be able to work."

George was given an apartment for two or three weeks and put under the care of Dr. Kennedy. When he was feeling better Mr. Page sent him out to the farm. He was temporarily put into the boys' tent. Jess Davis, fourteen years old, was the youngest of the older boys. There was no room for another bed so George was given the bed Jess slept in. A hammock was stretched from the the framework of the tent for Jess. The boys were immediately fond of the humble giant. In fact, everybody loved him.

George got up every morning at four o'clock to catch the early train. He sat in Mr. Page's office through the day, running errands now and then and returning to the farm on the four o'clock train in the evening. He always went by the Post Office and picked up the mail for the farm folks and brought them newspapers and magazines as well. When it was clear that he wasn't going to use drugs anymore, George was moved into a house Mr. Page owned. He remained faithful to God and to his promise to Mr. Page. He became a leading member of the Salvation Army. At every opportunity he testified as to what God and Mr. Page had done for him.

With workers hard to find, Mr. Page and Mr. Breeding started writing to relatives offering them a job if they would come. One day Mr. Page's sister, Elizabeth Rowena, who had married Morland Monsell, came to see what her younger brother was up to. Mr. Page took her out to the farm, but he couldn't stay long. He told Mr. Breeding to show her around and that he would come for her in the evening.

Mr. Breeding gave her a tour of the place. Puzzled at seeing all the tents, the old people, and the children, she asked, "What does all this mean? What is Charley doing? Why is he doing all this?"

"It's not something that everybody would understand," said Mr. Breeding. "And you may be sure, I've been asked these questions before. Charles Page is a very complex man. Unique is a good word for him. One man once described him as a hard headed, hard handed, intensely practical man, but a man with a very big heart. That's true. Businessmen, especially the oil men, know him to be one of the shrewdest and hardest traders in the industry. He has great foresight. He is a quick appraiser, capable of making instant but wise decisions that involve thousands of dollars. He is the most unassuming rich man I have ever met. He is kind and compassionate with those who need help. He is especially fond of children. And they love him too. In fact, they call him Daddy Page. Even my children call him that sometimes."

"Someone in town told me that he was doing this to get a tax break," said Mrs. Monsell. "They didn't know I was his sister."

"I've heard that too, but I suppose you have to expect such as that. You start with a vision. You try to do good but there are always those who will say, he has a motive. But you needn't worry."

"Ma would be proud of him," said Mrs. Monsell.

It wasn't many days after she left, that Mr. Page's nephew, Anthony Wayne Avery, came. Mr. Page called him "Bub." Bub rode out on Mr. Page's horse, Buster. He looked everything over and went back to town.

It was about this time that Mr. Breeding asked Mr. Page if he could take a vacation. He wanted to spend Thanksgiving with his folks in Manhattan, Kansas.

"There's a boys' industrial home in Topeka, Kansas," he told Mr. Page, "and I'll go by there and see how they run things. Maybe it would help me with the boys."

Mr. Page told Mr. Breeding not to worry, that he would get Bub to take charge while he was gone.

Mr. Breeding hadn't been gone more than a day, when Bub took inventory of the groceries in the store. He found that a large round of cheese was missing. He questioned the boys who had helped him in the store.

"Old Bull Frog Breeding took it with him," said one of the boys.

Bub had worked for the Pinkerton Detective Association, and he decided to do a little detecting. The boys had seemed a little too eager to help in the storeroom, and too quick to answer when he asked them about the cheese. While they were in school he searched their tent and found the round cheese box and what was left of the cheese under one of the boys' cots.

When Mr. Breeding returned from vacation, he told Mr. Page what he had learned about the boys' home. Mr. Page didn't seem interested.

"Lucy, I know you like Cap, and I do too. He's a good man. But I'm going to let Bub run things out there. He has come all the way from Wisconsin because I promised him a job when he got here. I can't ask Bub to lay railroad ties, dig ditches and things like that. Maybe with both him and Cap, things can go faster."

"Mr. Breeding isn't going to like being demoted, Charley. It's going to hurt him."

"I know, and it isn't going to be easy for me to tell him. That's what's bothering me. I'm trying to think of it as strictly business. What is best for business is what you're supposed to consider, but I'm very fond of Cap and this is going to be very hard to do." He sat down in his chair and opened the newspaper. "In fact I think I'll let Bub do the telling. That can be his first assignment. Cap can see to the needs of the people and their problems. That's what he's best at. He has no business sense. Bub can take care of the business and manage the workers. Cap says he has too much to do. This way we can get things done faster."

A few days later, Mr. Breeding and Leonard Nolen were taking inventory of the supplies in the storage basement when Bub Avery rode up.

"Cap," he said, "I never hated anything so badly in my life, but Charley has asked me to manage things out here."

It struck Mr. Breeding like a bolt of lightening. All the pent-up anxiety swelled up within him. He stood in shock for a moment. Then anger engulfed him.

He threw his pencil across the room and blurted out, "I have offered my life in the service of humanity. I wanted nothing for myself and this is my reward! If I ever do such a dumb thing like this again I want someone to kick me off the face of the earth. I QUIT! I'll tell Mr. Page how I feel about this in the morning."

24

Forfeit the Dream

That night, Mr. Breeding lay thinking of what he would say to Mr. Page. Finally, exhausted, he succumbed to sleep.

The next morning he caught the early train to Tulsa. As he made his way up the back steps to Mr. Page's apartment the smell of bacon frying and coffee brewing meshed with the smell of the O'cedar floor-sweep on the stairs.

"Come in," called Mr. Page, when Mr. Breeding knocked.

Mr. Breeding knocked again. He wasn't going to open the door and just walk in. Mrs. Page came to the door. She had just set Mr. Page's plate of bacon and eggs before him.

"Sit down Cap, have some breakfast," said Mr. Page, waving him toward a chair next to him at the kitchen table.

"No thank you, I'll stand," said Mr. Breeding. Then words failed him. A large lump in his throat prevented him from articulating. Mr. Page had a strange power over him. He stood momentarily as though hypnotized. Thoughts floated vaguely through his mind as to what he had intended to say, but he was unable to capture the right words. He felt like a school boy who had been called upon to recite before he had learned his speech. Heat began to rise in his face as it grew red. He knew he had to speak or lose his courage altogether.

"You are dissatisfied with me and I quit," he stammered.

Mrs. Page quietly left the room. Mr. Breeding turned his hat in his hands as he continued. "We had a gentleman's agreement. I was willing to spend the remainder of my life without financial consideration other than the needs of my family be supplied. I gave my body and soul to do what good I could and it makes a man feel like a miserable failure when he works for his room and board and can't give satisfactory service."

"Aw, Cap, you haven't done so much," Mr. Page answered as he continued eating. "If it wasn't for your father-in-law, Mr. Smith, and your friend Lindsay, you wouldn't get anything done."

Mr. Breeding hadn't expected this insult. "Well at least I surround myself with good people," he blurted out at random. "That's more than I can say for you. I don't see how Mrs. Page stands some of the characters you associate with." He hadn't meant to say that. But it was said, and he wasn't going to apologize.

There was no anger in Mr. Page's deep voice, and it was disconcerting. It was like fighting someone who refused to hit back. "Aw, Cap, you're crazy," he said. "I treated you in good faith. I supplied all your needs and you fared better than when you were with the Salvation Army. I even gave you forty acres of prime land."

"That land isn't mine," said Mr. Breeding. "There is a serious question as to whether the quit claim deed is worth the paper it's written on. I'm going to deed it back to you."

Mr. Page wiped his mouth with his napkin. "Cap," he said, "I didn't fire you. You know that we've been writing for relatives to come help us out. Bub came, and I had to give him a job."

"You don't have to fire me. I quit." said Mr. Breeding. "I don't want to work for somebody who is dissatisfied with me."

"Cap, you're a good man. You are trustworthy, you are respected by the people and I believe you love children. But you don't have as much business sense as that girl Lindsay does. Bub is a businessman. He knows how to get things done. You're too nice. People take advantage of you."

"I worked hard."

"You work hard, but you're not too good at getting others to work. I can tell that your attitude is, 'what's the hurry?' every time I try to urge you to get more done."

He put his knife and fork across his plate and shoved it out of the way. "Lucy says I don't understand you. Perhaps she's right. Maybe I do expect too much of you, but with Bub in charge you wouldn't have as many responsibilities. There is so much to be done and so little time. Things have to move faster."

"Nobody could work as fast as you can think," said Mr. Breeding. "We'd just get one project started and you'd have another one lined out for us to begin. You expect too much from a person who is just working for room and board."

"Cap, would it make you feel better if I paid you for your eighteen month's service, deducted your expenses and sold you the forty acres?"

"That would suit me fine," said Mr. Breeding.

"What do you consider your services were worth?" asked Mr. Page.

"I don't think fifty dollars a month is too much for all I did," said Mr. Breeding.

"All right. Fifty a month for eighteen months comes to nine hundred dollars," said Mr. Page. "Now let's figure the family's expenditures and you'll see that I have been fair."

Mr. Breeding figured twenty-five-dollars a month was a fair estimate of the family expenditures.

"That comes to four hundred and fifty dollars," said Mr. Page. "Let's call it four hundred. That leaves me owing you five hundred dollars difference," said Mr. Page. "Would you like that to go on the land, or shall I give you a check for the five hundred, so you'll have something to live on, and let you owe me for the land."

Mr. Breeding nodded consent, a little embarrassed that he hadn't realized that he wasn't working for nothing.

The price of the forty acres was set at fifteen hundred dollars. "Now, Cap, do you see what kind of a businessman you are?" asked Mr. Page. "You weren't thinking right. You came out with a thousand dollars less than I had given you."

Mr. Breeding hated to admit that anger sometimes erases reasoning. Mr. Page would have loaned him the five hundred to live on. "That's all right," he said stubbornly. "I'll pay for what I get. Then I'll know it's mine."

Mr. Page picked up the phone and called Claude Tingley, his secretary. "Claude," he said, "Cap is coming up there with the deed to some land I'm selling him. I want you to prepare mortgage papers for him. Make the payments small and don't let them start until the first of the year."

He wrote a check for five hundred dollars and handed it to Mr. Breeding.

"Cap, I think you can get enough lumber where I buy mine for about thirty dollars, to build you a small house to make out with for awhile. You are welcome to stay in the house on the farm until you get something to move your family into," he said, as he handed Mr. Breeding the check.

Mr. Breeding thanked him and left. When the door clicked shut behind Mr. Breeding, something inside him clicked shut with it. A sadness engulfed him. It had been hard, but exciting, working for Mr. Page, planning and seeing things happen. A feeling of finality gripped him. He would no longer be a part of the dream.

Mr. Breeding straightened his shoulders and breathed deeply of the crisp, cold air. He refused to entertain any regrets to his action. It was the first day of December 1909, and the first day of freedom to go his own way. He was his own man now and not obligated to anyone except his family.

As he walked down Main Street his thoughts went back to his childhood. Was there ever a time when he had really been free of obligation to others?

The Breeding family, of Welsh-English descent, had originally come from Virginia. On coming to Kentucky the large family homesteaded thousands of acres in Knott County, Kentucky. He recalled with nostalgia, the hill country, drained by a creek known as Breeding's Creek, a tributary of Rock House Creek which emptied its waters into the North Fork of Kentucky River. His father, Samuel H. Breeding a country doctor, was a graduate of two of Louisville's highly credited institutions of medicine. Mr. Breeding thought of his mother, formerly Annie Hale. She had been the first postmistress in the county. Mr. Breeding recalled the little post office in the corner of their living room. It was called "The Lucus Post Office." The doctor's office also occupied a couple of rooms of the home, with its own entrance. Dr. Sam Breeding had practiced medicine for twenty years at Camp Branch, in the hills of Southeastern Kentucky.

Mr. Breeding thought of the name, Brinton Flint, his mother had given him. The name suggested strength. He was born July 26, 1875, in Carter County Kentucky, the first of three sons born to Dr. Sam and Annie Breeding.

Brinton was six years old when his mother died. He had the responsibility of keeping his little brothers out of mischief. It seemed that he had never been a child.

He was in his early teens when his father remarried and another son was born. In 1891 when Brinton was sixteen and feeling the call to be a preacher, his father sold the homestead, loaded whatever they could get into two covered wagons and an old black hearse that his father drove and the family headed for Texas. They settled in what they thought was Texas, but they were actually in the dust bowl area of the Oklahoma Territory, fourteen miles from Quana, Texas.

Mr. Breeding recalled with sadness the two years they spent wrestling with the sandy soil, trying to get something to grow. They had spent the family fortune building a house, barns and fences. At last, broken in health and spirit the doctor admitted defeat. On September 16, 1893, the day of the opening of the Cherokee Outlet they loaded everything into the two covered wagons and the old black hearse again.

"Don't look back, Brinton," his father said, as Brinton, now eighteen years of age, climbed into the seat of the lead wagon. One of his brothers rode with him. His sixteen-year-old brother rode in the second wagon with their stepmother, and the baby. His father followed behind in the hearse.

Being on the day of the run for land, Mr. Breeding recalled that as they moved northward, they met the homesteaders from the north. The swollen Washita River held them apart, as they all waited for the waters to subside enough to ford the river. He recalled that one man, in a hurry, decided to take the risk. He, his wagon and horses were swallowed up in the raging waters. Who he was, nobody seemed to know.

The Breedings stopped at Yukon, west of Oklahoma City, where his father, broken in spirit and health, died within two years.

Their stepmother remarried, leaving Brinton to fend for himself and his brothers. He worked laying railroad ties, and did a little preaching on the side. What he wanted to be was a lawyer and an evangelistic preacher. He had done some evangelistic work with a friend by the name of Means.

He was 22 years old, and his brothers on their own, when he entered Lane College at LeCompton, Kansas. He worked at a tree nursery to pay for his education and found a place to board in the home of Mr. and Mrs. Millard Smith, who had two daughters, Elsie and Ethel. Brinton and Ethel were later married. The Smiths were active in the Salvation Army, a new selfless religious organization, and at age 23, he joined, taking the three years Salvation Army training at Chicago to earn his Captain's rank. He did not regret any services he had rendered to the church. The work had been very rewarding. But still it was good to be free.

Most of Breeding's forty acres had already been cleared. The trees left in the valley would give them an abundant supply of wood for cooking and heating purposes. Mr. Breeding bought a wagon and a team of horses. Thirty dollars worth of lumber to build him a 16' x 32' two room house was loaded into his wagon and hauled out to his land.

When the Smiths found that the Breedings would no longer be working for Mr. Page they also resigned. They purchased a piece of land from Mr. Page which joined the Breeding's land.

The Smith's property already had a house on it and they moved into it right away. Mr. Smith helped Mr. Breeding build his house.

On December 29, 1909, the Breedings moved into their new home.

The winter of 1909-10 was bitter cold. As soon as the family was settled in, Mr. Breeding set about chopping trees for firewood. He became ill from working long hours in the cold and was crippled with lumbago and unable to get out of the house for several weeks.

There was no school near where they lived, but while confined to his chair, Mr. Breeding taught his children their lessons so that they would not fall behind when they went to school the following year.

Things were not going well with Mr. Page, either. Bub Avery was quick to admit that it took a man with rare talents to deal with so many women and children. He decided that he had neither the patience nor the desire for this unusual job. He told Mr. Page that he would give him until spring to find someone to take his place.

Remembering his mother's idea that in keeping the village schoolmarm in her home, she was giving her children an extra learning advantage, Mr. Page decided to obtain a teacher to take Bub's place. He asked Mr. Ashbrook, the teacher of the little Pleasant View School if he wouldn't like to have the job. Mr. Ashbrook declined, saying that he and Mr. Breeding were friends and that he wouldn't feel right taking the job.

Dr. Calhoun came to serve as the resident physician in February of 1910.

The children's home was finished in March of 1910, and what a lot of excitement ensued, as forty children, each carrying his or her their own personal belongings, scurried into the beautiful three-story, white, frame building with wrap-around porches on the two lower floors.

The first thing they saw, above the stairway of the large entry, was Mr. Page's motto, "think right."

The rooms of the first floor were for the attendants of the home to occupy. The girls carried their things to the second floor, where their matrons met them and directed them to their rooms. The boys marched on up to the third floor.

At noon the children were escorted to the large dining room in the basement. Besides the kitchen and dining room, the basement had a boiler room and an attendant to be sure there was enough hot water not only for the use of its occupants, but to to keep the steam radiators going to warm the rooms above.

The basement also contained storage rooms, and an office for Bub Avery, or whoever was in charge. Out back just a few feet from the kitchen was a small stone smoke house. The smell of hams smoking, filled the air.

When the children were moved out of the little cottages on the hill, Dr. Calhoun and his small son occupied one of the houses. One house was used as a nursery for the children. Another was used as a library, and another as storage room for the school supplies. Bub and his family lived in the Breeding cottage.

Mr. Page's relatives had started to filter in soon after Bub Avery arrived. Bub's sister, Mrs. Hawkins, was made head matron, in charge of purchasing clothing and other needs for the children. Another relative, Mrs. Slack, an elderly woman, was put in charge of the babies. Miss Lindsay was promoted from cook to housekeeper. Mrs. Herd was the new cook. Mrs. Coppage was still the piano teacher. Mrs. Burgess was seamstress; Miss Newhouse, Mrs. Heater, and Miss Ender, who was also a nurse, were employed as matrons.

But Miss Newhouse didn't stay long. She nursed Joe Davis back to health when the doctor thought he would die with tuberculosis, and then she left.

1909. *Grandpa Williams sits between an elderly woman and Mrs. Webb with a cancer on her nose.*

25

The Drouth of 1910

WITH THE SPRING CAME HIGH HOPES. THE WARM DAYS MADE MR. BREED-ing feel somewhat better. By planting time, with the help of his wife and the Smiths, he was able to plow and plant a small garden spot. The soil was rich and he expected a good harvest. The tender shoots came up, but there were no spring rains. By late June the plants had withered and died, and so had Mr. Breeding's hope of making a living with his garden.

A drouth had hit the countryside. Crops died, creeks and streams dried up and everyone complained of the sweltering heat. The Arkansas River was a series of sand bars traversed by weak trickling streams. Water had to be brought in by train so the oil men had enough to drill their wells, and keep their drill bits from getting overheated.

Mr. Page's hopes were dashed too, concerning vegetables to can for the winter, and for crops to feed his animals. He had leased some of his farm land to sharecroppers for one dollar a year and one-third of their crops, hoping to get enough feed for his herds of animals. But there were no crops.

However, the crop failure was more serious with Mr. Breeding. His five hundred dollars were depleted. Mr. Smith found a job in Tulsa as a rough carpenter, and he shared with the Breedings or else they would have gone hungry. Neither the Smiths nor Breedings had seen the need to can food the year before they left the farm, and all foods had to be purchased in town.

It was a depressing time, almost unbearable for Mr. Breeding. Having to rely on his father-in-law was humiliating. He loaded his wagon with wood and took it into town to sell, but he had little luck. Everybody used coal or gas for cooking and heating.

On June 11, Governor Haskell was to speak at the Tate Brady Hotel in Tulsa. Mr. Breeding was always interested in public affairs, but he really decided to go to the meeting because he knew Mr. Page would be there. All the oil men had great interest in what the governor had to say.

The latest excitement was over where the permanent capitol of Oklahoma should be. The temporary capitol had been established in Guthrie, where the Bureau of Indian Affairs was located. Guthrie wanted to keep the capitol seat, but Oklahoma City was making a bid for it. That day there had been an election, and everybody was eager to learn whether Guthrie or Oklahoma City was to be the new capitol of the state.

The crowd began to gather. Mr. Page came in with three other men. When he saw Mr. Breeding he nodded from across the room as the meeting began. The governor announced that Oklahoma City was to be the new capitol. Everyone cheered.

Mr. Breeding listening with half an ear tuned to the governor's speech, had his mind on the difficulty of swallowing his pride and asking Mr. Page for a job.

Suddenly Mr. Tate Brady burst into the room. He interrupted the Governor's speech with the news that the Guthrie officials had declared the election was illegal. The process servers were on their way to serve an injunction against the Governor. The news caused quite a stir. The meeting broke up, and people were on their feet moving about the room highly excited. Some of them went home. Mr. Breeding tried to catch Mr. Page before he left, but he couldn't get through the crowd in time. Mr. Page had already gone.

Mr. Breeding paused and followed the crowd to see what Governor Haskell would do about the injunction.

Haskell, determined that Oklahoma City would be the capitol of the state, telephoned W.D. Anthony and his assistant Paul Nesbitt. The Governor told them to hide the State Seal in a suitcase and meet him in Oklahoma City. When Mr. Breeding left some of the oil men, caught up in the excitement of intrigue, talked about chartering a train to accompany the governor to Oklahoma City. They even mentioned strapping on their guns in case the governor needed protection.

William Stryker, of the *Daily Democrat* newspaper, who went along on the chartered train, reported the next day that the train ran at top speed to outrun the process servers. It was daylight when they got to Oklahoma City.

"Haskell seems to have won," said Mr. Breeding, as he read the account in the paper. Oklahoma City is to be the new state capitol."

"Who were the ones who accompanied him on the train?" asked Mrs. Breeding. Mr. Breeding read the names.

"Tulsa's mayor; L.J. Martin; former mayor, John O. Mitchell; Mr. B.J. Losier, one of Mr. Page's partners; Mr. and Mrs. Galbreath; and William Stryker,"

Mr. Page, more interested in finding the right person to be over his children, finally persuaded a Mr. Short, a Tulsa high school teacher to take Bub Avery's place. Mr. Short was a fine looking young fellow, unmarried and considered a good disciplinarian. He also taught a class in the little Sunday School. Miss Lindsay was elected the Sunday school superintendent and song leader.

But Mr. Short didn't stay long. Mr. Short's brother, a young man with a wife and a child, was persuaded to come and take his place.

Mr. Breeding missed the children terribly. Now and then he rode one of his horses over to see them. When he did, he held a prayer meeting, encouraging the children to memorize meaningful poems, which he quoted readily. He sometimes had them write stories which he let them read aloud. Before he left, he would gather the children around and pray for them. They looked forward to Tuesday evenings when he came.

The children still ran out to Mr. Page's buckboard when they saw him coming up the road, and sometimes they mentioned that Mr. Breeding had come to see them.

Mr. Page's main concern right now was getting a railroad through to Tulsa, and starting up his brick plant. He brought in some Mexicans who knew how to run a brick plant and lay railroad ties. Some of the black men who had borrowed money from Mr. Page to buy homes were given jobs clearing the right-of-way for the railroad tracks to be laid.

In the fall of 1910 Mr. Page asked for, and got, a permit to lay tracks for his railroad. He then sent Frank Avery, son of Bub Avery, to Omaha to learn to be an engineer for the electric motor cars that would be used as passenger cars. Mr. T. H. Steffens was borrowed from the Frisco Railroad Company to get the railroad business organized. Mr. Steffens liked what he saw of the pioneering venture, and when Mr. Page offered him the position of president over the railway company he accepted.

Mr. Breeding watched with interest as the land was being cleared. The tracks would run right past his house, as Mr. Page had promised. His children would have a way to go to school. As he watched, a longing to once more be a part of Mr. Page's dream engulfed him.

Mr. Page always had so many things going at the same time it was impossible for anybody else to keep track of what all was going on. But not for him. He had the ability to keep track of everything and knew everybody by their first name who worked for him. He often called people by their last name, but he knew what their first name was.

With everything else going on, Mr. Page was also in the process of building a home for Lucile and himself on the northeast corner of Third and Olympia. He purchased a lot from Mr. Crosby, an oil man who owned a great deal of land in Tulsa. This section of land was called "Crosby Heights," and was the first addition in Tulsa in which sewer and pavement were included with the purchase. The lots sold for $300 to $900 dollars each.

Mr. Crosby was buying Billy Roesser's home on Boulder Street. It was the showplace of the town. Billy had made millions in the Glenn Pool, had lived well for a few glorious years, but now he was broke. He was selling his showplace home and moving to St. Louis. Mr. Page bought some of the fine furniture and valuable oil paintings that Billy had paid such a high price for. For the children's home, he bought an elegantly beautiful sideboard for the dining room of their new home.

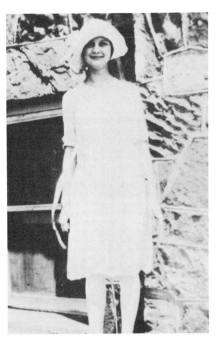

1921. *Frona Johnson, Charles Page and Gertrude Jean Bennefield.*

Mary Page, during her teen years.

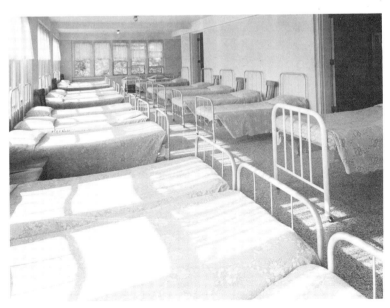

Each child had a bed of his or her own in the new Home.

The Charles Page Mansion built in 1915.
It stood at 810 Main Street in Sand Springs.

The race riot of 1921. A scene from the corner of Main and Archer street.

1920s. *Shell Creek dam.*

This house was built over the spot where Galloway had his temporary work shop. He later lived in this house. Then when Home children, Elizabeth Moore and Leonard Nolen, married, they lived in the house. Still later, it was called Lindsay Hall for older Home girls to live in. Paul Galloway is seen on the pole.

The flood of 1923. Above: *51st Street, west of Vern Station. The Arkansas went out of its banks, washed out the railroad tracks and stranded hundreds of people. Mr. Page sent mattresses and bedding to the buildings in the park, and took care of the people until they could return to their homes.* Below: *The washed out tracks at Bruner Station, 65th Street. They hooked four cars to steam engines for four days and ran them on the Katy tracks while Page's tracks were being repaired.*

Spinning room of the Sand Springs Textile or cotton mill. Built in 1922.

Sand Springs in the early thirties.

Sand Springs Children's Home built in 1918.
You can see the nursery penthouse on the roof.

1988. *Charles Page Children's Home. Jim and Opal Clark out front.*

1937. *Home children and their children at the Home on "Home Coming Day," which used to be on Thanksgiving Day.*

1941. *Thanksgiving Home Coming Day.*

Miss Minnie Bell Verbeck and her piano recital of 1937.

1940s. *Miss Verbeck and her girls in their annual spring piano recital.*

1945. *The Luce family was one of the largest families ever admitted to the home. L-R: Wilma, Judy, Leon, Brooksie, Richard, Quell, Allen, Ella and Robert. Their mother, Zena Hall Luce, (far right) died of cancer two months after entering the children into the home.*

Homecome Day, 1985: *The Luce family pose again. Robert is absent. They are one of many families of Home children that represent the excellent high values that Mr. Page wanted for all his children.*

1938. *Home boys' band.*

1947. *Home children and grandchildren on "Home Coming Day."*

1950s. *Children of the Home.*

1950s. *Mrs. Ruth Farnum and those who took part in the annual music recital. The little Home children got a front seat. Captain Cathcart, Home Superintendent, is at the right behind the older boys, Mr. Breeding is to the right.*

Dr. Calhoun in his office over the Rexal Drug Store.

Mr. B.F. Breeding

1965. *Girls of Lindsay Hall.*

1964. *Boys of Breeding Hall*

An artist's rendition of the new Widows' Colony and Sand Springs Home.

1958. *Mrs. Charles Page's photograph when she was
inducted into the Oklahoma Hall of Fame.*

Mrs. Charles Page's later home, now owned by former home boy, Hurley Lane.

173

*Raymond Stamps, a former Home boy, George Campbell,
and Mr. Breeding at a gathering of Home children.
Mr. Breeding was about 95 years old.*

*Dr. Wendell Sharpton, superintendent of schools,
looks toward Charles Page High School.*

Sand Springs Home Trustees, Memorial Day, 1956. L-R: B.F. Breeding, Jack S. Babbitt, Paul E. Estill, S. Neal Johnson, H.C. Jones, E.J. Doerner is not pictured.

PHOTO TAKEN BY OPAL CLARK — 1988.

Lynn Klopfenstein and one of the lions that Galloway carved to guard the park entrance. The lions now guard the entrance to the Charles Page children's home.

175

The five original members of the Board of Trustees: (back row) T.H. Steffens, P.E. Estill; (front row) Claude Tingley, E.M. Monsell, Edwin Page.

Present members of the Board of Trustees:

Joe Williams, president

Bill J. Brown

R.A. Weese

26

Railroad to a Briar Patch

EARLY IN 1911 MR. BREEDING WAS APPOINTED TOWNSHIP TRUSTEE AND served as assessor for the western part of Tulsa County. The job lasted until he had visited each residence in that area. For this he was paid three dollars a day.

When planting time came, he plowed and planted. His hopes were high as the seeds began sending tiny green shoots above the ground and the first rain came. More spring rains came, but they were light. Disheartened, Mr. Breeding watched his sparse garden wither and die, knowing he would have to look for work elsewhere.

The grading for Mr. Page's interurban railway was started in March 1911 and within forty-three days a single line track was laid from Third Street to the "Home Station," just west of the big spring.

On May 10, the train made its trial run. Mr. Breeding heard it coming and called to the rest of the family to hurry out on the front porch to watch it pass.

Mr. Page was on the train. Seeing the family he waved from the train window and yelled, "What do you think of it, Cap?" Mr. Breeding couldn't hear what he was saying, but he waved to Mr. Page.

There had been many hardships and many problems in dealing with the people on the hill, but right now all that came to Mr. Breeding's mind was the excitement of the pioneering venture. He longed to be working with the boys and the people who had become his friends.

That evening when Mr. Smith came from work he stopped by the Breeding's house. Mr. Page had given a tour through the train.

"They called it a 'Fool's Enterprise,' when he started this project. What do folks think of it now?" asked Mr. Breeding.

Mr. Smith grinned. "They said 'who, but Charley Page would spend three hundred thousand dollars to build a railroad out to a briar patch?'"

"One of these days they will see," said Mr. Breeding.

Finding an odd job now and then but nothing he really cared for, Mr. Breeding decided to swallow his pride and ask Mr. Page for a job.

It seemed like old times when he paused at the office door and waited for Mr. Page to ask him to come in.

"Cap, how have things been going?" asked Mr. Page, turning from his desk. "I figured you'd pick up where you left off in the Salvation Army. You didn't."

"I thought I could make a go of it as a vegetable gardener, but with the drought two years in a row I gave up that dream."

"It has been bad," said Mr. Page. "We have a little corn from an early planting, but that's about all. But I can't complain. We've been doing a booming business with our water bottling plant. It paid for itself last year, with enough profits to feed my kids. I figure God's lookin' out for these kids. That's why He directed me to buy the property with the spring on it. He knew this was coming. Two years of drought means three years without any canning done. That spring will have to feed my kids for three years."

"And your animals too?" asked Mr. Breeding.

"Them too," said Mr. Page with a nod. "I put in a new canning factory that will can in gallon cans this year hoping we'd have a big garden but we'll have to bring vegetables from areas not affected by the drought if we're to can anything this year."

There was an awkward silence. Finally, Mr. Breeding said, "Mr. Page, I'd like a job if you have anything I could do. I'm not asking for the job I had. I'll work at anything."

"Sure, Cap," said Mr. Page. "I can always use a good man. Go talk to Mr. Short. He's in charge out there now."

Mr. Page seemed glad that Mr. Breeding was coming back. "Cap, what did you think when you saw my train pass your house?"

"I was very excited for you. Your dream is coming true. You deserve it."

"Well, I don't know about that, but I said I'd run the train past your house and I kept my word, didn't I?" Mr. Page pulled his watch out of his pocket and checked the time against the big clock on the wall, as he added, "Now your kids will have a way to get to school."

Mr. Breeding looked surprised. "How did you know my children weren't in school last year?"

"Oh, I have ways of finding out what goes on." He looked down at Mr. Breeding's leg. "How is your lumbago?" he asked.

"I'm all right now, but I had a miserable time with it."

"Did Dr. Kennedy charge you for his visits?"

"No, he said that he heard I was sick and as a friend, he thought he would pay me a visit. He wouldn't take any money. He said the welfare department would pay him."

Mr. Page gave a hearty laugh.

Mr. Breeding grinned. "I guess he should have said Mr. Welfare Department would pay him, for I have a feeling you sent the doctor out."

Mr. Page waved as though to change the subject. "What do you think of our motor car?" He thumbed through some papers on his desk. "It's a

McKeen motor car. The most luxurious cars manufactured so far . . . all steel construction, self-propelled and gasoline driven. We have two of them. They consist of an engine-room, baggage car, smoker and parlor cars." Mr. Page's eyes were twinkling with excitement as he added, "This interurban car is for transportation back and forth to Tulsa, but when I get around to it, I'm going to add shipping facilities for hauling freight. With transportation and shipping facilities available, we should have little difficulty interesting merchants and industry in locating in the area."

"How often will your cars run?" asked Mr. Breeding.

"Every thirty minutes from each terminal. The fare, going either way between Tulsa and the springs will be ten cents...five cents if you get on the car between terminals."

"That's cheap enough," said Mr. Breeding.

Mr. Page drew a match from his pants pocket, struck it with his thumb nail, and lit his cigar. He blew the match out and laid it in a dish containing several cigar butts and burned matches. He squinted one eye as a curl of smoke drifted toward his face. Then continuing his conversation he said, "Home kids, and any child under school age and widows can ride free. So can you, your family and all my employees."

"You won't make any money giving everybody a free ride," said Mr. Breeding. "Your fare is cheap enough."

Mr. Page shrugged. "Just so we make expenses. But I'll make some profits when the park opens. I'm counting on freight from industry to take care of my kids needs. I'm working at it."

Mr. Breeding noticed that Mr. Page was wearing a new suit. He had looked neater since he had a wife to care for his clothes. But even with nice clothes, being a big man, his pants lost their press easily.

"Cap," said Mr. Page, ignoring the ashes that fell on the front of his clothes. "I've got my town all platted and several families are out there living in tents while they build themselves a house." He raised his eyebrows, and smiled.

"Good," said Mr. Breeding. "I knew you'd do it."

"Guess who was first to finish their house out there?" He didn't wait for an answer. "Anna Cullins and her daughter Maybelle. Their house was finished the first part of June. It's built of slab lumber from our new sawmill along Adams Road. I persuaded Mrs. Cullins to build out here to serve meals to the men who were clearing the right of way and for those running gas and water lines and other construction work."

"Mrs. Cullins is a nice lady." said Mr. Breeding. "I don't know what we would have done for water when we moved to Tulsa if it weren't for Mrs. Cullins. She made us welcome to get water from her well."

Mr. Page had a double row of drawers across the top of his desk. He drew some folded papers from one of the drawers. "Cap look at this," he said. Mr. Breeding went over to his desk. Mr. Page spread the paper before him. "This is just a rough sketch." He leaned back and smiled. "It's the lay-out for my town. I got Mr. W.H. Henderson of the Tulsa Engineering Company, who surveyed the railroad for me, to plat the town. I had hoped the town could be all platted by my birthday, June second, but we ran into difficulty and it wasn't finished until a couple of days ago."

"That would be June 17, 1911. I hope you wrote that down as a day to remember. At least I will," said Mr. Breeding, "for that was the day you saw your dream come true."

"It's only the beginning." Mr. Page gave a deep sigh. "But it's all coming together at last. Sometimes I find it hard to believe, but it's happening, Cap. It's happening. But it takes money. I've been spending so much money I nearly went broke. Earlier this year, I sold seventeen hundred acres of land and my big Taneha well. That well was producing about 2,000 barrels of oil a day." He sighed. "But I had to have ready cash to continue what I had started. I wasn't ready to give up my kids nor my town. I sold to Clifford B. Harmon, William Grahm and other New York associates, for a million dollars."

Mr. Page laid his cigar down. He got up and went to the water cooler. He took a flat paper cup from a box on top of the five gallon bottle of spring water, turned upside down in the cooler. Mr. Breeding watched the bubbles rise to the top of the bottle, making a little gurgling sound. Mr. Page handed the filled cup to Mr. Breeding and filled another for himself.

"The railroad alone cost me $300,000." he said, tossing the empty cup into the metal wastepaper basket. He sat down and started telling Mr. Breeding about some of the things he had accomplished while Mr. Breeding was away.

The next day, June 20th, Mr. Breeding rode one of his horses out to the farm. Mr. Short sent him to the field to cut corn with the boys. When the boys saw him coming they ran to meet him. Their warm greeting made him happy. The boys had grown quite a lot during his eighteen month absence. There were also some new boys.

Mr. Page continued to prod everybody to get things done and things were happening. The convenience of transportation to and from Tulsa made moving out to the area more attractive. But the place had to have a name. There were suggestions that the place be called Pageville, Page Addition or perhaps Page City, but Mr. Page shook his head.

"The town is not mine. It belongs to the people. I'm just giving it a start. As to a name for it, I think the Indians have already named this town Sand Springs."

Mr. Page had men at work constructing an amusement park, simultaneously with the railway construction and the platting of the town. The park was near completion and was scheduled to open on the Fourth of July with a grand celebration. It had been well advertised and much talked about around Tulsa.

Mr. Page was making plans to extend the tracks to loop around Main Street and past the park, but that would come later.

One evening Mr. Page came to the Breeding home. "Cap" he said, "we're putting up some little sheltered waiting stations along the line between Sand Springs and Tulsa where the interurban will make stops to pick up passengers. We've got to have names for these little stations. I thought you'd like to go along and help me name them."

Nine-year-old Eva Breeding wanted to go along.

When they had seated themselves in the front seat of the buckboard, Mr. Page handed Mr. Breeding a pencil and some paper for him to write the names down, so that the painters could paint them on the shelters. They started at PARK STATION. LAKE STATION was so named because the water now held within the lake had been a succession of small pools of water covering this area. The dam now held most of the water from the hills. The remainder had been taken care of through drainage into the river.

There was a cotton field beyond Lake Station, and that stop was called COTTON PATCH. But no one used that stop, and it was soon discontinued.

All the low lands, from what was to be called BRUNER STATION to the big spring, lay in pools of water during the rainy season. This land was the allotment of Creek Indian Billy Bruner. The road south of where Billy lived ran through these shallow pools of water to a long stretch of higher ground near the center of the river. Going south it wound around back to the wagon trail and on to Sand Springs.

"This is the place where I spent the most frightful night of my life," said Mr. Breeding, as he told Mr. Page of the time he spent the night on the wagon load of lumber in the middle of the river while Mr. Green went for help.

The waiting station would be near Billy Bruner's house. Mr. Page gave Billy a lifetime pass to ride the interurban. He rode often, and was often drunk. But Billy was harmless. He loved children. Children came to expect him to slip a penny or a nickel into their hands as he walked up the aisle to a vacant seat. Mr. Bruner lived to be a very old man.

The name chosen for the next station was LAWNWOOD. With transportation provided, little settlements were already springing up along the line. A few people had settled in this area hoping to start a little town of their own, but the Governor vetoed their request. He claimed that the financial expense of building a school in the area would throw the school system's budget off balance.

The station nearest the Breeding's home was about midway between Sand Springs and Tulsa. "How does the name midway sound?" asked Mr. Page. Mr. Breeding wrote the name down.

Eva had been learning a few French words. "Medio is the French word for midway," she said.

"Good, we'll call it MEDIO," said Mr. Page.

There was a farm at the next stop, that had a sign over the gate posts which read, "Mistletoe Glenn." The Elm trees were full of mistletoe. Mr. Breeding suggested that Mistletoe Glenn be the name of the station.

"That name is too long to paint on the station," said Mr. Page. "Let's call it GLENN." This was agreeable. However, when the men painted the signs on the stations they mistakenly painted the name GLENNWOOD on the station. It was corrected at the next paint job.

VERN, was the name chosen for the next stop, and following that came the station called HOME GARDENS, because Mr. Page had gardens there.

The next stop was at a place where they switched cars off onto a side track that ran through a field, past a corn crib. The brakemen had been calling it CRIB SIDING.

"We don't want to call this stop Crib Siding," said Mr. Page. "What is a good name for it?"

"How about naming it after my mother Annie Hale Breeding. Hale is a short name." The station was named HALE STATION.

The next stop was at the place where Mr. Page's pipe ended when he miscalculated the amount needed to carry the spring water from the spring to Tulsa. An old Indian by the name of Joe who lived in the area had passed away recently, so Mr. Page decided to honor him by naming the stop JOE STATION.

The name PARKVIEW was chosen for the next station, for the want of a better name.

Mr. Page reined his horses to a stop near Newblock filtering plant at the outskirts of Tulsa. "NEWBLOCK STATION," said Mr. Page, and Mr. Breeding wrote it down.

From that point the tracks ran along a lower level, parallel to the Frisco tracks, passing under the Third Street viaduct. There was a stop just before the interurban passed under the Third Street Viaduct. This stop was a little different because it had a stairway leading up the side of the bank to the upper level to Crosby Heights where Mr. Page lived. From there the tracks looped around the north side of town to Main and Archer to the Sand Springs Interurban depot which housed the management offices upstairs. The last stop was at Greenwood, the town of Tulsa's black residents.

And that was how each station was named. As the areas built up, each settlement would take on the name of its station.

1910. Laying the tracks for the railroad. See tracks behind the horses. The second peach orchard in the background.

27

A Dog Named Jim

THE PAGES' NEW HOME WAS A MODEST THREE BEDROOM, TWO-STORY, frame house, gleaming white, with a wrap-around porch.

His stepson, Will, whose dental office was in the Alexander building, purchased a home next door to Mr. and Mrs. Page.

"What we need now is a dog to run in this big back yard," said Mr. Page, who liked animals.

Will inquired around and found a puppy, which he gave to Mr. Page as a present. Bowser, the pup was little more than eight weeks old.

One day as Mrs. Page was sweeping the back steps, she paused to watch the tumbly little pup play in the backyard. Suddenly a strange dog who was frothing at the mouth, came running around the house. He headed straight for the little pup. As the dog bit him on the nose, Bowser yelped. Mrs. Page beat the dog off with the broom. Picking the puppy up, she carried him to the basement and put him in the sink. She scrubbed him with a brush and lye soap, putting iodine where the dog's teeth marks were. Then she hurried to the telephone.

"Charley," said Lucy, "Bowser has been bitten by a mad dog. What shall I do?"

"Aw Lucy you wouldn't know a mad dog if you saw one," he said. "There aren't any mad dogs around here."

"The dog's mouth was covered with white slobbers," Lucy insisted. "It was mad all right."

"Dogs slobber when they've been running," said Mr. Page. "I'm busy now, Lucy, and you stop worrying. That pup is going to be fine."

Lucy's heart was pounding. What was she going to do? She was sure that it took more than lye soap to rid the pup of the danger. How was she going to keep the puppy away from Charley? Maybe she could keep him in the basement.

That evening when Mr. Page came home, Lucy told him again that she was sure the dog that bit the pup was mad. "He was frothing at the mouth," she declared.

Still not willing to believe a mad dog bit the pup, Mr. Page opened the door to the basement and looked down at Bowser, who was yipping to come upstairs. He smiled as he watched the chubby little short legged pup try to mount the first step.

"Here, Shorty, let me help you," said Mr. Page. He went down the steps and picked Bowser up by the back of the neck. He brought the pup upstairs and slid him across the linoleum floor toward Lucy.

"Please, Charley!" cried Lucile in panic. "Don't handle him! Leave him downstairs."

"He's lonesome down there," said Mr. Page, as he sat down at the kitchen table and began to do card tricks for Lucy.

Days passed. Mrs. Page fed Bowser in the basement every day to get him accustomed to staying down there.

One Sunday afternoon Bowser was whining in the basement and Mr. Page suggested they let him go with them to see his kids.

"Charley, it's about time for Bowser to begin to show signs of going mad," said Lucy in protest. "That's why he's whining. He doesn't feel good."

"He's whining because he's lonesome down there alone in the basement," said Mr. Page. "There's nothing wrong with the pup."

When Lucy knew she was defeated, she wrapped the lap robe around the squirming puppy, making sure that his head was turned away from Mr. Page. She didn't want her husband to reach out and pet the dog as they drove along.

When the children saw the buckboard coming they began to run down the hill squealing, "Daddy Page! Daddy Page!"

Mr. Page always stopped to let the children climb aboard. Before Mrs. Page could warn them, seven children had been bitten. This alarmed Mr. Page. He had to admit that Bowser was behaving strangely. He turned the buckboard around and went back home with the pup.

Mr. Page called Will to come over and see what he thought about the dog. They sat on the basement steps and watched Bowser for awhile.

"I think he's going to be all right," said Mr. Page. "He just got cranky because he didn't like that long ride wrapped so tightly in that lap robe Lucy had around him."

The next day Lucile called. "Charley, you've got to come home. The little dog is frothing at the mouth and falling down when he tries to walk. He won't eat. He's acting strangely."

Mr. Page came home bringing Will and Dr. Kennedy with him. Dr. Kennedy confirmed the fact that the dog was mad and must be put out of his suffering immediately. Mr. Page went upstairs and got his gun, but he couldn't shoot the little dog. Neither could Will. Dr. Kennedy said that he would do it. Upstairs, Mr. and Mrs. Page and Will waited sadly. The shot was fired and Doctor came upstairs with the puppy wrapped in the lap robe. Bowser was buried in the back yard.

Neither Dr. Kennedy nor Dr. Calhoun knew how to give rabies shots, so Mr. Page sent Dr. Calhoun to Kansas, to learn so he could give the shots to the children who had been bitten.

When people heard about the dog going mad, friends convinced Mr. Page that he should take the shots, too. If he had had a scratch, the saliva from the dog might have infected him too. Rather than take a chance, he packed his bags and made ready to go to Kansas to take the rabies shots. He wanted Lucy to take them, but she refused. She tried to spare him the painful ordeal, insisting that she had watched carefully to see that the puppy kept away from him and that he need not worry. But he took the shots anyway.

When the news got around to relatives about the loss of the little dog, one of Mr. Page's sisters sent him a registered German Shepherd puppy from Alsase Lorraine, France, where Mr. Pages' mother had lived before coming to America. The registration papers stated that the dog's name was Jim.

"I don't want a dog," was Mr. Page's reaction. "One mad dog is enough." He walked out of the kitchen where the little pup stood looking up at him. Jim followed him into the living room and lay down beside his chair, with his head on Mr. Page's foot.

"Now, Jim," said Mr. Page, looking down at the dog. The dog's ears went up at the sound of his name. Mr. Page grinned. "You don't need to think you can win me over. You're going back where you belong." Jim wagged his tail as though he had just been told that he was a good dog. Mr. Page slid him off his foot and turned his attention to the evening newspaper. When Lucile announced dinner, Jim followed Mr. Page into the kitchen and again lay at his feet.

Mrs. Page smiled. "They say that a dog chooses his master, and I believe Jim has chosen you."

Mr. Page frowned. "Now don't get attached to that dog, Lucy. We're not having another dog in this house." As he looked down, Jim got to his feet. The little dog's ears were up, and he turned his head this way and that, expectantly. Mr. Page had to grin.

"Now, Jim," he said, "if you're trying to get on the good side of me, you might as well forget it because you're going back to where you came from." Jim wagged his tail.

"Go to Lucy, Jim, I don't want you," said Mr. Page. To his surprise Jim went over to Lucy and stood waiting for the next command. Mr. Page looked at Lucy. "He knows who you are already," he said. "He's a very smart dog." He paused. "But he goes back tomorrow before we get attached to him."

After Mrs. Page had fed Jim, he went back to lie under the table at Mr. Page's feet. For two days Jim followed Mr. Page wherever he went. The third morning he lay at Mr. Page's feet in the kitchen.

Mr. Page liked sitting at the kitchen table as Lucy prepared a meal. He always had a deck of cards handy, and after a few card tricks, he would settle down to two or three games of solitaire. If he won, he figured his luck would be good that day. Sometimes he made decisions based on that theory. This morning, Mrs. Page had a feeling that Jim's destiny would be decided according to the way the games went.

"I won both games of solitaire," said Mr. Page, as his wife set his breakfast before him. "That means good luck." He looked under the table at Jim. Alerted, Jim immediately stood to his feet. He turned his head this way and that, as if to say what is it you want?'

"He can almost read your mind," said Mr. Page "He'd make a good watch dog."

When Mr. Page went to work that morning, he took Jim along. Jim became a constant companion to Mr. Page. He lay beside his master's chair at the office, and if Jim growled at anyone who came into the office, Mr. Page judged that man to be up to no good, and he got rid of him as quick as he could.

"Jim is a good judge of character," Mr. Page would say, "He's just a dog. He has no axe to grind. His concern is for his master, and his keen instincts tell him whether a man is on the up and up, or if he's a crook. I trust Jim."

December 1909. *Home not finished. Girls hold Christmas dolls. Mr. Page on the porch. Railroad spur for building supplies in the foreground.*

Not a Vision Anymore

28

Not a Vision Anymore

Mr. Page's project was no longer being call "A Fool's Enterprise." People were beginning to take notice. Now a pat on the back with a compliment at his foresightedness was more often given. Many were caught up in the excitement of the pioneering venture and wanted to become a part of it. Mr. Page was so eager to get his town populated so he could draw the attention of industry, people could buy land at just about any price. He wanted even the poorest to be able to own a piece of land. He sold twenty-five foot lots as single lots so all could afford to buy. Fifty-foot lots were called double lots.

Mr. Short had been given the title of "Superintendent of the Home and Farms," doing what Mr. Breeding had done. He had a private office in the basement of the children's home.

The children no longer roamed the hillside like a colony of ants. There was now a place for everything and everybody. The Home had been built to accommodate fifty children and their attendants. There had been about thirty-one children when construction began, but by the time the building was completed there were forty-three children and attendants.

Mrs. Emma Hawkins, a sister to Bub Avery, had been hired as girls' matron after Miss Newhouse left. Mrs. Hawkins was in charge of purchasing clothing and various needs for the children. But Mr. Page said he wanted no uniforms on his kids. They were to dress as well as other children. They were not poor little orphans. They were his. He forbade anyone calling the childrens' Home an orphanage.

Mrs. Trippet and Miss Frieda Ender, a nurse, had been engaged as matrons while Mr. Breeding was gone. But Miss Ender and Dr. Calhoun, who had become resident doctor in February 1910, were married May 2, 1911, by Reverend Baird in the Presbyterian church in Oklahoma City. They now occupied the Jones cottage as their home.

The other two cottages were used for a library and a day nursery for under school age children.

Nelle Heaton had taken Miss Ender's place as assistant matron. Miss Margaret Lindsay was now the housekeeper, keeping things shining bright and spotless. Mrs. Hurd was the cook, Mrs. Burgess was the seamstress and Mrs. Coppage was still the girls' piano teacher.

The attendants' rooms were mostly on the first floor of the Home. The girls were on the second floor and the boys occupied the third floor, with the exception of the older boys. Rooms were added to the house that had been built for the Breedings to live in, and Leonard Nolen, Luther Nolen, Bert Evans, John Durham, Jesse Davis, Joe Davis, and Calvin Moorey were moved into it. A Methodist minister by the name of Kensit was in charge of older boys. They all took their meals at the Home.

It wasn't long after Mr. Breeding returned that Mr. Short resigned, and Mr. Breeding was asked to take his place until Mr. Page could find somebody else. He was to be paid fifty dollars a month. However, Mr. Breeding insisted that his salary be raised to seventy-five dollars a month beginning January of 1912.

Mr. Breeding now the superintendent, with a private office in the basement, didn't choose to be too private. Mr. Page's idea of leaving the door open as a welcome sign appealed to Mr. Breeding, and he too left his office door open.

Mr. Page recognized the dignity of labor and believed everyone should learn to work with hands, head and heart. So the children were always alloted duties to perform without pay, after which work could be offered for pay. They were always eager to go to the canning factory, or gardens because they were paid.

"Always save some of your money," Mr. Page had said, and most of them did.

The canning factory was south of the Katy tracks on Adams Road, within walking distance from the Home. It had been enlarged, updated and equipped to can food in gallon cans. But the drouth of 1910 continued through 1911. Without gardens and field crops, the cost of feeding the children and the many animals was astronomical. Gratefully the money from the spring water fed the children for three years as Mr. Page had predicted.

Mr. Breeding was saddened to hear that Mrs. Webb had passed away the year before and was laid to rest beside Mrs. Jones and the widow's four-year-old son in the little lake side cemetery.

Mr. Rust, who had come while Mr. Breeding was away, was employed to do farm work, but he liked flowers. He terraced the trampled hillside and planted beds of flower seeds. With water from the springs, the plants survived the dry summer. Before long the hill was alive with a delightful array of colors. Mr. Page was very pleased. This hill was the first thing people saw when they got off the train. Mr. Page hired Mr. Rust to plant flowers around the Home and along the walkways of his beautiful eighty-acre amusement park, not yet open to the public.

Eight grades being taught in the one room, Pleasant View School was now so over-crowded that there was talk of building another school. To alleviate some of the problems, Mr. Page improvised a private school for his children. Desks and other school equipment were installed in the basement storeroom of the store. The daughter of Lou North, now Tulsa county commissioner, was hired to teach in the private school.

The number of children in the Home continued to increase. Before the end of the year there were fifty-seven children in the Home. Visitors coming, dubbed the fifty-seven children, "57 varieties," after the Heinz label. And indeed they were.

Mr. and Mrs. Page remained faithful to spend Sunday evenings with the children. The children looked forward to seeing them. After supper, Mr. Page liked to sit on the front porch and talk to them. He told them many stories of his childhood and entertained them with funny little songs which he made up on the spur of the moment, inserting the names of this child and that, as he went along. To add to the rhythm of his songs he stomped his heel and made a funny sound by squashing the air between his palms. The small ones climbed into his lap, rode his foot and they all crowded so close they nearly smothered him at times.

Earlier, Mr. Page and Mrs. Page had been Sunday night dinner guests of the Breedings. Mr. Page now gave the Breeding family an invitation to have dinner with him each Sunday at the new children's home. They accepted the standing invitation.

Mr. Page also brought other guests with him every Sunday. Some of the guests brought their children along to play with the Home children, which to them was a special treat.

Through the years, Mr. Page delighted sitting at the table with his guests, and explained as he passed the heaping platter of chicken, turkey, pork, or beef, "this is the product of our own herds, or flocks, raised on our own farms, fed from feed grown on our own land, processed in our own processing plant or preserved in our own storage." It was his desire that his town and his farms be self sufficient and self maintained.

Shortly after Mr. Breeding returned to work for Mr. Page, a revival was held at the little school house, by home missionary Reverend Duncan. Several of the Home children were converted, and Mr. and Mrs. Breeding were admitted as members of the church on restatement of faith. Although Mr. Breeding had been responsible for getting a Sunday school organized for the children, neither he nor his wife had taken their membership out of the Salvation Army organization. So they were not listed as charter members of the community church.

Mr. Breeding was elected as an elder. Miss Lindsay was already the song leader and Sunday school superintendent. It wasn't long before she also became head matron of the Home.

Sarah Davis, one of the Home girls, wanted to teach a class, but she was afraid. Patiently, Miss Lindsay taught her the lesson at night, so that she could teach the children on Sunday.

Things were running as smoothly as could be expected with fifty-seven varieties of children, but the new excitement was the town of Mr. Page's dreams. Things were coming together, and his enthusiasm was soaring.

Clarence Harvey Tingley of Tulsa, began construction of the Municipal Power and Water Plant on April 26, 1911, and within three weeks had completed the storm and sanitary sewers for the town. A supply of gas piped from Mr. Page's gas wells was offered for a very low price as an incentive to build in Sand Springs. The electric plant consisted of two large Delco systems placed on flat cars. Water from the spring was piped to the childrens' Home, but a well drilled earlier to supply water for the cattle was sufficient to supply the town for a few years.

News was getting around that Mr. Page's dream of an industrial town was beginning to materialize, and people were coming to see what was going on. Mr. Page did the rest. He had something for everybody. For those who preferred country life he platted ten-acre tracts, "Upon which a family could establish their own little kingdom, living free and independent," he told them.

Mr. Page always gave prospective buyers a tour of the children's Home when he brought them out. He explained that THINK RIGHT had been his motto for years, and he wanted to pass the concept on to his "Kids."

"If they keep their thinking right, they're going to act right, and do what's right," he explained.

Mr. Page often took his guests through the kitchen in the basement where he stopped to treat them to a glass of fresh churned buttermilk, explaining that it was his favorite drink. He would stop at Mr. Breeding's office door, introduce his guests, and move on to show them the lovely dining room. Mr. Breeding would smile as Mr. Page called attention to the beautiful, highly polished solid oak sideboard that he had purchased for his Kids, when his friend Billy Roesser, an oil baron, sold the expensive furnishings from his mansion. Mr. Page would lift one of the delicate china bowls from the dainty sideboard shelves, and flip it gently with his finger to hear it ring.

"The finest of china," he would say, "from Billy Roesser's collection." Everyone knew that Billy had collected only the best.

The value of these extravagant gifts was lost on the children, who didn't know the difference. But this touch of elegance was symbolic of what Mr. Page wanted for his children. Nothing was too good for them.

After the tour of the Home and its grounds, Mr. Page would take his guests on a walking tour of his town. He would explain that he had reserved the land nearest the river for industry. Colored-town lay between Highway 64, the Katy tracks and downtown business district.

The numbered streets ran east and west. The streets from north to south, except Main Street, were named after presidents of the United States: Washington, Lincoln, McKinley, Main Street, Garfield, Roosevelt, Cleveland, Wilson, Grant, and Franklin.

The business district seemed destined to be centered around Second and Lincoln streets. The first grocery, owned by Al Sherrow, was on Lincoln Street, and W.B. Hickson's general store was soon to follow. But the sand was so deep people could hardly walk in it. Mr. Page decided he was going to have to extend the railroad tracks to loop around the town.

Mrs. Anna Cullins' boarding house on east Main Street between First and Second was a welcome aid to the workers in the vicinity. She and her daughter, Maybell White, served good food, family style.

One of the first structures on Main Street was the Kingsberry building at Second and Main. The Clute's Drug Store occupied the first floor with the post office in one corner of the drug store.

A.W. "Bub" Avery was the town's first postmaster. Mail was mostly general delivery, but post office boxes were installed on November 21, 1911, and Charles Page's younger brother, Edwin Adelbert Page, was first to rent a box. The number of the box was 48. By 1912 there would be twenty boxes rented.

Mr. Page was building several houses scattered about, mostly on Lincoln, Washington and Main streets. He named his real estate company "Townsite Real Estate" with Ross Rayburn, his wife's younger brother, as manager of the company. Ross' office was room three on the second floor of the Kingsberry building.

The water, gas and electric company also had its offices on the second floor with one person in charge of collections. Only a little over thirty-six dollars was collected the first month. But it was a start.

J.O. Brown opened a carpenter shop on the present site of the Kahn building. Al Sherrow opened the first butcher shop on North Lincoln Street.

The Sand Springs Amusement Park was being created almost simultaneously with the town. A grand opening was planned for the Fourth of July.

The twenty-acre lake, fed by springs, had been dammed at the south end, to make the water rise. It was stocked with fish, and a flotilla of row and motor boats were purchased for fishing or for a romantic ride downstream. Diving boards were installed, the beaches were sanded for bathers and a large bathhouse was built.

The flower beds that Mr. Rust had planted throughout the park added to the beauty of the shadowy woodland retreat.

The park proved popular since Tulsa was lacking a good recreational facility. Two of the magnificent McKeen motor cars made the runs from Tulsa to the park every twenty minutes, and they were filled each trip with no standing room left. The park had been well advertised and people came from a hundred miles or more for the gala occasion.

The park was divided into four sections. There was the playground area, the main park area, the zoo, and the lake area.

The playground was equipped with swings, slides, giant-strides, manually operated merry-go-rounds, exercise bars, teeter-totters and even a tennis court. There was a picnic area large enough for the Indians to hold pow-wows. The public was invited.

The section between the playground and zoo was the main amusement park. The lake was beyond the zoo. The main park was equipped with electric rides such as merry-go-round, ferris-wheel, Ride-Em-Dodge-Em cars, the whip and many other amusement facilities. The fare for each ride was ten cents, but free to the Home children.

There was an opera house, dance pavilion, skating rink, picture gallery, shooting gallery, penny arcade, crazy house and more. Dozens of rustic huts with picnic tables in them were scattered throughout the park. Concession stands operated exclusively by widows, to give them a chance to earn a little extra money, were in abundance. A whole beef was barbecued for the grand opening, and sandwiches were free.

Mr. Breeding chaperoned the older boys and the matrons took the other children to the park, and the adults had as much fun as the children.

The children especially enjoyed the penny arcade building where everything cost a penny. A player piano played automatically. There were moving pictures seen through peep machines. Looking down into a mirror at one end of the building one child could see the face of another child at the other end of the building. You could shoot a gun, get an electric shock, and many other fun things for only a penny.

The crazy house was a house of crazy mirrors.

There was a round wheel called a Roulette wheel. It measured about sixteen feet in diameter and was propelled by an electric motor. The object of the game was for people to sit in the center of the wheel which was started by the motor in a circular motion, increasing in speed, until all slid off against the padded curbing. The center of the wheel was covered with metal which had an electric attachment. If anyone stayed on too long, a light shock was produced which put them off in a hurry. Mr. Breeding was especially amused at seeing the boys try to stay seated on the wheel.

There was a live orchestra later in the evening at the dance pavilion. At nine o'clock, as the music wafted through the air, the crowd gathered at the lake where benches were provided to watch a grand display of fireworks from the opposite side of the lake. It was an experience that would have people talking for days, and eager to go back again.

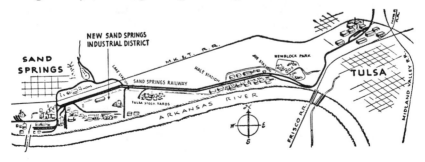

29

Baby Mary Ann

WHETHER IT WAS BECAUSE OF ALL THE GOOD DEEDS OR PERHAPS because Mr. Page had so many relatives calling him Uncle Charley is not certain, but others started addressing him as Uncle Charley.

"Uncle Charley," said a friend one day, "you always seem like a happy man."

"Make others happy and you'll find happiness for yourself," said Mr. Page.

But there was a void in Mr. Page's life. He longed for a child of his own. He loved his Home Kids, but it wasn't the same. He wanted a child of his own to live in his home. A child to cuddle, to love and cherish. A child to run to him when he came home from work each night.

In January of 1912, Charles Page and his wife went out of town, and when they returned they had a little newborn baby girl.

"I named her Mary Ann. That was my mother's name," said Mr. Page when friends and relatives came to see the tiny infant.

"How old is she?" asked one.

"Mary Ann was born January 9, 1912," said Lucy, smiling down at the baby in her arms.

"There's a place in Kansas where babies are adopted. Charley, did you get her there?" asked someone. Mr. Page looked disturbed and almost angry.

"Don't mention adoption," he said, as he took the baby out of his wife's arms. "She is my own, and I hope she never hears the word adoption." He encircled his arms around baby Mary as though shielding her from a cruel world. "She is not adopted. She is my very own child." The subject was never mentioned to him again.

Each evening when Mr. Page came home from work he ask, "How's the baby?" Then heading straight for the nursery, he carried her about the house talking to her.

"Charley, you're spoiling her," Lucy warned.

"Every child needs lots of love," he would say, holding her close and rocking her as he sang, "Oh, my baby, oh my baby."

He lay her tiny hand in his big hand and marveled at the the perfection in every detail. He kissed the two little hands that had wrapped themselves about his heart. When the little fingers curved over his big finger, he exclaimed, "She's holding on to me!" When she smiled, he looked at Lucy. His eyes twinkled. "She smiled at me! She likes me," he said.

Lucy smiled. "How could she not love you, Charley?"

His happiness was complete. As he rocked, he sang, "Go to sleep my baby, go to sleep my baby." As baby Mary closed her eyes in sleep he spoke in hushed whispers to Lucy, who was busy sewing baby clothes.

"Lucy, God is good to me."

"You're a good man," said Lucy. "You promised your mother that you would help widows and orphans, and you have. You've kept your promise to God that you would give your tithes to helping others less fortunate, and you've more than honored that vow. You deserve happiness for yourself."

Mr. Page rested his head on the back of the rocking chair. "We're getting to see my dream of an industrial town develop, Lucy, and now we have a child of our own."

A few days later Mr. Breeding went to his office to see him about something. Mr. Page was standing at the window looking down at the street below. He waved Mr. Breeding into his office.

"Cap," he said, "I've been thinking about how good God has been to me. I split my income with the Big Fellow, not thinking about getting any rewards, and He has heaped his blessings upon me more than I deserve."

"That's the way God is," said Mr. Breeding, "but you deserve it. Many a man who calls himself a Christian should take lessons from you."

"Well," Mr. Page said, "I can't call myself good, as I've told you often, Cap. I've never had a great awakening as I've heard some describe it, so I guess I can't call myself a Christian, but I'm not afraid to meet the Lord face to face." He looked out the window. "If I saw God standing across the street over there, I'd go up to him and shake his hand."

"And I don't believe God would turn away from you," said Mr. Breeding.

A short time later a mother came to Mr. Page with three little girls. "I can't work and take care of my girls," she said, "and I thought maybe you would let me put them in the Home?" Mr. Page sent her to talk to Mr. Breeding.

There were children now in the home whose mothers, who for one reason or another, couldn't care for them. Mr. Breeding agreed that under-school-age children should not be left alone in the home to fend for themselves. He accepted the children.

Three weeks later the woman came for the girls. There was a man with her, whom she introduced as the girls' new father. Two weeks passed and she came bringing the girls back, saying that the marriage had not worked.

"Things like that happen," said Mr. Page, when Mr. Breeding reported the incident to him on Sunday evening.

When the mother returned three weeks later with another man and introduced him as the girls' new father, Mr. Breeding called Mr. Page and asked him what to do, Mr. Page was upset. He talked to the mother.

"Children are human beings with feelings and emotions," he said "They are not boom-a-rangs to be thrown out and grabbed back. They need stability and security. If you take them this time you can't bring them back. It's up to you. Which is it going to be?" The woman left the girls in the Home.

Mr. Page knew he was going to have to do something to protect the children from being snatched back and forth from relatives, and never having a feeling of permanency and belonging, never being able to adjust to either situation. He began legal proceedings that would give him full custody of the children. This way, he would be the one to make decisions as to their welfare. Rules were made that a parent could take a child from the Home once, but she could never bring the child back.

On May 21, 1912, Sand Springs was incorporated by the unanimous vote of forty-one legal voters. The interests in which Mr. Page wanted to engage for the town were so many and varied, it took a special act of the State Legislature to include them all in the organization he planned.

Although Charles Page was the founder of the town and provided water, light and power, sewers, and other municipal facilities he never "bossed" the town. He had neither the time nor the inclination to run the internal affairs. He insisted that the town belonged to the people. He had all he could do to take care of the needs of his Kids, provide jobs for the people, and see to his park and railway system.

In order to handle to better advantage the crowds attending the Sand Springs Park it was decided to electrify the line. This work started in 1912 and for a number of years three classes of power were used — steam, electricity and gasoline. However, the McKeen gasoline motor cars were not practical as interurban cars to carry passengers to and from the park. The McKeene cars were sold. The interurban tracks were completed to circle through the town and electric cars were purchased to be used as interurban street cars.

In the early part of 1912 the name Sand Springs Interurban Railway Company was changed to Sand Springs Railway Company. The construction work was pushed to the utmost by Mr. Page, until the line was connected with the Santa Fe, Midland Valley, M.K.&T. and Frisco railways. With this connection the Sand Springs line was in position to render a belt line service giving to the industries the advantage of a four-way inlet or outlet which was of value to large receivers and shippers of freight.

With freight service now established, Mr. Page really had something to offer as inducements to bring in industry.

The Neodesha Bottling Works was the first plant to locate in Sand Springs. The attractions were cheap supply of gas, the right types of sand, a free plant site and a cash bonus.

When the railroad tracks were run through the town, the business district began to shift from Lincoln to Main Street.

Hotels were being built to accommodate the overflow of people. One hotel on Main Street was the Cart Hotel. The Budd Hotel and the Gray Hotel would come soon after, as the town continued to grow.

Despite the fact that the Home children were taken out of the little Pleasant View School, it was still too crowded. The townspeople knew there had to be another school built. They went to Mr. Page. Mr. Page traded the school system a piece of land on Fourth Street, between Garfield and Roosevelt Streets, on which to build their new school in exchange for the little Pleasant View schoolhouse property.

Classes for the public school children were held in two bungalows at Fifth and Lincoln streets until their school was completed. "Central," as the new two-story brick school was called, contained classrooms for all grades.

The Pleasant View school was used as a private school, third grade and under for the Home children, with Mrs. Flora Wiggins as their teacher. She remained through the year 1921, when she retired and the school was closed.

The little school came in handy for other uses as well. On Saturday the girls took piano lessons. The boys used the school building evenings, for boy scout meetings. Mr. I.P. Nelson, a fine looking Indian gentleman, was the boys' scout master.

At this time the Community Church, later to become Presbyterian, had a new church the members had built on 4th & Main streets. Dr. Seth Gordon, a scholarly white-haired Presbyterian minister, had been forced to give up his large pastorate in Pennsylvania because of poor health. He had moved to Tulsa to become president of Tulsa's Kendall College, but was happy to come to Sand Springs to pastor the new church.

The town was really becoming organized. Clarence Harvey Tingley, superintendent of the municipal power and water plant, was elected as the first[1] mayor of Sand Springs.

Mayor Tingley was also the first to own an automobile in Sand Springs. He bought a Maxwell in 1912, and E. Morland Monsell soon was the proud owner of a Ford touring car.

Mayor Clarence Tingley was also father to the first white boy born in the town of Sand Springs. Dr. Calhoun's daughter Margaret, was also born in Sand Springs in 1912, which made her the first white girl born within the city limits, although Margaret Breeding had been born in 1909 on the Home grounds.

As for now, Ross Rayburn was elected town clerk, and Robert "Bob" Fleenor was elected town marshal.

Fleenor was the only member of the police force. His main duty was to keep drunks off the streets after payday. Alcoholic beverages were forbidden

[1]The mayor-council form of government, would be superseded by the commission type government in 1916, but would be adopted again in 1963, with John M. Hess as councilman of a city manager form of government.

in all of Oklahoma, but bootlegging was going on in the backwoods. Liquor was still being smuggled into Sennett at the little Indian trading post only a few miles up the river. Men drunk on the elixir would come into town in a "shoot-em-up" frame of mind and people were getting hurt. But Marshal Fleenor got tough. He swore to stop the lawlessness. He raided the liquor joints and announced that anyone found carrying a gun or any concealed weapons in Sand Springs would be arrested and punished to the limit of the law.

The town had no jail, so Mr. Page donated a small building on Fourth and Main streets to be used for that purpose. Looking more like a smokehouse, the 8x10 rock and cement structure was so small that the officer was forced to do his guarding outside. The cot and stove inside for the prisoner took up all the space.

Mr. Page established a bank in Sand Springs in 1912 for the convenience of his people. The bank had a capital stock of $10,000. Being a frugal man, Mr. Page believed in utilizing every space to its fullest, so a supply of farm equipment and tools were displayed in the back of the bank.

The bank would be reorganized in 1913 and given the name "Sand Springs Bank."

A cotton gin was ready for operation in 1911. Bub Avery suggested that farmers scattered about Sand Springs and beyond plant cotton. But they refused on the grounds that there were practically no roads, and it was impossible to drive wagons in to the gin. But when Mr. Page talked to them and guaranteed a market for the product, they agreed. Mr. Page had someone take a picture of the loaded wagons as they rolled through town. In 1912, there were 1180 bales of cotton ginned.

A new M.K.& T. and Sand Springs Railway depot was built on Main Street, and on December 15, 1912, the American Express Company opened its office in the depot.

Marshal Bob Fleenor owned the only transfer business in town. The mail came to the railway station every afternoon at 2:00 p.m. Marshal Fleenor used a hand cart to deliver the mail from the station to the post office in Clute's drug store. He also delivered ice, which was sent to the depot from Tulsa.

The telephone lines that had been strung on railway posts for the use of the Home folks in 1909 were extended to serve the town in 1912.

Mr. Davis, the telephone operator, had a strict ruling that there would be no service after 10:00 p.m. except for emergencies. On Sunday Mr. Davis sang in the choir, so service was discontinued between the hours of 11:00 to 12:00 a.m.

Sand Springs would not have a phone directory until 1914. By then three hundred names would be in the book.

There was now a broom factory in Sand Springs, owned by John Johns, a blind man who went door to door selling his handmade brooms.

Mr. Page had a saw mill by 1911, but by 1912 he had a hardwood lumber company on Adams Street, and they were doing a good business because of all the building going on. There was no more burning of valuable wood. Hardwood stumps sold for more than the body of the tree. There was black oak, red oak, water oak, and curly walnut, to name a few.

The Neodesha Bottling Works, that had been the first industry to locate in Sand Springs, was not doing well. The company manufactured bottles of various types, mainly whiskey flasks. However, Oklahoma, the first "dry" state, ever, was protected by the Enabling Act which prohibited the sale of liquor in any form. Men managed to get liquor when they wanted it, but there was no real demand for the factory's product in Oklahoma, and the company was going broke.

In scouting for possible industry for his town, Mr. Page learned of Alexander Hewitt Kerr, who had a business in Altoona, Kansas, making glass canning jars. The shortage of gas was forcing Mr. Kerr to relocate. Mr. Page got in touch with him, and made him an offer he couldn't refuse. He gave Mr. Kerr a free site for his company, an abundant supply of gas at three cents per thousand, with the convenience of railway facilities.

Mr. Kerr brought his factory to Sand Springs in 1912. Mr. Page talked him into buying the failing Neodesha bottling plant and converting it to make five gallon water bottles for Mr. Page's spring-water sales.

Mr. Kerr moved his family to Tulsa and purchased a home across the street from Mr. and Mrs. Page, who lived on the northeast corner of Third and Olympia. The two families became friends. Mr. Kerr had a dignity and sophistication that made the Pages wonder if he wasn't of nobility.

Ruth Kerr would joke, saying to Mr. Kerr that he had married her to get a mother for his son Tom, but the Pages knew better. Ruth was a beautiful eighteen-year-old christian girl, much younger than Mr. Kerr. She had been his secretary, and a very smart girl. She continued to help him at the plant. She was of Pentecostal faith and Mr. Kerr had joined her church. She was a very dedicated christian and sometimes preached. In every box of fruit jars, she sent along a bit of scripture reading.

The Kerr family multiplied rapidly. It was a familiar sight to see three maids pushing three baby buggies down the street.

One Saturday afternoon Mr. and Mrs. Page sat on their front porch reading the newspaper. The three maids came out of the Kerr's house pushing three buggies. They headed down the Third Street viaduct toward town.

"They are shopping for shoes today," said Mrs. Page.

"How do you know?" Mr. Page asked, looking away from his paper to watch them depart.

"Because Ruth told me," said Mrs. Page. "Anyway, about the only ready-made clothing they have in Tulsa is for men. We women have to make our own and our children's clothes."

The Kerrs were a great asset to the town of Sand Springs.

"Think of all the jobs he gives to our people," said Mr. Page. "And even our widows can find work there — inspecting, and filling boxes with fruit jars."

Things were going well, both at the town and at the childrens' Home. But a cloud of gloom fell over the Home folks. The elderly man who had been nicknamed Governor Williams, and later affectionately called Grandpa Williams by the children, died in his sleep. Seventy-eight-year-old Grandpa Williams, still insisting on earning his own living, had worked in the garden that day. The summer of 1912, he and the boys had harvested a fine crop of sweet potatoes. He had suggested that they would keep through the winter if there was a good root cellar to keep them in. Mr. Breeding had the men make one. When the cellar was completed, Mr. Breeding went to seek Williams' approval on the finished structure. Getting no answer to his knock, Mr. Breeding went in to check on him. He found that Mr. Williams had died in his sleep.

Mr. Breeding conducted the funeral. He was the last person buried in the little cemetery beside the lake.

Mr. Page donated land for a cemetery north of town in a beautifull woodland area. It was called "Woodland Cemetery."

Long line of oil tank cars coming from the Pierce —
later Sinclair Oil Refinery, Sand Springs, Oklahoma.

30

Fastest Growing Town in the Midwest

THE YEAR 1913 SHOWED UNBELIEVABLE GROWTH AND PROGRESS FOR THE town of Sand Springs. Using simple but encompassing logic, Mr. Page had the power of vivid persuasion and vision to light the flames of imagination that drew people with a compelling force. Sand Springs was said to be the fastest growing industrial town in the midwest.

Mr. Page owned the *Tulsa Tribune* newspaper which had once been called the *Tulsa Democrat* newspaper. The Tribune could be purchased at the Sand Springs Greenhouse. But on February 21, 1913, Sand Springs had its own newspaper as *The Review* published by Fred Badger. It was printed in Tulsa for the first three issues, but on March 7, Mr. Badger announced that he had purchased a B. Franklin-G. Washington "armstrong" hand press. The next paper would be printed in Sand Springs. The annual subscription price was one dollar. Mr. Badger installed the press in the basement of the Kingsberry building.

The Kingsberry building is an example of how every bit of space was utilized in that day. The second floor contained offices for Ross Rayburn's Townsite Real Estate Company, the utilities offices, and Dr. Calhoun's office. The street floor of the building which contained the Clute's Drug Store with the post office in the corner at the front of the building, now also had a furniture store in the back with a side entrance from Second Street. The basement of the building housed The Shepherd Brother's Plumbing Company, a sheet metal shop, Fred Gray's barber shop and poolhall, and now the *Review's* press.

An article in the February 28, 1913, *Review* reported that Mr. and Mrs. John Davis had purchased the tent of Mr. Thomas on the hill and that they would move there soon. Transactions such as this were common.

The announcements and advertisements in the *Review* kept everybody in touch with what was going on in the town.

Sand Springs was to have a bank of its own in the new Dalton building on the second lot on the northwest corner of Second and Main streets, diagonally across from the post office. The capital stock was $10,000. Charles Page's younger brother, Edwin Adalbert Page, was made president of the bank. Mr. E.L. Orr was vice president and T.W. Spillman was cashier.

Mr. Page was building an outdoor theater in the park. But the *Review* called it an "Airdome" when they made the announcement. The seating capacity was 1,200 people. The entertainment was high-class vaudeville and motion pictures.

"One or two new attractions will be added to the park each year," said Mr. Page.

Mr. Page asked the Tulsa County Board of Directors for an electric lighting franchise for Sand Springs and got it by a four to one vote. His large electric system was now making enough electricity for his town, thousands of lights throughout the park, and for his interurban cars, which the people called street cars.

The cars ran every twenty minutes. After they carried 15,000 people to the park on the fourth of July, eight more electric cars were ordered.

Mr. Page worked relentlessly bringing factories and industry into the town to provide jobs for his people. He also gave inducements other than factory sites — cheap gas, electricity and freight services. The March 7, 1913, issue of *The Review* stated that Mr. Page had finally landed the $2,000,000 Waters-Pierce refinery. But the people didn't know that he had also given Waters-Pierce $35,000 to get them to locate in Sand Springs. Such a plant would employ from 500 to 700 persons when in operation, and 400 men for the year that it would take to build the plant. Jobs would become available to make the needed by-products such as storage tanks and other oil field equipment.

The town had been incorporated hardly a year and it already had four hotels and other eating establishments. Various shops supplied the needs of home builders. There was a saw mill, two lumber companies, a plate glass company, a sheet metal company, two general stores, a butcher shop, a bakery, a Nu-Flake cereal company, the Kerr's two glass factories, a cotton gin, a cleaners, a tailoring shop, the greenhouse, and others, including two oil refineries, Waters-Pierce which was later purchased by the Sinclair Oil and Gas Company, and the Chestnut and Smith refinery. 1913 was a good year.

The new $40,000 Central school building opened with 363 students enrolled in 1913.

Because of the Jim Crow law, a Negro child could not attend the schools for the white children. The district school system declared that there were hardly enough Negro children of school age to require a school in "Colored Town." Representatives of the black community went to Charles Page. He gave a donation, and a lot on Oak and Elm streets. They built a Baptist church which also served as a school. It was 1914 before the school district would decide there were enough children to warrant a school.

Jim Rust, manager of Charles Page's greenhouse, was doing a lot of landscaping about town. He was also in the process of building a nine-room house on Lincoln Street.

The Kingsberry building was getting pretty crowded and Mr. Page started drawing up plans for a building of his own south of the Dalton building on the corner of Second and Main streets. The various "Home Interests," as he called them, would be on the second floor over the bank.

With all the excitement of the booming new town, *The Review.* reported the sad news of two deaths. Sias Buttons, who had sold his and his wife's allotments upon which the town was platted, passed away in late April 1913. After Sias sold his land to Mr. Page, he moved close to relatives near Sapulpa where Sias was later buried.

The other death was a drowning tragedy. Sand Springs had no bridge which made it difficult for people living across the river south of Sand Springs to shop in town. There was a school south of the river, but little else in the way of supplying the needs of these residents. They had to drive several miles to Sapulpa by wagon or buggy, or cross the river by ferry, or by row boat, which was very dangerous.

Grace Haney, who died March 1, 1913, was the daughter of Mr. and Mrs. O.C. "Cap" Haney, well-known residents of the community south of the river. The newspaper stated:

> The young woman, a teacher of the Limestone school, and Professor Ashbrook, the Limestone principal were crossing the river at Wekiwa at night when the boat overturned. It was a most painful ordeal, and Grace caught pneumonia from the exposure in the water. She died within a week. Professor Ashbrook blamed himself for the accident and became so distraught that he closed the school.

Grace Haney's brother was married to the daughter of Lincoln Postoak and Grace was buried in the Postoak cemetery.

The Sand Springs residents began talking about the possibility of having a bridge built to span the river. But at the time they didn't have the money for such an endeavor.

Meanwhile, the town progressed. Marshal Bob Fleenor, elected Fire Chief in 1913, had a volunteer fire department. In March of that year the bucket-brigade was replaced when the city purchased a hose reel with 500 feet of hose. When Mr. Page heard, he donated 500 feet more of hose. When someone yelled "FIRE," Bob quickly removed his team from his wagon to the fire wagon. Having nowhere to house the fire wagon, he simply left it wherever he was. Sometimes he forgot where he left the fire wagon, causing panic when a fire broke out.

Tulsa still had no water except the brackish river water. It was hardly fit for bathing or even washing clothes, let alone drinking. Therefore Mr. Page still sold spring water to the 10,000 residents of Tulsa. He extended the water line that had ended at Joe Station in 1909 when he ran out of pipe. He moved his water bottling plant to Third Street, at the end of the viaduct, and across from where he lived. He changed the name Osage to Sand Springs Water Bottling Company.

In keen competition at the 1913 State Fair, Mr. Page's spring was awarded the gold medal for having the purest water.

Feeling strongly that children needed a Christian upbringing, Mr. Page encouraged the building of churches by offering a free lot to anyone wishing to build a church. Mr. Page had given a lot to the Community Church. By 1913 the Community Church had become mostly Presbyterian, causing members to pull out to start other churches.

The First Methodist Church was given a lot on the corner of Fourth and Main streets. The church was dedicated February 1, 1914, with Rev. J.C. Henderson as their first pastor.

Rev. Archie Kinion, among the first to receive a free lot, built the Church Of God on Fourth and Grant streets. Rev. Kinion pastored the church forty-five years.

Automobiles were getting a little more common, but still weren't practical for driving on the deeply rutted wagon trail between Sand Springs and Tulsa. Sand Springs voted a $16,000 bond to build a road to Tulsa, and to put sidewalks along the unpaved streets because of the knee-deep sand traps.

In searching throughout the United States for industry for his town, news spread that a man by the name of Charles Page was building a town to support an orphanage. Newsmen came from as far as New York for this unusual story. They were not disappointed. The story was greater than they had imagined, of what one man was doing because he loved his fellow man.

That newsmen came clear from New York to see what Mr. Page was doing was in itself news and brought attention closer to home. Excitement was growing. People were pouring in from all around thinking something big was about to happen, and they wanted to get in on it. One man related his experiences this way:

"I attended a convention in Muskogee, and while there met a prominent man from Tulsa who told me about Charles Page and his town. I was interested from the start and decided to visit Tulsa on my way home and take in Sand Springs. I rode to Sand Springs on an open car with long rows of seats. When the conductor called Sand Springs, I got off. On the corner I saw a drugstore — went in and asked for a sody. While drinking I fought off the flies and inquired about business. The bystanders were real boosters for their town.

"I crossed the street and went into the bank. In the lobby stood a huge stove with several loafers sitting around. In the back of the bank farm machinery was piled high, and business was not rushing. Green grass grew between the street car tracks, and an old woman was leading a cow down Main Street in the center of the tracks. A pink frame building stood on Lincoln Street. A grocery store, J.E. Lawless Grocery, was next to the bank.

"I walked on around the curve of town and sat on the steps of a brick cottage across from the street car waiting station. I emptied the sand out of my shoes and decided to look around. The C.C. Spillman home on the corner of Fourth and Lincoln was under construction. A little farther up I saw two rather attractive frame cottages painted green and the brick bungalow of Tom Spillman. At the top of the hill I could see several small homes dotted here and there.

"The jack oaks were plentiful. It was getting late and I walked back to the street car line. I went back to my hotel in Tulsa, but bright and early the next morning I again took the interurban for the Sand Springs Park and the Sand Springs Home. I thoroughly enjoyed the day in the park. My visit to the Home was an inspiration. The freedom of the country — the idea of pioneering and making new friends thrilled me. I returned to my home, and in the course of a few months I had disposed of my business and was making plans to cast my lot with the pioneers of Sand Springs."

A personal note from one subscriber in the *Review* gives an attitude as to what the people thought of Charles Page. It was in the form of a thank you note from P. C. Shipton to Mr. and Mrs. Clute for their aid and thoughtfulness during Mr. Shipton's recent illness. He ends his thank you note with, "May this Charles Page kind of kindness be ever present in Sand Springs."

One of the electrically powered street cars
at the Sand Springs waiting-station in Tulsa.

31

A Widow's Colony

THE YEAR OF 1914 WAS A YEAR OF MANY HAPPENINGS, ONE OF WHICH would again draw far reaching attention to Charles Page.

When Sias Buttons sold the piece of land that had his log cabin on it, he moved to a lovely wooded area that was so full of squirrels that it was called Squirrel Hollow. Sias built himself a nice five-room house, a barn and a saddle-and-harness barn. But his health was failing, and he sold this last piece of land to Mr. Page and moved close to relatives near Sapulpa.

*In 1912, during all the building going on, Mr. Page had built a row of forty three-room cottages, some with screened back porches. They stood behind Washington Street, in the lovely wooded area of Squirrel Hollow. The row of houses faced the five-room home Sias had built.

Squirrel Creek, a clear sandy-bottomed stream, shallow enough for children to play in, trickled through the forest just a few yards behind the Sias Buttons' house.

Being confronted with many people asking for help, Mr. Page's first thought was to provide temporary assistance to people in need until they got on their feet.

These little cottages, comparable to small apartments, would be rent free, with free gas, water and electricity. There was a row of hydrants in front of the colony of houses and a private privy for each in the back-yard.

All the people who had been early residents living in tents on the hill below the Childrens' Home had been dispersed throughout the town to various houses Mr. Page owned or built, but more had come for help. A woman with a blind son was permitted to occupy one of the houses. A widow, with a widowed mother to support was given another. A man released from the penitentiary was allowed to rehabilitate with his family there, and widows, single women, and anyone needing a place to stay were given one of the cottages to live in.

Mr. Page, who considered all cases, was too busy and too trusting to check on all the applicants for the colony and soon ran into trouble. His good intentions were abused. Sometimes, upon hearing of such a place, women deliberately conspired with their husbands to become separated in order to

---

*Correction on the date the Colony was started.

gain all these benefits and additional support for their family. Some husbands moved in, claiming to be only visiting the children. Things got so out of hand that the colony turned into a brothel where men hung out. Women were getting venereal diseases. The gossip finally reached Mr. Page's ears and he knew that something had to be done. His aunt Fanny had a suggestion.

"Charley, why don't you move everybody out except widows. Get a man to check on those to be admitted to make certain they are truly deserving. Have very strict rules to protect the names of those who live there and to keep the place decent. If they are not willing to cooperate with the rules, they probably don't really need your help anyway."

Since Mr. Page had a particular interest in helping widows, this idea appealed to him. He knew only one man who had all the qualifications for such a job. Mr. Breeding was a disciplinarian who believed in strict rules, yet he was patient, understanding and kind. He had high moral standards and could be trusted to deal with women without getting involved with any of them. But would Mr. Breeding accept the job? He had expressed a desire to be free to try his luck at truck-farming, and Mr. Page had even been obliged to raise his salary from fifty to seventy-five dollars a month to get him to stay on.

When Mr. Page talked to him, Mr. Breeding reminded him that he had been hired temporarily, and that nothing more had been said about it becoming a steady job. He also told of his fear of being replaced as soon as Mr. Page found someone more qualified for the job, as had happened in the case with Bub Avery.

"Ah, Cap, you know you don't have to worry about that," said Mr. Page. "I don't know anybody else who would have the patience that you have in dealing with women and children. In fact, I'll put it in writing that you have a lifetime job if it'll make you feel better."

"Well, I'd feel a little more secure," said Mr. Breeding.

Mr. Breeding was to be superintendent of the Home and Colony. He was given a raise in salary and made a member of the board of trustees for the Home Interests which met each Monday morning in Mr. Page's office.

Any widow or divorcee coming for help was told to go talk to Cap Breeding. If he deemed her worthy, a private detective would make an investigation before consent was given for the woman to move in.

All women were to have a physical examination as a safeguard against spreading communicable diseases. No men were allowed past the first cottage in the colony, which was designated as a parlor where fathers could visit their children, or where the women could, with a chaperon, meet a gentleman friend to go on a date. She was expected to return home at a decent hour.

Mrs. Friend, a gentle, refined, middle aged widow with a young son, Halton, was given immediate charge over the widows. She was to reside in Sias' five-room house, facing the row of cottages. She would see to the needs and complaints of the widows and report anything she couldn't handle to Mr. Breeding.

Knowing that a mother couldn't leave small children alone while she worked, Mr. Page built a nice day-nursery just north of where Mrs. Friend lived. The large playground was fenced and equipped with swings and teeter-totters to play on. Mrs. Gould, a widow with two little girls, Mildred and Elsie, was put in charge of the nursery.

The nursery had a row of pigeon hole shelves along one wall to hold the personal belongings of each child. Their names were written on surgical tape and taped to the square. Each child had his own tin drinking cup with his name on it. A series of hooks along the wall held coats and caps. There were two long low tables with little chairs for the children. A large cabinet held crayons, pencils, blunt scissors and a stack of Big Chief tablets. An ice box was provided with free milk for the bottle babies. At one end of the room was a large gas heater.

Just outside the door leading into the play yard was a large white box, waist high, with legs and a heavy lid. Square pigeon holes lined the inside of the box, labeled with names of babies still in diapers. Each baby's soiled diapers were placed in a tagged space, for mothers to pick up as they came for their children. Mothers were expected to give information as to where they worked and how they might be contacted in case of accident or illness of their children.

The saddle-barn that Sias had built was converted into a kitchen and dining room. Mrs. Willhour, a widow with four children, was hired to do the cooking. Free meals were provided for nursery children while their mothers worked to earn a living.

Certain rules were established. A widow with a mother to support was eligible, and a widow or divorcee with two or more children to support, if the oldest child was under twelve years of age.

Mr. Page was a strong believer that work was good for you. He was against giving total charity to those able to earn at least part of their living. Charity, he said, robbed one of self respect and pride. A mother was expected to support her children.

She was welcome to stay in the colony until she became self supporting or one of her children had sufficient earning capacity to help provide or watch after the younger children while the mother worked. When able, she was encouraged to leave the colony and resume her place in society, giving room for another family who needed assistance.

However, Mr. Breeding discovered that providing all this was still not sufficient in many cases. Some women were going to the Tulsa Humane Society for additional help. He reported the situation to Mr. Page, who agreed that he had to do more for these families. To prevent panhandling, he forbade any of them to seek help from any county or state organization. She was given one quart of milk a day for each child, surplus vegetables from the

Home gardens and an occasional baking hen. Ice brought in from Tulsa via rail was delivered free of charge, and all medical help was provided with Mr. Page paying the bills. He expected mothers to work and earn the rest.

On Thanksgiving and Christmas a large hen and a bushel of groceries were sent to each family in the Colony, to every Negro family, and any other needy family in the town.

But regardless of how much he did for people, there were always those who complained. One of the rules laid down to follow was that the women must take their children to church at least once a week. Some of the women rebelled at this. Mr. Breeding was unsympathetic, stating that children needed to be taught about God, and that Mr. Page was thinking about the children when he made the rule. One of the mothers decided that Mr. Page would be more understanding so she went to him with her complaint.

"What harm would a bit of religious training do to you or your children?" asked Mr. Page.

"Well, I don't have clothes good enough to wear to church," said the woman.

"Well what do you want me to do!" he exclaimed. "Do I have to have gowns made for all of you so you can outshine everybody, just to get you to take your children to church? Children need to learn to trust in God."

Mr. Page had a little frame chapel built down at the colony so that there would be no excuses. Mr. Breeding preached there every Wednesday evening and Sunday afternoon. Families could attend another church if they wished, but most preferred the convenience of going to the little chapel. The little church burned in 1915, and Mr. Page had a stone church built in 1916.

After the Widow's Colony was established, only complete orphans were accepted into the Home except in rare cases where a mother was not physically able to work and provide for her children. A mother with children was housed in the Colony.

Galloway's table with 9,999 pieces in it.

32

More than a Craftsman

IN THE SUMMER OF 1914, MR. PAGE WAS WALKING UP MAIN STREET IN
Tulsa on his way to his office when he saw an unusual carving displayed in the
Drug Store window. He went in to inquire where the carving came from.

"Who made this?" asked Mr. Page, going over to the carving for a closer
look.

"I did," said a young man standing at the counter. He held out his hand.
"I'm Nathan Galloway," he said, "and I know who you are." He held out his
hand. Mr. Page was amazed. The young man not only looked like Will
Rogers, but his speech and mannerisms were much like the famous humor-
ist. Young Galloway rested his hand on the head of the gigantic snake curled
around the giant sycamore log.

The piece was nearly two and one-half feet in diameter and stood over six
feet tall. The huge snake appeared to be coming from a hole near the base of
the log and was wound five times around the log, holding a large fish in its
mouth. Practically every known type of reptile from alligators to frogs were
carved on the log, with a huge turtle at the base appearing to be carrying the
carving on its back.

"How did you ever get into this kind of work?" Mr. Page asked.

Mr. Galloway explained in a slow measured drawl. "I spent several months
working for the government in Japan and in the Philippine Islands where I
became interested in Japanese art. In studying the wood carvings, I decided
to try my hand at the art."

The druggist came over to where the two men stood. He told Mr. Page
how Galloway had been discovered as a master carver.

"Galloway worked in the Springfield Wagon Factory in Springfield, Missouri. Whenever he could get away from his work he went fishing. While
waiting for the fish to bite, he would take his pocket knife and carve on any
limb or log that happened to be near. Some businessmen from St. Louis who
fished in the same stream saw one of the carvings. They recognized it as a
wren. 'Who carved that bird?' they asked about town. 'An odd young man by
the name of Galloway does things like that all the time,' said one of a bunch of
fellows standing on the street corner. They told the men where Galloway

could be found. One of the men went to talk to Galloway. 'Did you carve that wren on a log?' asked the man. Galloway replied, 'The wren was in the knot on the log. I just cut the knot away to let him out.'"

"Did the man just want to see what the carver looked like?" asked Mr. Page.

Galloway smiled his slow, amiable smile and answered. "The man offered to secure space for me to display my work at the Panama-Pacific international exposition to be held in San Francisco in 1915. I was to represent Missouri. He wanted me to produce twenty carvings of large size in the same quality of workmanship as the wren he had seen at the fishing hole, tablets with the busts of the twenty-eight presidents of the United States, a collection of a thousand different colors of wood from within the state of Missouri.

"I selected and cut trees from forests all around the state and had them shipped back to Springfield. I rented a building set up my shop and started working." Mr. Galloway shifted his weight from one foot to the other while he was talking.

"The plan was to work on all of the pieces and bring them to near completion to show what the wood looked like before I started the carving. I was to take them to San Francisco in a group and finish some of them during the exposition. I had worked on them for four years. Twelve were ready, and the rest nearing completion when a fire broke out in the building. The pieces were heavy and I was only able to save this piece, and a caged lion, which I could roll out the door."

Looking down at the floor Galloway shook his head with regret as he continued. "I had over $8,000 invested, not counting my labor. All was lost except the two pieces I had saved. They happened to be carved from sycamores that grew on the banks of the James River, near the mouth at Finley. They were each carved from one piece of wood. I carved the lion inside a cage with bars around it."

"Are you saying that you carved the cage, and through the bars you carved out the lion?" asked Mr. Page, in awe.

"That's right," said Mr. Galloway.

"Where is that caged lion?"

Galloway sighed. "The lion did guard the entrance to the cave in Doling Park," he said. "The last I heard, it was at Zoo Park in the administration building. I suppose it's still there." Mr. Galloway ran his hand lovingly over the head of the large snake with a fish in its mouth.

"I had to sell the lion. This piece is for sale too," he said, "I'm trying to get enough money together to put in another shop. I've offered it to Mr. Sinclair for two hundred dollars, but he hasn't agreed to the price yet." He turned to Mr. Page. "Would you like to buy it?" He continued to rub the smooth finish of the snake's head and body.

"I think you should keep it," said Mr. Page, "It's all you have left. Anyway, two hundred dollars would buy a lot of food for my kids. How would you like to come into the country to my children's home and teach a class of boys that kind of work? I'll set you up a shop."

"I'd like that very much," said Galloway. He didn't ask if he would get paid, or just have the privilege of using the shop. To him, money was not important.

One of Galloway's relatives summed it up about right when she said, "Galloway hates money. He cares only for the bare necessities of life. He just wants to spend his time doing what he likes to do."

The next day Mr. Galloway had friends to help him. They laid a wagon on its side and rolled the big carving into the wagon. They raised the wagon back up on its wheels and sent the carving to Mr. Page. A note was stuck on the piece that read. "To Mr. Page, for his children's home."

When Mr. Page was told that there was a present for him downstairs he went down to see what it was. He refused to accept it as a gift. He sent George Nye with a message that he would keep the piece for Galloway, in the Home, until he had a place for it. Galloway never asked for it.

That morning Galloway went to see Mr. Breeding. Mr. Page had been notified that he would be there. Just across the road north of the childrens' home was a platform about twenty-four by twenty-four-foot square that had been used for the children to run and play on. Mr. Breeding asked Galloway if he could build his shop on the platform. Mr. Galloway went to work immediately.

Galloway got slabs of wood from the saw mill and built the walls of the wood shop. With native lumber and shingles he put a roof over it.

Two years later, in 1916, Mr. Galloway built a manual training shop directly north of the little school. It was one of the largest and best equipped buildings for shop work in the southwest. The building was a two-story sandstone structure with each floor measuring 36 by 70 feet.

The boys undertook the repair work about the Home. They made some of the garden tools, rakes, and other devices such as wheelbarrows and carts. Later they mended the furniture. Many became so good at it that thereafter they built most of the furniture for the Home. At Christmas time each year they made cedar chests, inlaid sewing boxes and various gifts for the girls of the Home to receive from Santa. They also made many fine elaborately carved articles.

Mr. Galloway taught the boys how to carve sandstone without it chipping. He carved two large sandstone lions weighing ten tons each which were placed at the entrance to the Sand Springs Park, and later moved to the entrance to the Sand Springs Home.

Galloway liked boys and the boys liked him. In fact, everybody liked Galloway. He often had forty or so boys training at the same time. He taught them safety in working with tools. Even an eight-year-old could run a lathe and turn out simple articles such as tool handles, kitchen articles and bowls. After work, Galloway took the boys swimming at the lake. He taught them all how to swim, and how to save a life. He took them hiking, explaining the different woods and what they were best used for. He, his wife, and their small son, Paul, took the boys boating, camping, and fishing. They often brought Mr. Page a mess of fresh fish, which he enjoyed very much. One time they took him a twenty-five-pound cat fish.

Various state institutions were interested in Mr. Galloway's work and offered him inducements, but his educational qualifications didn't meet their standards, so he stayed with the Home for many years. Many of the boys who received his instructions found that the craft could help them work their way through college.

Mr. Breeding worked with the boys too, but he always said, "Galloway has the unique ability to lift others above and beyond themselves." 'Work on your imagination,' Galloway would say.

*Mr. Galloway beginning the carved piece that sits
in the living room of the Sand Springs Home.*

33

Continuing the Care

THE POPULATION OF THE TOWN BY 1914 WAS 4,000. FACTORIES AND industries were now providing 1,400 jobs for the people, and the number was growing.

A man by the name of McFall, founded the *Sand Springs Leader* weekly newspaper on May 19, 1914. It was a small press and he had a hard time meeting the competition of *The Review,* until Fred Badger received a legacy and quit printing his paper.

In 1914, Mr. Page piped gas from a big gas well near Bruner Station that his men had brought in the year before. He gave residents living in Osage County the advantages of cheap fuel.

Mr. Page's bank building was completed in 1914. His offices were all moved to the upstairs part of the building. Mr. Farmer and his son hauled Mr. Page's furniture from his Tulsa office to Sand Springs in a wagon. Jim rode to Sand Springs with Mr. Page every day, always lying beside his master's desk.

Dr. Daniel White and Dr. Peter Cope White, eye, ears, nose, and throat specialists who had been employed in the Indian Service in Oklahoma, came to Mr. Page and offered to examine the children. They had earlier done surgery on two of the girls' who had trachoma, a disease of the eye. Other children had infected tonsils and adenoids, and surgery was necessary. Most cases were taken to Sapulpa and some to Tulsa. Operations were performed in the doctors' offices set up in their own residence. Patients were, as Mr. Breeding put it, "dragged home terribly sick."

One instance as an example, was the case of Elizabeth Moore who became seriously ill with pneumonia. Fluid had filled one lung and the doctor advised immediate surgery. Mr. Breeding carried Elizabeth, who was ten years of age, down the hill to the street car line and took her to Tulsa. The operating room was nothing more than a room in the doctor's home with a table in it. It was very disturbing to Mr. Breeding that the child had to be "dragged home," as he put it, in her condition.

Mr. Page agreed that something had to be done. Once more the store's basement storage room was put to use. Mr. Page had it equipped as an emergency operating room. Mr. Galloway and the boys made the cabinets and an operating table. This relieved the situation somewhat, until Mr. Page's generosity made things too complicated.

Indians, who were patients of the doctors, came for operations and treatment. Others, not able to pay for the operations were taken care of in various ways at the childrens' Home. So many operations became quite a problem. The Home was already short of bed space. The matrons complained at having extra duties in caring for the sick, and Miss Lindsay complained that it upset the routine of caring for the children.

"I guess I'll have to build a hospital," said Mr. Page, and he began drawing up the plans.

The hospital was barely started when an epidemic of smallpox broke out. Pest houses had to be built to quarantine the people who were afflicted with the disease. Everybody helped. Mr. Page donated the land and one of the houses. Lumber companies furnished building materials and citizens of the town donated the labor to build two additional houses. One house was for the men, one for the ladies, and one to serve as a mess hall for both. A dray wagon was used to haul the patients to the pest houses and then away when they died.

Dr. C.E. Calhoun, the health commissioner, did all he could for the sick and the well. He vaccinated everyone who would be vaccinated and took care of the sick and dying. This kept both him and his volunteer helpers busy. There were 125 people suffering from smallpox at the same time.

As the hospital building progressed, Tulsa doctors became very interested, but Mr. Page had invested his money and was loath to part with its supervision. He thought of turning it over to doctors White and White, but they wanted it under Catholic supervision. This didn't suit Mr. Page. He then employed a Mr. Miller, who had been trained in Battle Creek Sanitarium, and specialized in hidrotherapy, the use of water in the treatment of disease. Water tubs were installed, but this treatment wasn't satisfactory. Mr. Page then wrote to Dr. Clay Campbell, a surgeon with a practice in Anadarko, Oklahoma. Dr. Campbell was married to Mr. Page's niece, Elizabeth Monsell, daughter of Elizabeth Rhoana, Mr. Page's sister.

Dr. Campbell came to visit the Pages with his eight-year-old son, George Morland Campbell. Mr. Page drove them out to Sand Springs. He stopped first at the spring house where the dairy products were kept.

Mr. Hensley who, with his wife, now had charge of dairy products, was Mr. Breeding's cousin. They were proud to show Mr. Page their infant son, Zenus, who was born in the living quarters on the upper floor of the spring house.

Mr. Hensley knew that Mr. Page often stopped by, sometimes bringing guests, for a glass of fresh churned buttermilk, and he had fixed a little shelf with clean glasses for him to use, and a bowl for Jim.

Little George watched with interest as Mr. Page took the long-handled porcelain dipper from a nail on the side of the shelf. He lifted the lid from a ten-gallon milk can, stirred the milk, then filled three glasses with buttermilk. Then he filled Jim's bowl.

"Fresh churned buttermilk is my favorite drink," said Mr. Page, wiping the milk from his mustache. He poured each of them another glass.

Mr. Hensley told Mr. Page that he had whittled out the little flower that was in the butter mold so that he could carve the words "Sand Springs" into the mold. "When I had finished, I packed the butter into the mold tightly to make the words plain and clear. When I pushed the butter from the mold," he said, "I discovered that the words 'Sand Springs' were wrong side out."

Dr. Campbell liked the hospital and agreed to close his practice in Anadarko. He was put in charge of the hospital. Dr. Fred Glass, Tulsa County's leading surgeon, soon joined Dr. Campbell. The team was hard to beat. One of the doctors was left handed and this worked out fine. They could work side by side without getting into each other's elbow space. The hospital had the largest X-ray machine anywhere around. It seriously burned the fingers of both doctors.

Mr. Page's friends and relatives from Wisconsin continued to come to Sand Springs and he gave them all jobs. To some he gave homes, but he had a special fondness for his great-nephew, George Campbell. He often took George to the farm. The boy liked animals and Mr. Page gave him a pony of his own. Mr. Page had a bob-tailed horse that he rode a lot, and together they rode about the farm, Jim enjoying these sprints as he followed close behind.

One day Mr. Page called to see if George could run an errand for him. When George got to the office Mr. Page stuffed a fat manila envelope into the boy's inside coat pocket.

"George, my boy," he said, "I want you to get on the street car and go to the First National Bank in Tulsa for me. You'll see a tall white-haired man there. He's expecting you. I want you to give him this envelope."

When George delivered the envelope the man counted the money in it and asked George if he knew what was inside the envelope. George said, "No."

"Well, young man," said the banker, "you had eighty-five thousand dollars in your pocket. Who would have thought that an eight-year-old boy would be carrying that much money?"

Mr. Page had his eye on this bright boy and hoped that he could someday use George in his business. He said "George, get a good education, then let's talk about your future."

Mr. Page wanted to incorporate the Home so that business could be transacted and property owned by the corporation could provide for the perpetuation of the Home. The question in his mind was who would be responsible for his kids at his passing. He could select the trustees, but who would select their successors? Mr. Page at first thought of the Catholic Church, and invited certain Catholic authorities to visit the place; but he changed his mind when they became too eager to take over the organization. Things stayed as they were with the original trustees, C.F. Tingley, C.H. Buckner, Edwin Page, B.F. Breeding, and Charles Page as president.

However, Mr. Page attended an Oklahoma Methodist Church Conference held in Enid under the direction of the late Bishop McIntyre, and decided that the Methodist Church would be a safe organization on which to place this responsibility. The Sand Springs Home was to be recognized by the church as a part of the work in which a Methodist minister could be engaged. The Bishop sent Methodist Minister Kinset and his family to Sand Springs to learn what Mr. Page had in mind. Mr. Breeding got along fine with Rev. Kensit, but Mr. Page thought the man was in too big a hurry to take things right out of Mr. Page's hands.

Rev. Kensit stayed four months and then asked the Bishop for an appointment in the church. He left on February 29, 1914.

No extravagance for his family or his kids was too much, to Mr. Page, but for himself he found no need for elegance. He contented himself with the simple things of life. He had his same scant office furnishings brought to his Sand Springs office. Every morning when he came to work he found a line of people sitting in chairs outside his door waiting to see him. He ushered them into his private office about nine at a time, and seated them in dining-room chairs placed in a semi-circle around his desk. The rest waited in the outer office, also seated in plain dining-room chairs. No immediate secretary shielded him from the crowds of people who descended upon him daily. He liked the personal association with people. He believed that the gift without the giver, was was not enough. You had to give of yourself.

"Who gives himself with his alms feeds three, Himself, his hungering neighbor and Me"
author unknown

When Mr. Page had seated himself at his desk, with Jim at his side, he would turn to those seated in the nine chairs. One by one he listened as each need was stated, while he considered how to meet their needs. When all nine had stated their needs, he would already have made up his mind as to what to do. If it was a widow seeking a place in the colony, he would tell her to go see Cap. Some needed a job. Others sought loans. If he approved the loan, that person was sent downstairs to the bank with a call from him to approve the loan.

Many needed money to start a business. One such case occurred when Mr. "Doc" Harvey asked for a loan to open a barber shop.

"Are you a good barber?" asked Mr. Page.

"Well, I like to think so," said Mr. Harvey. "I've been barbering for twenty-three years."

"Well if you're a good barber and you've been in business that long, what did you do with all the money you made?"

"I spent it on wine and women," came the reply, in jest.

Mr. Page laughed heartily. "Well at least you're honest," he said, and lent Mr. Harvey the money.

Another man came with a crooked money raising scheme. Mr. Page had already been warned by Jim's growl that the man was a crook, but the man was allowed to speak his piece. When he was through, Mr. Page took the cigar out of his mouth, and squinting one eye, he gave the man an answer to his scheme.

"Mister," he said, "you're a crook, and I want you out of my office. You work your side of the street all you want, but don't you ever cross over to my side of the street."

Mr. Page had great faith in Jim's ability to judge character. If Jim stirred and looked nervously at anyone coming into the office, that man was questionable. If he growled, that meant the man was bad.

"Jim knows," Mr. Page would say. "He's just a dog. He doesn't have a complicated mind as humans do. He has no ax to grind, nothing to gain or lose. His one thought is to protect his master. He instinctively knows a good man from a bad man."

Going fishing wearing men's basketball bloomers. **L-R:** *Mrs. Galloway, Myrtle Durham, Elizabeth Moore, Ethel Kelly, Mr. Galloway, Goldie Barnett, Gertrude Benefield, Frona Johnson, and Anna Moore.*

34

San Francisco Here We Come

THE YEAR WAS 1915 AND THINGS WERE GOING WELL FOR MR. PAGE. THE factories and industries that he had persuaded to locate in Sand Springs to give jobs to his people were also giving a volume of business to his freight line, which he had designated to be the support for his kids. Although his oil business was mostly gas wells, and he sold the gas for only three cents per thousand cubic feet, he was seeing some profits. He now had gas and electric lines to many surrounding towns, including Tulsa.

In the year 1911, Mr. Page had purchased several hundred acres of land in the Euchee Creek valley. By 1915 the rough raw land, cleared and cultivated, proved to be very rich productive soil. Its fertile fields were now yielding abundant harvests of every kind of grain to feed his livestock.

His herds of pure-bred Holstein cattle shipped from Wisconsin were magnificent, and he was proud of the increase. He now had large pig, turkey and chicken farms, and some of the finest horses and mules. The dream of his farm becoming self-supporting was being realized. Now worth six million dollars, his dreams were growing as well. He decided it was time he built his family a home in the city of his dreams.

He built a gracious home for them, at 810 North Main Street. Although he could be content in a two-room shack, he deemed nothing too good for his family. The house and grounds occupied an entire block. The beautiful three-story house, red brick, with a red-tiled roof, boasted a sunny rounded solarium with ceiling high windows. At the semicircular end of the long room, rose red drapes hung to the floor, cheerful with the afternoon sun behind them. Large plants stood in attractive settings between the tall windows. To the west end in a raised alcove Mrs. Page had her desk. Mr. Page's study was to the right of the east front entrance.

Hanging on the walls of each room were large paintings from famous artists, some of which came from Billy Roesser's fine collection. Two excellent, smaller paintings hung in the entry. One of an old man with his hands on the table, giving thanks before breaking bread.

Each morning as Mr. Page passed the pictures going to work, he would salute the old man with a squashing sound with his hands, and he would say things like, "take care of everything until I get back, old man." Sometimes he teased his wife, pretending to be jealous at having to leave her alone with the old man. Then after kissing Lucy and little Mary good-bye, he and Jim would be on their way.

There wasn't too much going on in the way of entertainment in those days, so the Pages gave bridge parties two or three times a week in the beautiful solarium of their home. Mr. Page enjoyed playing bridge.

"Are we playing bridge tonight?" he would ask. When Mrs. Page told him they were, he would say, "Good." The game seemed to relax him and get his mind off other things. But he hated to lose, even in a card game, and especially couldn't stand to see his wife lose.

"Lucy, give me those cards," he would say, trying to help her.

"Charley, it doesn't hurt for me to lose," she would answer. "I want to play my own cards. After all, it's only a game."

Things were going very well for the children of the Home, except that the dormitory was so crowded that there was talk of building on to the Home. The children were sleeping two to a full-sized bed, and one family of children was boarded out. Their mother, a semi-invalid, was unable to work and care for her children. The children had been left with different families until something was decided about building on to the dormitory. Meanwhile, things went on as usual.

On June 2, 1915 Mr. Page's birthday, he decided to celebrate the coming year by doing something special for his kids.

"How would you like to go California?" Mr. Page asked. This brought squeals of delight from the children crowded around him.

Mr. Breeding and Miss Lindsay cautioned him at making such a promise. But he continued to discuss such a plan with the children, although Miss Lindsay and Mr. Breeding saw it as impractical, if not impossible.

"You've got to think big," said Mr. Page. "There's no challenge in thinking small."

Each Sunday, as the children crowded around him, he talked about all of them going to the San Francisco World's Fair when school was out. The children would ask questions. To him it was a nostalgia trip. He planned to stop at many places where he had experiences that he had told the children about. He answered the childrens' questions in a way that fired their imaginations. Mr. Breeding and Miss Lindsay were very concerned. The whole idea seemed so impractical.

The Breedings, the matrons, Mrs. Page and whatever guests the Pages brought with them, always sat a little distance from Mr. Page on the porch, to give room for the children who crowded around him. Off to the side, they spoke their concern to Lucy Page.

Lucy smiled. She had made herself a promise never to interfere in any of her husband's business. She had learned that others thought many things ridiculous, preposterous, and impossible, that Charley had been able to achieve. She had great confidence that Charley could do anything.

"If Charley says he can do it, I'm sure he had a way figured out before he ever mentioned it," she said with confidence. "Furthermore, I want to go," she added, with a smile.

But Miss Lindsay wasn't one to give up easily. She shooed the children out to play, and discussed the matter seriously with Mr. Page. Mr. Breeding backed her all the way.

"Mr. Page, there are so many things the Home needs," Miss Lindsay began. "Think of the cost of such a trip for so many children. The money could be better spent adding a wing to the dormitory for one thing. We are so overcrowded that it makes things very difficult. This home is only equipped to handle fifty children, and we have sixty." Children are sleeping two in a bed, and there is a family of four being boarded out because we can't possibly squeeze them in."

"Lindsay, these things will come in due time," said Mr. Page. "If we do that first, the Fair will be over and the children will have missed it. I want them to have a grand vacation. You and Cap will enjoy it. I'll see that you have help with the kids."

Mr. Breeding intervened. "Mr. Page," he said, "I know how much you love these children. I know you want to do everything you can for them, but it is so impractical to crowd sixty children and their attendants into a pullman car that is designed for fewer than thirty people. The younger ones would derive no benefit from such a trip. They would get tired and cross. If you have your head set on such a trip, why not take the older children, and we can plan something less tiring for the younger ones."

Mr. Page thought a moment, then he agreed to compromise. "Well, maybe you're right, Cap," he said. "We'll take the older girls and boys, and plan something closer to home for the younger ones. Maybe a camping trip."

And so the plans were made. "Cap, bring your family along." said Mr. Page. "They need a good vacation, and you can look after the boys. Lindsay can see to the girls."

Eagerly the children waited to learn which of them would go. Finally the names were posted where the children could read them. Bert Evans read the names as they all gathered around. "Leonard and Luther Nolan, John Durham, Jess Davis, Bert Evans, Martha Davis, Sarah Davis, Nancy Davis, Clarissa Davis, Rosalee Davis, Inza Arnold, Bertha Casey and Anna Mosley."

"That's thirteen," said one of the girls, "an unlucky number."

"I think we are thirteen lucky numbers to get to go," said Bert. "If you're superstitious, you stay home and there won't be thirteen." He punched the girl in the shoulder.

On July 10, the pullman car on the siding near the greenhouse was loaded with supplies from the canning factory, the commissary and the garden. Mr. Page, as usual, had everything organized for their trip.

Mr. Lot, the Negro chef, a porter, and Johnny Lane, an old friend of Mr. Page's, who had been a railway conductor, were placed in charge of the car.

The children all had new clothes made for the trip. This would be the only time in the girls lives that they would wear anything resembling a uniform. Their blue dresses could easily be spotted should they stray in a crowd.

At ten o'clock at night, Mr. and Mrs. Page and Mary, age three, Mr. and Mrs. Breeding and their two daughters, Eva, now thirteen years old and Margaret soon to be six, all boarded the train. Harold Breeding, age eleven, chose to stay at home with his grandparents. Miss Lindsay soon came aboard with the Home children, making a total of twenty-five, a comfortable number for one pullman car.

One of Mr. Page's steam engines took them to Tulsa, leaving them on a siding near the Frisco depot for a passenger train bound for Kansas City to pick them up.

As they waited, the town's people heard about the trip and came into the train to see for themselves. The children also talked to people through the open windows. "What will Charley Page do next?" they heard somebody say.

Mr. Page still owned a hotel in Denver, Colorado, and he wired ahead that they were coming. They arrived in Denver on July 12 and were shown to the rooms reserved for them. While everybody else rested, Mr. Breeding and the boys decided to take in the town, visiting the state capital, and the mint, exchanging old money for new.

Mr. Page routed the trip through Colorado Springs where he had started one of his real estate ventures. They stopped at Cripple Creek, where they ate lunch high above the clouds, and listened to Mr. Page tell of his gold digging and real estate ventures in Cripple Creek. After lunch the children looked for gold and gathered bits of rocks with shining specks in them.

The train took them up the Arkansas River through the Royal Gorge to view the beautiful scenery. They went to Salt Lake City, where the boys swam in the salt lake. The salt and sun burned their faces. They visited the Morman Temple and Tabernacle, and listened to the unusual pin dropping stunt.

The party arrived at Oakland, California, on Saturday, July 17. During their stay in San Francisco, they left the pullman and went to the Washington Hotel. Rooms had been reserved with a luxury suite especially prepared for Mr. and Mrs. Page and Mary. When the bell hop showed them to their rooms the Breedings were given the luxury suite. Mr. and Mrs. Page were given an ordinary hotel room with a bed brought in for Mary. Mr. Page realized the mistake but he just let it go.

"Cap looks more like a millionaire than I do," said Mr. Page, "let's let him enjoy it. I can't wait to see his face when they hand him the bill."

The group spent five days both at the fair, and taking in the city. When checking out the clerk handed Mr. Breeding the bill. He looked at the paper wondering what the man was handing him. Mr. Page, standing aside, smiled as he chewed on his cigar.

"What is this?" asked Mr. Breeding.

"It's the bill, Mr. Page, is there something wrong with it?"

"I'm not Mr. Page," said Mr. Breeding, as Mr. Page stepped forward and held out his hand for the bill. The clerk looked from one man to the other, not knowing what to say. He began to bow and scrape and apologize for giving the luxury suite to Mr. Breeding. The Breedings were very embarrassed to learn that the Pages had spent nearly a week in cramped quarters while they had enjoyed the luxurious suite.

"Think nothing of it," said Mr. Page. "We've slept in worse places. It didn't hurt us, did it Lucy?" Lucy shook her head. "Besides, it was worth it to see Cap's face," Mr. Page added.

They visited Catalina Island and stopped to take in all the sights along the way.

When time came to go home, the Pages decided to stay in California a while longer. Miss Lindsay and the Breedings escorted the children home, with much to dream and talk about.

1915. *Mrs. B. Lassley and Mrs. Nellie Hinkle with Home children.*

35

The Tommy Atkins Case

On January 12, 1915, Harry Bartlett of Sapulpa driller for the Gypsy Oil Company, brought in a big gusher on the Tommy Atkins lease, and there was a scramble for leases all around the well. So began the Cushing field, one of the richest and most famous in the entire state of Oklahoma.

A dispute arose over the validity of the lease to the property on which the big well came in. When large amounts of money were involved, lawyers appeared on the scene pointing out the possibility of large profits in lawsuits. Many leases were tested in hopes of finding a technical flaw that would make the hold on the lease invalid and fair game for grabbers.

After Gypsy Oil had proven the value of this certain section of land, two large oil companies had their lawyers check the lease.

Preliminary investigations indicated that the acreage specified was the allotment assigned to Tommy Atkins, an Indian boy, infant son of Minnie Atkins. The lease was signed by Minnie, who had inherited the property from her deceased son, Tommy. The contract for drilling rights was properly drawn and witnessed. The woman's authority appeared to be sufficient and the title valid.

Still not satisfied, the lawyers talked to the Indians. It was common knowledge that when the Indians received their allotments some Indians were known to get in line twice, and some claimed an extra child in order to obtain an extra 160 acres. Lawyers pointed out that should Minnie be guilty of either of these actions, the land would go back to the tribe and the eventual millions with it.

The leaders of the tribe thought it over. They later brought witnesses who testified that Tommy Atkins never existed, that Minnie had borrowed a child from her sister to pose as her own. A suit was filed against the Gypsy Oil Company, stating that the lease they held was a forgery. It was up to the Gypsy to prove otherwise, or lose the lease. In order to do this they had to find Minnie. Her tribe didn't seem to know where her family had gone, but word was that they had traveled westward.

Since the land had proven to be of such value, the Gypsy decided it was worth the expense of locating Minnie. Months passed as the search continued.

In the meantime more oil and more money were pouring in from the Cushing field. The Tommy Atkins lease was growing richer every day, but nobody could touch the money until the case was settled.

In discussing the case with Mr. Breeding, Mr. Page thought the situation was unfortunate that so many who had so much were trying to get what rightly belonged to a poor woman who reportedly made her living as a cook.

"I understand that the Indians share of profits from oil found on their lands is one eighth, and that they retain mineral rights even though they've sold their land. Is that right?" asked Mr. Breeding.

"Something like that," said Mr. Page. "Anyway, with a well such as that is, Minnie would be a very rich woman."

It was Sunday, and Mr. Page had brought his cousin, Bub Avery to the Home as his dinner guest.

What is the latest news on the Atkins case?" asked Bub. Has the Gypsy Oil Company found Minnie?"

"No. They've spent a lot of money looking, but they're about to lose because they can't prove the lease without Minnie. I can't understand why they haven't found her," said Mr. Page.

"You would have found her by now," said Bub. Then he turned to Mr. Breeding. "Cap," he said, "did you know that Charley and my dad were once detectives in the famous Pinkerton Detective Association?"

Mr. Breeding shook his head. "Mr. Page has worked at many trades, but I don't believe he ever told me about that."

Bub nodded, "Dad told me that Charley never failed to get his man. He quit that job because he didn't like bringing a man in to be punished."

Mr. Page chuckled. "I was very young. I even tried to get the Pinkerton Association to let some men go, after I had brought them in. I argued that every man deserved a second chance. But they told me that was up to the judge."

"Charley, I'll bet you could find Minnie. Why don't you give it a try?" said Bub enthusiastically. "Make a deal with the Gypsy, and maybe they'll cut you in on their millions."

"Don't bet any money on that one," said Mr. Page. "These oil companies are strictly for themselves.

There was a long silence, as the men sat on the front porch of the children's home, watching the children play on the front lawn.

Mr. Page removed the cigar from his mouth, and snuffed it out on the sole of his shoe. Tossing the cigar butt into the flower bed, he said, "Bub, If I should do such a thing as find Minnie, I wouldn't even let the Gypsy know I was doing it. They could have someone tailing me, then claim they found her so they wouldn't have to split with me. I know where they've already been, searching for Minnie, so I know where not to go. But if I found her, I'd make sure I could prove she had a son Tommy, then go to the Gypsy and try to BUY the questionable lease from them. Then I'd bring Minnie in, prove my case, and Minnie and I would both be rich."

"You're already rich," said Bub. "But you give it all away as fast as it comes in."

"But this Cushing well would make me very rich." Mr. Page looked at Mr. Breeding and winked. "Cap, if I had all that money I could enlarge this Home for the kids." He leaned back dreamily. "I might even take my kids on another vacation."

A few days later Mr. Page called Mr. Breeding and told him that he was going to take a vacation. He couldn't let him know where he could be reached because he might be on a river bank somewhere fishing, but he was sure Mr. Breeding could take care of any situation that arose concerning the Home or the Colony.

Mr. Breeding had never known Mr. Page to go fishing. He suspected that he was going to hunt for Minnie but didn't want anybody to know what he was doing, in case he failed to find her.

The word got around that Mr. Page had taken George Nye on vacation with him. George had told Mr. Page that he was having trouble with his stomach and that the doctor had put him on goat's milk. He had to stay home where he could get goat's milk.

"Don't worry," Mr. Page was reported to have told George. "I'll see that you get your goat's milk every day."

The next day Mr. Page drove up in front of George's house. He had a goat in a crate on the fender of his shiny black Cadillac, and bales of hay and goat feed in the back seat.

When Mr. Page returned home, he was feeling good. He liked old hats, but was sporting a new ten-dollar Stetson that he was very proud of. He took it off and turned it in his hands to show Mr. Breeding. Then he cocked it at an angle on his head, and changed the subject.

"Well, Cap, I found Minnie," he said, smiling broadly. "I searched throughout the southwest, even going into Mexico, inquiring as to an Indian woman, Minnie Atkins, who made her living as a cook. I followed a lead that took me into California. There I found her cooking in a mining camp."

"Did you bring her back?" asked Mr. Breeding.

"No, I told her to wait until I sent for her. I"ve got to get the Gypsy Oil to sell me the leases. Then I'll get Minnie to come here, and we'll go to Cushing. She will show me where her son Tommy is buried, and we'll win the case."

"It sounds like a sure thing all right," said Mr. Breeding. "Now what I'd like to know, is how did the goat fare on the trip?"

Mr. Page laughed. "Oh, you heard about that, did you? Well, old Nanny did all right. When we went through the hot desert she rode in the shade, inside the car with her feed."

Mr. Page talked to officials in the Gypsy Oil Company. Realizing their legal claim on the lease was extremely tenuous, they agreed to sell. But Mr. Page didn't realize the price would be so high. He had to reimburse them for all they had spent on the development of the well, the expense of the search for Minnie and their attorney fees. It took all the money he could scrape together, including mortgaging most of his land and business interests. But ever optimistic, he was sure the case would be settled in a short time.

When Mr. Page sent for Minnie, she came, bringing her husband Harry Folk, and her older son, Charles. But when they went to Cushing to show where Tommy was buried, they couldn't find the grave. The trees had all been cleared from the area, and nothing looked familiar to Minnie. Minnie's sister, Nancy was sent for to vouch for Minnie, but it was only their word against that of the other litigants. It was a complicated case.

The other litigants had the well shut down, demanding that Mr. Page put up bond. He had to deed some of his remaining land to his brother Edwin, so that Ed could qualify as his bondsman.

Mr. Page tried to be optimistic. He didn't like being any other way, but as he told Mr. Breeding, if he lost the case, he would lose about everything he had. His business was in the hands of receivers, the land that wasn't tied up had to be sold to meet expenses. He was going into debt as expenses continued.

"I'm afraid the courts will take my kids because I can't support them if something doesn't break soon," he said. "I just don't know what to do."

The wagon bridge, built by the oilmen in 1905, was a toll bridge.

36

Difficult Decisions

Mr. Page always had drillers on his lands, but luck hadn't been with him lately. Each evening when the men returned from the oil fields they reported their progress. So far there had only been dry holes.

"We should know by tomorrow whether you're a rich man or a poor man," said the men who had been drilling on a lease directly across the river from the Childrens' Home.

That night Charles Page tossed and turned. Finally, unable to sleep, he got out of bed and went over to the window. Jim raised his head from his paws and watched his master pace back and forth from window to bed. As Mr. Page stepped out on the balcony, he could hear a coyote calling to his mate. Jim followed to investigate the noise.

Standing motionless, gazing toward the heavens, Mr. Page's voice was barely audible as he said, "I need your help, Lord. I'm gonna lose my Kids if things don't get better for us. . ."

Jim walked over to the banister and looked out over the grounds below. He stiffened, ears alert, as something moved in the shadows. A rabbit from the near by woods came into view and disappeared again into the shadows.

Mr. Page stood silent gazing at the boundless canopy of sky. The vastness of God's universe was awe-inspiring. Both dog and man watched the stars twinkle like flickering candles. An owl hooted from within the trees and shrubs that bordered the moon lit lawn. Jim stiffened again and gave a low bark, drawing his master's attention. Mr. Page patted the dog on the haunch.

"Now Jim, don't you go scaring those little creatures. They've got rights too," he said. He knelt down and rubbed Jim's fur. "I've been disturbing your sleep a lot lately, haven't I, old buddy?" Jim licked his cheek. "Yeah, I know, you're trying to tell me that you like your old master. Well Jim old boy, it's mutual. Now let's go in and get some sleep. We've got to get up early in the morning to see what it's going to be with that well." He gave Jim an affectionate pat and opened the screen door.

Lucy rolled toward him as he crawled back into bed. Sleepily she threw her arm across his chest. "Charley, have you been walking the floor again?" she asked. Then, pressing her cheek against his shoulder, she dozed again.

Morning seemed to come too early. As he sat waiting for Lucy to fix breakfast, Mr. Page opened a drawer and got his deck of cards out.

"I feel lucky today," he said, as he spread the cards before him. "I want to see what old Sol has to say about it."

"Charley, winning a game of cards has nothing to do with luck," said Lucy, "except that you won the game."

"Sure it does," said Mr. Page. "You wait and see. I'll win two games out of three this morning. I'm gonna be lucky today."

Mr. Page played three games and lost two. "Old Sol isn't going to discourage me," he said. "As you say, it's just a game. It doesn't mean anything."

Mr. Page ate hurriedly. Then he and Jim headed out across the river. Going down the long narrow lane leading into the oil field he came upon a wagon blocking the road. The wagon was loaded with heavy casing for a well. When Mr. Page honked, the driver of the wagon motioned for him to go around. The ground was wet from a recent rain and he didn't want to get stuck in the mud at a time like this. He opened the car door and stepped aground. He held his hand up to his mouth and yelled.

"Hey fellows, will you pull over and let me pass? I'm in a hurry."

"Can't do it," said the driver. "If I got stuck in that mud with this heavy load, I'd never get out. Old man Page is counting on these wells to pull him out of a bad spot. He'd be mad as hell at the delay."

"What's your name, young fellow?"

"M'name is Lute Bond, sir."

"You're a good man, Lute. The kind of man I like working for me. I'm old man Page." He got back into the car and pulled cautiously around the wagon. As he passed he called from the window, "You're gonna have a job for a long time, Lute."

Mr. Page arrived at the well just as the men were lowering the bailer to take a soil sample. As he watched them work his pulse quickened as the bailer was drawn up. Just then he thought he heard a noise coming from below. His pounding heart reverberated in his temples as he leaned over the hole. The noise was getting louder. Almost afraid he was only hearing his heart beat, he looked at the bailer, then at the men. They were smiling.

"Boys, I believe we've got something down there," he said.

The gurgling and surging grew louder as they all stood transfixed gazing at the thin gaseous stream that began to spew out of the hole. It was followed by an increasingly forceful column of oil. Jim ran from the platform, barking for his master to follow. The men began to whoop. They retreated from the platform as the plume of oil rose higher and higher. Mr. Page ignored the warnings to stand back. He stood where he was, watching the fountain of oil. With a sudden blast, oil shot up to the top of the derrick, over the crown block and high into the air spraying everything around the well. It filled the brim of

Mr. Page's new hat, then spilled down on his shoulders. He took his hat and waved it in the air, as the black gold washed down his face.

"Thank You, God, thank You," he said. Then waving his hat toward the Children's Home across the river, he shouted, "Kids, we stay. We're gonna be all right."

After the big gusher came in, Mr. Page was able to pay some of his debts and get a release on most of his business interests. But 1916 was by no means a year without problems. The lower courts were unable to settle the complicated Tommy Atkins dispute and sent the case to a higher court.

Mr. Breeding and Miss Lindsay were also often faced with problems. Most could be handled without bothering Mr. Page; however, one problem persisted. The Children's Home was so overcrowded that the larger children had to sleep two to a full-sized bed, and four to a bed for the smaller children. Cribs lined the stairway hall. Miss Lindsay refused to accept another child into the Home until something was done about the overcrowding.

"Mr. Page, when are you going to build a wing onto this building?" she had asked again and again. But she knew with his financial problems, he couldn't do any building. Maybe after the big well came in, he would. But his answer was no more encouraging.

"Lindsay, girl, I haven't forgotten," he had said. "But I can't decide just how to do it. If I enclose a portion of the porches, that would do away with the windows in the present bedrooms, and adding on always ruins the looks of a building."

An idea to build another dormitory to the north of the Home had been considered, and work was even started, but that idea had been abandoned by the time the foundation and flooring was laid. This platform was later used as Galloway's temporary wood shop. The problem of overcrowding remained.

Meanwhile, Mr. Page kept sending Mr. Breeding to see about more children who had been reported to him as having no parents, and no place to call home. Most had relatives who agreed to keep the children until room could be made for them. But the Bennefield children had no nearby relatives, so Mr. Page paid various widows of the Colony to care for the children until room could be made for them at the Home.

One Sunday, at the close of the service Mr. Breeding always held at the Colony, two of the women asked to speak to him.

"Mr. Breeding," said one, "when we agreed to care for the Bennefield children, we understood it to be only temporary. Several months have passed. An extra child in a small house is very difficult."

"I understand," said Mr. Breeding. "You've been very patient and we appreciate what you've done for us. But off hand, I can't tell you how soon we will take them. You see, Mr. Page is out of town, and he usually makes such decisions. However, I assure you we will do something."

Mr. Breeding asked Miss Lindsay if she could possibly crowd the children into the Home, but she shook her head with an emphatic no.

"We could possibly crowd the boy in, but we'd have to move somebody out to make room for one more girl." She paused. "That's not such a bad idea. Some of these older girls are getting too big for their britches anyway. They are earning a wage. They are capable of taking care of themselves."

"Then that's what we'll do," said Mr. Breeding. "They are no longer helpless dependent children. We need to think of those unable to fend for themselves. I'll go down to my office and check the register to determine which girls are the oldest."

"Wait," said Miss Lindsay as he turned to go. "I know. Sarah Davis and Ona Shockley are eighteen, and Nancy Davis is seventeen."

"Seventeen is a little young," said Mr. Breeding.

"With her older sister she will do all right," said Miss Lindsay. They will all do fine. If anything happens Mr. Page will help them."

When the girls got home from work the next day, Miss Lindsay sent them down to Mr. Breeding's office. Mr. Breeding explained to them that it was time they spread their wings and tried to fly. He suggested that they try to find a place where they could all stay together for awhile until they felt more secure to go their separate ways. "You are no longer dependent children," he said. "You are fine responsible young ladies qualified to take care of yourselves. We must make space for others in need."

"Hurt at being asked to move, the girls moved out the next day. Insa Arnold decided to move out with them.

Joe and Martha Davis had moved out earlier. Martha was taking nurses' training at the Sand Springs Hospital, and slept in the nurses' quarters. Joe had a job and promised to help his sisters all he could.

The four Bennefield children were brought to the Home, happy to be together again. Gertrude was eleven years of age, Haskell was ten, Beulah was eight, and Opal was four years old.

When Mr. Page returned, he wasn't too happy to learn that some of his girls had been moved out. But the girls were getting along all right, and he acknowledged that Mr. Breeding had done the best he could under the circumstances. He also agreed that an age limit of 18 years should be set in order to make room for more dependent ones. Should a child wish to go to college, the cost would be paid by Mr. Page.

That spring, Mr. Page decided to find a suitable place for summer vacations for the Home folks. Coin Harvey, a politician who had once run for president of the United States, owned a summer resort in Monte Ne, Arkansas. Mr. Harvey's resort consisted of rustic cabins, a store, and other conveniences. But the main attraction was a lake and several Italian gondolas which he had shipped from Italy.

Mr. and Mrs. Page were among one group of vacationers who got off the train, and were escorted to the fancy boats waiting for them. They drifted dreamily down stream for about two blocks distance where they entered a big glassy lake. When they came to the resort grounds, everyone was deposited on shore to climb a hill to the popular lodge hidden deep within the beautiful Ozark mountains.

Mr. Page, fascinated with the resort, wanted such a place for his Kids. He purchased land from Mr. Harvey, and sent Mr. Galloway and a number of his wood shop boys to build a few rustic cabins, where a few at a time could enjoy the magic of the beautiful Ozark forest hideaway. Mr. and Mrs. Breeding, Mr. and Mrs. Galloway, and Miss Lindsay and Mrs. McDonald, each took a turn with a group of children until everyone, including Mr. and Mrs. Page and their daughter Mary, had a good vacation.

However, in visiting the camp during the various groups' stays, Mr. Page had not been pleased with the consideration the children received. They were not allowed to ride in the gondolas or use the lake for any purpose, because they were not renting cottages from Mr. Harvey. Mr. Harvey ran them off every time he saw one of the children on his lodge grounds. This hurt Mr. Page. When vacation time was over, he sold the property.

Meanwhile, things around Sand Springs were looking very good. Three years earlier the town fathers had purchased a lot on the corner of Broadway and McKinley for the purpose of building a city hall. Mr. Page had donated a second lot; however, they had not been able to raise enough money to build the city hall until 1916.

Being a member of the Tulsa Chamber of Commerce, Mr. Page learned that Tulsa was going to remove the Eleventh Street wood and steel wagon-bridge that the oil men had built in 1905. It would be replaced with a wide concrete bridge. Being ever on the alert, Mr. Page bargained for the old bridge, had it taken down in sections and floated down the river on rafts. Cables and wires were used to string the steel sections across the river where they were re-assembled. New wood flooring was added, and Sand Springs had its first bridge in the year 1916. The bridge has been replaced twice since then.

On June 2, 1916, Mr. Page's birthday, he announced that his his good deed for this year's birthday, would be to build a new home for the children. Everyone was excited.

"The new home will be at a select site independent of this home. We'll turn this place into a school for deaf children. I have a doctor friend who lives in Tulsa. He has a little girl who can't hear. He says there are no schools around here for him to send his little girl to. So I decided to turn this place into an oral school as soon as I get your new home built.

He picked up one of the little ones leaning against his chair and sat the child on his knee. "You're going to get a new home, right on the top of that hill," he said, pointing toward the northeast. "It's just opposite the little five-acre peach orchard.

Everybody was excited as Mr. Page told of his plans. "This home will accommodate at least two hundred children, with room for expansion." He stood the child down and took him by the hand. "I'll show you exactly where the new home will be." He motioned, and everybody, including the matrons, followed.

When he arrived at the site, he asked, "How's this?"

"It should be a little farther north," Miss Lindsay suggested. "That would give more room for a big driveway."

Mr. Page stepped back a few more paces. "Right here?" he asked. Miss Lindsay backed him up until she was satisfied.

When the architects and engineers came to establish the corners for the basement, they advised moving twelve feet farther north, due to the lay of the land. A tree stood right where the front door would be. Instead of turning a shovel of dirt to celebrate the start of the project, the tree was cut. Everybody who could lift an ax took a whack at the tree. Later the older boys and Mr. Galloway finished the job. Soon the work on the home began.

Mr. and Mrs. Breeding and their two daughters, Margaret and Eva, at the waiting-station in front of their house.

37

A World at War

It was now 1917, and Americas chances of staying out of the war that had been raging in Europe since 1914 were growing more tenuous every day. American merchant ships were being sunk by German submarines in neutral waters. On October 7, 1916, a German submarine appeared off the American coast and sunk a British passenger steamer. It was discovered that Germany had diplomatic representatives in the United States plotting against the Allies to ruin the relationship between them. There was also evidence that plots had been laid to destroy American lives and property and to stir up the people with riots and strikes. Ships bearing food and materials to the Allies were sunk at the rate of 600,000 to 800,000 tons a month by the Germans, hoping to starve the countries into submission.

On April 6, 1917, the United States declared war on Germany. Posters placed in conspicuous places announced that all males between the ages of twenty-one and thirty were to report to the polling places in the election district in which they resided. They were required to register in accordance with the president's proclamation on Tuesday, June 5th, between the hours of 7 a.m. and 9 p.m. The first American troops were sent to France.

Joe Davis was the first of the Home boys to enlist. He shaved his head, much to the distress of his sisters. As he prepared to go he gathered his sisters and brothers together for a family photograph to take with him. "We may never all be together again," he said, "and we should have a picture made for each of us to keep."

Jess Davis, Luther Nolan, Calvin Morey and others joined the armed services. Burt Evans joined the navy, and Dr. Calhoun served as a doctor.

There was a terrible flu epidemic throughout the country during the war, and many people died. All the hospital rooms were crowded, and beds lined the corridors. Martha Davis, who was going to be a graduate nurse in a few days, caught the flu. She was told to go to bed upstairs in the nurses' quarters. But knowing that she was needed, she stayed, helping with patients until she collapsed and was carried to the nurses' quarters. She died two days later.

Luther Nolan was the first of the injured to be sent home. He had been badly shell-shocked and had a nervous breakdown. He would never completely recover from it.

Germany's assurance that with the use of a great fleet of submarines in a ruthless warfare would force a peace within a few months was a disappointment when America entered the war.

Letters from the boys of the Home told of the large guns directed at breaking up roads, railways and bridges, and of the large shells containing poisonous "mustard" gas being fired at the trenches. Joe Davis was among those who suffered from the mustard gas.

By the end of August America had over 1,500,000 men in France. The British began surprise attacks at one point, driving the Germans back, and France and the Americans attacked at another point.

On November 11, 1918, President Wilson issued a formal proclamation that Germany had surrendered, the Armistice had been signed, and the war was over.

There was much celebration throughout the towns. Sand Springs enthusiasts hung the Kaiser in effigy on a wagon, and paraded him up Main Street. Soldiers who had been injured and returned home from battle marched along behind the mule drawn wagon bearing the Kaiser. There was much cheering over the victory, as the mass of people followed. Up Main Street they went, around Broadway to the southwest corner of Jefferson Street to a large boarded-in area that was used for ball games, rodeos, the school's May Day festivals, and for anything else that needed a place to happen. Here in the center of the grounds, the Kaiser was removed from the wagon and burned at the stake.

The war was over, and the boys began returning home. None of the boys of the Home were more seriously injured than Luther Nolan.

One day Mr. Page decided to go to Washington D.C. to talk to authorities about his noted surgeons, and offer his hospital for returning soldiers needing surgery. Leaving Tulsa by train, he happened to sit next to a man who introduced himself as a Tulsa attorney, and was glad to meet Charles Page whom he had heard so much about. In the course of conversation, Mr. Page mentioned a concern that was always on his mind. He was constantly strengthening the organization of the Sand Springs Home to insure its perpetuity. He had selected the trustees he wanted to manage the affairs and the money of the Sand Springs Home, but he still worried over the appointment of trustees to succeed those he had selected when they too should die.

"Why don't you have the Grand Master of the Masons to appoint a suitable man to fill such vacancies?" the lawyer suggested. Mr. Page was not a mason. He knew very little about them. The man called a few names of men who were masons and giants of respectability. When he got through talking, Mr. Page had made a decision.

When Mr. Page got back home he sent for his cousin Ed Gottry, a prominent Wisconsin attorney. Ed's wife, Cosette, and their daughter, Amy, came with him. Mr. Page hired Ed as his attorney, and asked Ed to prepare a will for him.

Mr. Page called a conference of the Board of Trustees of the Home and the masons who were empowered to act at the conference, among whom were Henry S. Johnston, Grand Master; G.B. Bristow, deputy grand master; and C.A. Sturgeon, senior grand orator. He asked to have this stipulation made a part of the by-laws of the Sand Springs Home. Thus he felt assured that each succeeding trustee after his death would be selected with the same discrimination and care that he, himself, had used in appointing men to handle the affairs of the Home Interests.

Due to the war and the shortage of materials, the children's new home was not completed until December of 1918. The dedication of the Home was scheduled for December 25, 1918. There would be a feast fit for kings, and practically everybody was invited.

The Davis family. Taken in 1917, just before Joe and Jess joined the army in World War I. The last photo that they would all be together.

38

A New Home

As Christmas drew near, everybody was excited. Weeks earlier, the children of the Home had sent their letters to Santa. Each child was allowed to ask for two gifts, and a second choice in case Santa didn't have the first. Galloway and his boys became Santa's helpers, keeping the machinery humming in the manual training shop as they filled orders for such items as sewing boxes, cedar chests and doll beds for the girls. Some boys also made personal gifts for a sister or friend.

The older boys and girls did the decorating. A ceiling high Christmas tree was artfully decorated, and Merry Christmas banners, bells and bows were displayed conspicuously at windows doors and hallways. The older boys brought mistletoe and boughs of cedar from the woods, giving everything the smell of Christmas. There was a lot of giggling going on, as the girls tried to avoid walking under the mistletoe.

The motto THINK RIGHT had been brought from the old home and was proudly displayed in the entry above the wide marble staircase. Under the motto hung a large clump of mistletoe.

On the day before Christmas Mr. Page sent baskets of food to every home in the Colony, and to every needy family in town. Each child would receive a gift, and a large bag of fruit, nuts and candy.

On Christmas Eve night, the children of the Home gathered in the big living room where they would receive their gifts from Santa. Some had never seen Santa before, and they were tense with excitement as he made his appearance. Mr. Page smiled as the children ran to show him what Santa had brought them. They were amazed that Santa could remember the wishes of nearly one hundred children. Each child received five gifts. A big orange mesh bag of candy, fruit and nuts was given to all. This was a night Charles Page's children would always remember.

The next day was Christmas, and the day of the dedication of the new Home. The children were awakened by a big bell attached to a pole in the backyard. The bell had been taken from one of Mr. Page's trains. It rang every morning at six o'clock and at meal times.

At the sound of the bell, the children got up, made their beds, washed their faces and dressed for breakfast. When the second bell rang, they marched down to eat. Under the direction of Miss Lindsay, who believed in keeping boys and girls apart, the boys would occupy the tables on the south side of the dining room, and the more numerous girls were to be seated at the tables in the center, and to the north side of the room. Miss Lindsay often stood at the corner of one of the tables in the center of the room. She carried a small bell in her hand, which she tapped when she wanted the attention of the children. Everybody stood until grace was said. When the noise in the dining room got too loud, Miss Lindsay would tap her bell and call out, "STOP THE NOISE."

When breakfast was over the tables were cleared and made ready for the dedication feast. Much of the food had been prepared the day before, but the big kitchen in the basement was a beehive of activity with special chefs preparing the menu of roast bear with chestnut dressing, venison steaks and stews, roast buffalo, baked opossum with candied yams, mallard duck with chestnut stuffing, baked sirloin of elk with brown gravy, fried rabbit with cream gravy, quail on toast, salmon salad, and every kind of vegetable and dessert imaginable.

While all the cooking was being done in the kitchen, the dining room was being prepared for the dinner hour. Galloway and the boys had made all the solid oak dining room furniture from trees from the land. Each table had a white linen table cloth, and a vase of fresh flowers from the Sand Springs Green House.

The older girls, helping to put the food on the tables, were fascinated with the electric dishwasher and the dumb waiter. They all wanted to pull the rope that drew the dumb waiter laden with food from the kitchen below up to the dining room.

When everything was in readiness, Mrs. McDonald sent the girls upstairs to get dressed for the big event. The children, each dressed in his or her Sunday best, were kept upstairs out of the way until time for them to come down.

When guests began to arrive, the children were told to get in line. When the signal was given, the children marched silently down the winding stairs and into the dining room. The little ones leading the procession, paused inside the large double doorway. Mr. Page was visibly proud as a smile passed between him and his children.

A hush fell over the crowd as Mrs. Wiggins, teacher at the little private school, gave the signal. The voices of the children rose loud and clear as they sang in acapella harmony:

"Joy to the World, the Lord is come!
Let earth receive her King;
Let every heart prepare him room,
and heaven and nature sing, . . "

When the children had finished their song, the people held their applause. The children had another song for them. Smiles passed from one guest to another as the little ones at the front stood as they were trained to do, straight and tall, chin up, with eyes looking straight ahead, as they sang,

"All hail the power of Jesus' name,
let angels prostrate fall. Bring forth
the royal diadem, and crown Him Lord of all . . ."

When they had finished, Mr. Breeding returned thanks and the meal began.

After dinner the guests were led on tour through the Home. Mr. Page explained with pride that Mr. Galloway and the boys, not only made the furnishings for the dining room, but also many comfortable chairs and couches that were made of solid hardwood.

"They will last a lifetime," he stated.

He was especially proud of the beautiful inlaid tables.

"I'll wager that table has 9999 pieces in it," said Mr. Breeding, as he rubbed his hand across the smooth surface of the longest table. After that, when anyone asked about the table, he or she was told that it contained 9999 pieces, but nobody ever counted them. A piece of the tree cut in dedication starting the building of the Home was in the center of this beautiful inlaid table.

Mr. Galloway's masterpiece with the twining snake and the reptiles stood near the large fireplace. He had also hewn out another big log to keep brooms in with large fishes carved around the outside.

A grandfather's clock stood between the door to Mr. Breeding's office and a row of piano practice rooms.

Guests who exclaimed at the large bear rug stretched out near the fireplace, were told that they had eaten the bear at dinner. The animals for the dinner had been killed earlier and kept in the cold storage plant in the basement of the Home. The head and skin of the bear and the heads of the elk and deer had been sent to a taxidermist. The head of the elk would be hung above Billy Roesser's buffet in the dining room.

The deer skin was being tanned. "When it gets pretty weather we will have pictures made of the children, and together with photographs of some early scenes of the beginning of the Home, an Indian artist whom I have commissioned," said Mr. Page, "will draw these pictures on the deer skin."

The east end of the second floor was the boys' dormitory. The west end of the second floor was reserved for a library, and study hall, and a place for assembling for various occasions such as Mr. Breeding's Tuesday and Sunday afternoon worship services. The children attended the Presbyterian church on Sunday mornings.

The third floor was for the girls. Both girls and boys had long sleeping porches that wrapped around in a U shape at the east end of the building. The outdoor play porches stretched across the front and circled the west end of the building on all three floors.

The large French windows, completely surrounding the sleeping porches, made the room light and airy as the sun cast shadowy patterns across the rows of little white beds that lined the walls of the long room. No child would ever have to sleep two in a bed again. The older girls had private rooms with heavy maroon drapes at each doorway.

The matrons in charge of the children would change from time to time, but of those who would remain faithful to retirement age were Miss Margaret Lindsay, head matron; Miss Bimmy Rosebud Dobozy who came as girls' matron in 1921 and stayed to retire at old age. Mrs. McDonald, dining room matron, became head matron after Miss Lindsay retired; Mrs. McClain, boys' matron; Miss Darrow babies' matron; Mrs. Cheatham, seamstress, later to become girls' matron; Miss Minnie Bell Verbeck, piano teacher; and Mrs. Wiggins, private school teacher.

Miss Darrow and her under school age "babies" occupied the fourth floor. The nursery was like a penthouse, with a large play area. A four-foot-brick wall, topped with a high, wrought iron fence, surrounded the roof garden which contained slides and a gazebo for shade. Miss Darrow loved babies and had a good time with them. Galloway and his boys made small chairs and furniture for the nursery.

Mrs. McDonald was a jolly, heavy-set woman to whom the girls felt they could go when they needed to talk. Mrs. Cheatham, in charge of the sewing room was, from the south. The children loved her southern accent. "Cheatie," as she was affectionately called, didn't pronounce her Rs, and the girls were always getting her to say such words as "four hours." Then they would repeat "fowa owas." Sometimes she sang songs from the south as she sewed many beautiful dresses for the girls. She took pride in seeing to it that the Home children were the best dressed children in town. She also taught the older girls to sew. One time the girls were scolded for sewing up the legs of the boys' overalls. They were sent back to the sewing room, and the girls had to pick out all the stitching, so the boys got the last laugh. But they didn't mind having to pay for a good prank on the boys.

Cheatie had two children, Preston, and Helen. They lived in a house to themselves. Miss Verbeck, the girls' piano teacher, new at this time, was a refined soft-spoken, woman. She was a patient teacher and very quiet. She had a private room on the girls' floor.

Mrs. Wiggins, the private school teacher, lived in one of the original little houses on the hill. She had a son living in Tulsa, and preferred a place of her own, where she could entertain her son and his family when they came to see her. She had two grandchildren Doris and Jimmy Wiggins. Mrs. Wiggins was a nice looking, elderly woman with gray hair that lay in soft waves. She was an excellent teacher, who didn't hesitate to use the paddle if a student didn't get his lessons. Her third grade students were usually so advanced by the time they started to public school that they got to skip from four-B to four-A.

Mrs. Wiggins wrote two songs that would be handed down from one generation to the next. Seeing the love between Mr. Page and the children inspired Mrs. Wiggins to write the song, quoted in part, below:

"WHAT WOULD YOU TAKE FOR ME, DADDY PAGE?"

> What would you take for me Daddy Page,
> If somebody wanted to buy,
> And stacked all the bright shiny dollars
> In a pile up as high as the sky.
>
> Chorus
>
> They say you are good at a bargain.
> I know you're as wise as can be
> So what would you take for me Daddy Page,
> If someone made an offer for me.
>
> I don't think Miss Lindsay would miss me,
> Because I'm so much in the way,
> Except when she offers to kiss me
> At night when I kneel down to pray.
>
> Chorus

"There aren't enough dollars in the world to buy you," said Mr. Page wiping the tears from his eyes after the children had sung the song to him.

The other song Mrs. Wiggins wrote was dedicated to Mr. Page, Mr. Breeding and Miss Lindsay, is in her own handwriting.

The children often took advantage of Mr. Page's good nature. They knew that they were not allowed to go into the peach orchard just down the walk and across the road in front of the Home. When the pink blush appeared on the peaches, the temptation was too overpowering to resist. Those who were caught were punished either by a few lashes with the razor-strap, or a big dose of castor oil, or both. But Mr. Page didn't know this. One Sunday while he was visiting, some of the girls asked him if they could go into the orchard and pick some peaches.

"Sure girls, go ahead," he told them. "They are your peaches." The girls ran down the walk toward the orchard. Miss Lindsay came out on the porch just then, and Mr. Page turned to her. "Lindsay," he said, "I told the girls they could go into the orchard. I don't know what your rules are on it."

"Mr. Page," said Miss Lindsay, "If all these children were turned loose to plunder the orchard at will, there would be no orchard. They know that they cannot go into the orchard on Sunday." However the girls were not punished this time.

Miss Lindsay was efficient in whatever she did. She was very strict but not unkind. But she had some strange notions. She decided that no two children should have the same first name. She changed names, sometimes honoring one of the matrons by naming a child after her. In some cases, an entire family of children had their names changed.

The Kyler children for instance, whose parents died during the flu epidemic, were named Beulah, Opal, Leo and Mary Kyler. Beulah and Opal Bennefield were already at the Home when the Kyler children came, so Miss Lindsay changed Beulah Kyler's name to May. Opal Kyler's name was changed to Daisy. There was a Leo Simons, so Leo Kyler's name was changed to John. There was a Mary Barnett, so Mary Kyler was given the name Cecelia.

Some children resented having their names changed. When they were grown, they took their original names back. This was confusing to those who had always known them by the name they grew up with. However some rules were changed when Miss Lindsay retired and Mrs. McDonald became head matron. She allowed family members to sit together at one table, keeping the family ties closer. The children were also given an allowance.

But on the whole, the children of the Home were happy and carefree. Mr. Page insisted that they never be taught that they had to be beholding to him for anything he had done for them. He never expected a thank you. They were given many cultural advantages that few families could afford.

The First Presbyterian Church now sits where the little Pleasant View School once sat.

1 Tune – Battle Hymn of the Republic.

From the state of old Wisconsin,
   (With its trees of spruce and pine)
Came a man with wondrous vision,
   With a purpose most divine,
For a righteous cause, far reaching
   'Way beyond the present age
We call him: "Daddy Page".

            Chorus.

Glory, glory Hallelujah
   "   "   "   "
   "   "   "   "
His cause is marching on.

2 He came a man from old Kentucky,
   (Where the meadow grass is blue)
With the sunshine of that country
   In his face and manners, too!
He came to serve the children
   And the gospel to proclaim
B. F. Breeding is his name.

            Chorus.

3
4 From the rolling plains of Kansas,
   (Where the yellow sunflower grows)
Walked a maiden, tall and stately,
   Out amid Life's joys and woes;
She gave her youth and beauty
   For the cause she knew was good
Miss Lindsay understood.

39

Unto the Least of These

THE TOMMY ATKINS CASE WAS FINALLY SETTLED IN THE UNITED STATES Supreme Court in 1919, after having been tied up in litigation for four years. The case went down in history as a complicated fraud among the Indians. Winning the case made Mr. Page, the third richest man in Oklahoma. He saw that Minnie Atkins got her share.

Mr. Page had just received a call from his attorney telling him that he had won the case, when he heard a loud noise on the street below. He hung up the receiver and looked out the window. A Ford touring car had driven in front of the street car at the intersection.

Mr. Page recognized the car as belonging to Roy Simms, a young Osage Indian who lived at Shell Creek, about nine miles from Sand Springs. Roy was catcher on the Sand Springs baseball team and was also known to drink. Mr. Page figured Roy was probably drunk or he would have looked before crossing the intersection. How could he miss seeing a big thing like a street car? Roy helped his sister, Lottie, out of the car and a man climbed from the back seat. Roy pulled something from his coat pocket, raised his shirt and rubbed his side.

There were always several men loafing on the Rexall or the bank corner. Standing around talking was the way they spent their extra time. Several men rushed to the scene. When they saw that nobody was hurt, they picked up the Ford and moved it from the tracks. The street car went on its way.

Roy crossed the street toward the bank building. Mr. Page knew he would see him soon. He took his seat and waited. "What can I do for you, Roy?" he asked, as Roy came into his office.

Accustomed to being called uncle by people who were not related to him, Mr. Page nodded when Roy Simms said, "Uncle Charley, your street car ran into my Ford and banged it up. I want you to have it fixed."

"Was anyone hurt?" asked Mr. Page.

"Naw, but I had a new oil can in my pocket," Roy said, "and it made a print of the can in my side." He pulled up his shirt and showed his side.

Having just received the news that he had won the Tommy Atkins case, Mr. Page was feeling good. He didn't question Roy on his drinking. "Roy, my boy," he said, "go to the Home garage and tell them that Charley Page said for them to come and get your car and fix it up like new."

Roy grinned broadly. "Thank you, Uncle Charley," he said, and hurried out the door and down the hall.

Things were going well in Sand Springs. Harry Bartlett was elected mayor that year and during his 1919-1921 tenure the city established a commission form of government. The small city hall building was replaced in 1920 with space for offices, a jail and a fire station.

The town received the honor as having more industries for its size than any other town in Oklahoma, due to shipping facilities and through Mr. Page's hard work.

Villages that had sprung up along the so called "line," between Sand Springs and Tulsa were spreading in both directions with people coming to Sand Springs to work.

Mr. Page belonged to the Tulsa Chamber Of Commerce, and at one of the meetings held at Hotel Tulsa, Mr. Alf Heggem spoke in recognition of Page's contribution to Tulsa.

"We are using the vision of Charles Page in building up a mighty industrial zone along the Arkansas River and much of what has been accomplished is due to his faith, his constant effort and hard work," Heggem said. "Charles Page doesn't dynamite his way through. He does things quietly and effectively step by step with an indomitable spirit that carries him from one achievement to the other. He is always pressing ahead in his own quiet way with definite ideas and ideals in mind.

"It is not necessary to catalog his achievements. We all know of his efforts for big plants here and of his deep interest in building up this entire region, not just the city of his creation. As a result of his vision and labors we now have miles of industry along the Arkansas. It is an industrial strip the like of which is not found anywhere else in this region. All this exists because of Page's foresight in building a railroad for freight and a separate street car line for passenger service."

Around the clock service was provided for the 67 industries of Sand Springs, using the freight trains carrying cargo to and from the area.

The convenience of street cars running every twenty minutes with a fare of five to ten cents prompted many residents of Tulsa to ride to Sand Springs to work in factories there, or along the line.

However, all this convenience of transportation was detrimental to the growth of the downtown shopping area of Sand Springs. Tulsa had a wider selection of merchandise and many Sand Springs residents rode the street car to Tulsa and did their shopping there. Mr. Page was warned that no small town bordering a large city, especially "the oil capital of the world," could survive. He conceded that it would take a mighty effort, but he wouldn't even think of withdrawing the street car services. Perhaps a lot of the Sand Springs trade was going to Tulsa because of the transportation, and perhaps Tulsans were taking some of the Sand Springs jobs that the town's residents deserved, but if more people were served it had to be all right. He would just have to work harder providing more jobs. Anyway, it really worked both ways. Tulsa had more jobs for women in offices and clerking in the large stores, and until he could provide more jobs for women he was glad he provided cheap transportation to help women. In fact, widows, preachers, his employees, the children of the Home, families of the Colony and many more were given free passes to ride the streetcars whenever they wanted to.

Page continued to offer free sites, gas at cheap rates, and other inducements to get more industry into Sand Springs.

Sand Springs had three very nice movie theaters, but Tulsa's theaters were bigger and more elegant. Tulsa had everything in the way of entertainment except for an amusement park. People were riding out to Sand Springs' beautiful park at the rate of a million a year. The park had become one of the greatest recreation grounds in the entire southwest, with regular visits from fifty to one hundred miles around. Clubs and organizations held annual picnics in the park. Schools brought their children as a special holiday treat. The dozens of rustic huts with long tables, lunch pavilions with heat, water and electricity provided plenty of space for the largest of gatherings. A free band was provided three times a week for dancing or for listening pleasure.

Mr. Page continued to dream up innovative ideas to build the excitement of the park each year. All summer long the mystic and lilting strains of Hawaiian music floated throughout the park to sooth the tired parents and children who rested on benches in the shade of the spreading oaks between the lake and the main part of the park. The grounds of the park were well kept, and long flower beds lined the walks.

Indian pow wows were welcome in the playground area. These pow wows lasted for days. The last one held began on Mr. Page's 59th birthday, June 2, 1919, when a tribe of Lightfoot Indians from the north pitched their tents and tepees, cooked on open fires, and hung strips of beef across poles to dry. This was educational to the Home children, as they observed and enjoyed their visit with these Indians.

Mr. Page loved his park. He loved people and liked to see them enjoying themselves. He often went out in the evenings just to sit on a bench and watch the people with their children, having a good time. One day Mr. Breeding asked if he wasn't afraid to mix with the people, being such a prominent figure.

"I can take care of myself," said Mr. Page. "I like to be in the center of things. I like to have people come over to the bench and talk to me."

But sometimes people said things they shouldn't to him. If they were sincere they were met with sincerity. If not, he had no qualms about telling them what he thought. People also said things about him to Mr. Breeding.

Sometimes they asked Mr. Breeding if Mr. Page had dealt unfairly with the Indians when he bought their land. Mr. Breeding answered more than once that people always assume such things when they see someone buy something and make something of it that raises its value. Mr. Breeding knew, and the Indians knew, that Mr. Page gave the Indians a good price for their lands. They had laughed when he bought what they called dead worthless land. Most of the land he had purchased was a mass of tangled briars or swampy low land. It had cost him years of labor and thousands of dollars to get it in shape. Then people seeing it, without knowing what he paid for it, assumed that he got it at a rare bargain. But he often paid very high prices for land.

The number of children in the home was now 110. Mr. Page saw to it that they got to go to everything that came to town: the movies, the circus, the opera and whatever. Mr. Page's greatest concern was to be able to provide enough jobs when these children were ready to begin to work. He continued to launch industries and lease sites and buildings to create jobs and make traffic for the railroad, which was their main support.

Mr. Page used everything nature provided to create new industry. His chemical company even extracted salt from oil well water, making large salt blocks for animal licks. He had an eye to using products of Oklahoma fields and mines, or making something for which the region had a market.

The smelter and refining company's product was zinc dust and slab zinc. Zinc dust has a multitude of uses such as in paints, dyes, metalizing, and galvanizing.

His brick plant, about a quarter of a mile north of the lake, was doing a good business under the direction of Clarence Greer. Greer's son, Curtis Greer, had an automobile company on the corner of Lincoln and Broadway, and his building was built with bricks from the brick plant. This building would later be used as the Masonic Hall.

Many homes in Sand Springs were built of bricks from Page's brick plant, as was the *Tulsa Tribune* building, the K.P. building that housed Haliburton Abbot, and ten other buildings which Mr. Page owned in Tulsa.

Page no longer owned the *Tulsa Tribune* newspaper, once called *The Daily Democrat*. He sold the paper and the afternoon Associated Press franchise to Richard Lloyd Jones of Wisconsin in the year of 1919, carrying the mortgage himself.

Mr. Page owned property in Wisconsin and Wyoming, as well as at least fifty-nine different parcels of real estate in Tulsa and various parts of Creek County and throughout Oklahoma. He owned at one time 22,000 acres of land. Mortgages still unpaid on properties he had sold figured approximately half a million dollars. He still owned 1,245 lots in Sand Springs, many farms, oil and gas leases in Tulsa, Osage and Creek counties and in Texas.

Mr. Page had selected five men from the heads of departments of the Home's interests as trustees. The board of trustees met each Monday morning to discuss business. Mr. Page had things set up so that each transaction of importance must be signed and approved by every trustee. This kept each branch of business knowing what the other was doing, also giving the benefit of six men's expertise including his own. Mr. Breeding, who was also one of the trustees, said the prayer at the beginning of each meeting.

But Mr. Page sometimes found it difficult to get Mr. Breeding's signature. He was always sending Cap on one mission or another. Once Mr. Breeding and a carload of boys were on their way to a camp in the Ozarks when the car brakes burned out going down the steep Ozark hills. They stopped at a garage to have the brakes fixed and Mr. Breeding called Mr. Page to let him know what had happened.

"Well, when you get the brakes fixed, come home," said Mr. Page. "I'm finalizing an important deal and I need the signatures of all the trustees." Mr. Breeding had to return to Sand Springs, just to sign his name.

Later, Mr. Breeding and Galloway were taking some of the boys to Eureka Springs when Mr. Page had the police of Siloam Springs to stop them as they passed through the town.

"Cap," said Mr. Page, when Mr. Breeding called to see what he wanted, "I need your signature but I won't ask you to come home. When you get to Eureka Springs send a wire saying that you approve the business transaction I'm finalizing, and that will be sufficient this time."

A short time later Mr. Breeding received a letter from Mr. Page stating that due to the difficulty of getting Mr. Breeding's signature, that he would get somebody else to take his place on the Board of Trustees. Mr. Paul Estill was chosen to take his place. Mr. Page informed Mr. Breeding that he could attend the meetings when he desired, and that he would remain as chaplain to say the prayer at the meetings. The letter also stated, for the records, that Mr. Breeding would remain Superintendent of the Home and Colony for as long as he lived. A copy of the letter was filed with the business records of the Home Interests.

Breeding, Galloway and a group of Home boys getting ready to go fishing.

40

Disasters

THE POPULATION OF THE TOWN HAD GROWN SO MUCH MR. PAGE KNEW HE had to find another source of water supply. He purchased one hundred and twenty acres of land from Roy Simms, and as much from Lottie's husband, Skinner Anderson, also an Osage Indian. When the transaction was completed, Mr. Page handed Roy a hundred dollars extra because he had had the street car accident. Roy told folks what a fair man Uncle Charley Page was.

The land that Mr. Page had purchased from Roy and Skinner had a large creek on it. Mr. Page's plans were to enlarge the creek and build a dam. He ran a spur from the Katy railroad to Shell Creek to carry supplies, and with slips and mules, they excavated the creek and constructed a reservoir large enough to hold two billion gallons of water even in the driest year. He piped water clear to West Tulsa to Joshua Cosdin's oil refinery. He had hoped to furnish water for Tulsa as well, but when Tulsa's city fathers saw what Page had done for Sand Springs, they decided to have their own reservoir. They built the Spavinaw Dam, and that ended the sale of spring water to Tulsa.

The Sand Springs Water Utility Company was finished in 1921, and cost Mr. Page over a million dollars. Mr. Page stocked the Shell Creek dam with fish, and it became a favorite fishing spot for all. Cabins were built near the dam for a permanent vacation retreat for the children.

Mr. Page was constantly branching out in new projects that seemed to grow out of others. His business interests and philanthropical interests kept him busy providing for them all. He also sent checks all over the world to needy people he heard about.

He was interested in charities other than those he fostered. He contributed regularly to independent charities such as the Salvation Army, the YMCA and the YWCA of Tulsa, the Tulsa County Humane Society, Tulsa County Public Health Association, Family Welfare Association of Tulsa as well as for Sand Springs, the National Jewish Relief Association, St. John's Cathedral Girls' Home of Colorado, the American Red Cross Association and The Crippled Children's Hospital. He also gave building sites for such organizations as the Tulsa Boys' Home, furnishing temporary quarters until their building was completed and gave free lots to anyone wishing to build a church in Sand Springs. He gave a donation to anyone who asked, if he deemed it a worthy cause.

In the early days, Mr. Breeding tried to talk Mr. Page out of paying workers every night because it was so time consuming.

But when Mr. Page hired Mr. Gene Dickenson as his bookkeeper, Gene taught him a lot about letting his money work for him. Gene explained that as long as money remained in the bank, it was drawing interest. Where large amounts of money were concerned, one day's interest could amount to hundreds of dollars. Mr. Page let Gene take care of finances his own way after that.

The bills to run the Home were staggering, and Gene paid them on the last due date rather than at the first of the month. The employees started receiving their checks once a month, and came in person to get them. Those who delayed coming after their checks for a few days were just piling up interest for the company.

There were still some people who kept their money hidden away rather than trust it in a bank. If Mr. Page suspected that of somebody, he won them over by borrowing money from them with an offer of interest for the loan. He invested the money, making interest for both himself and the one to whom the money belonged. He paid the money back through a savings account in the person's name and explained to them that it would draw interest until it was drawn out. He gained a lot of new patrons by showing them how it worked.

Mr. Page always kept a silver dollar in his pocket for "good luck." He had been the only person attending a sale in Denver, Colorado, in which a hotel was to be auctioned off. The auction went on as scheduled, and since he was the only bidder and had only one silver dollar, he bid one dollar and got the hotel. He carried a silver dollar in his pocket from then on, calling it his good luck piece. But with someone always asking for money, he couldn't keep pocket change. He often borrowed from his friends, especially his closest friend, Mr. Breeding.

One evening Mr. Page drove up to the Home station just as Mr. Breeding got on the street car. He drove along the line out-distancing the street car, and when it stopped at Bruner Station he got on. He told the conductor to wait, and went to where Mr. Breeding was seated.

"Cap, lend me three dollars," he said. "My wife wants me to take her out to dinner this evening and the bank is closed."

The Clutes Drug Store now belonged to George Harrison and was called Rexall Drug Store. In the building in back of the Rexall was a three-chair barber shop with a Second Street entrance. D. O. Clark, who had worked in a high class barber shop in Tulsa's Mayo Hotel building, had been required to wear white shirts and white washable pants in the shop because they were more sanitary. When he put in his own shop at Sand Springs, he required his barbers to wear white also. No other barbers in town did so. Mr. Clark named his shop The White House Barber Shop.

Mr. Page was one of Mr. Clark's customers. His shaving mug sat on the shelf along with those of other customers, and each morning he came in for a shave. Once a week, or when the notion struck him, Mr. Page came for a haircut.

Mr. Clark was a good barber but he had a habit of leaving the shop to the other barbers when business was slow. Mr. Page didn't say anything, but he didn't like it when he had to let another barber cut his hair. They weren't "first chair" barbers. One day he came in for a haircut and Mr. Clark was gone.

"Where's Clark?" he asked, rather sharply.

"He just stepped out," said one of the other barbers.

"Seems to me he steps out too often," said Mr. Page. "A man with four children to support ought to pay more attention to his business. He got his shaving mug and took it to Harvey's Barber Shop. Mr. Harvey became his barber.

In 1921 there was a terrible race riot in Tulsa. The Jim Crow law forbade white and black persons from associating too closely with each other. This caused a lot of tension. On May 30, 1921, a white woman who operated an elevator in a building in the 300 block on South Main, reported that Dick Walden, a nineteen-year-old Negro youth had assaulted her in the elevator. She didn't know, nor did the town's people know, that many city officials were members of the Ku Klux Klan, and just itching for action. When the lady reported the incident it ignited the flames of hatred of the klan and Dick Walden was arrested.

Dick claimed that he had stumbled after accidently stepping on the woman's foot, and that he had bumped against her as he tried to balance himself. That it was all an accident. However, it was reported that he was lying to save his hide. A meeting was called at the klan's headquarters at Main and Easton streets. The name of their club was BENO HALL. None but the klan knew that beno meant "be no Negro, be no Catholic, be no Jew."

The news of the boy's arrest was in the paper that afternoon and mention was made that there was going to be a lynching. There had been a lynching of a Negro man for killing a white man in 1910. Everyone had been shocked that the police had done such a thing. But they watched it happen.

The jail was on the second floor of the courthouse. Between 9:00 and 9:30 p.m. on May 31, an angry group of klan members met at Sixth and Boulder on the courthouse steps. As they waited for other klan members, several car loads of Negro men arrived. Both sides were armed, and the fight began on the courthouse steps. Shots were fired, then all hell broke loose. By 11:00 things had gotten out of control. Rioters were running amuck down Main Street, shooting out the lights, breaking into stores and looting. As people tried to hide they were shot at. Bullets were whizzing, people were screaming, and men were cursing.

By 11:00 the chief of police realized that the Klan had more than they had bargained for. The rioters were running amuck. The dead and wounded of both Negroes and whites were strewn about. Buildings were burning, and the clanging of the fire truck bells that rang in the night could scarcely be heard above the screams and the crackle and roar of the burning buildings.

Shortly after midnight the sheriff and the chief of police sent a telegram to the governor, requesting help from the national guard.

At 1:00 a.m. Governor James Robinson ordered the national guard to the scene. But by this time the anger was at such a fevered pitch that they couldn't control the mob headed for the Black section of town, torching everything as they passed. The new Mount Zion Baptist church was not passed over. It was burned with the assumption that the blacks had an arsenal of weapons hidden in it.

"Burn little Africa, wipe them out," they cried as escaping Negroes hurried from house to house yelling for everybody to get their guns, that they were going to be raided.

Stunned by the gun fire, Blacks fled with nothing but what they had on their backs. Some were in their gowns and barefoot. Families were separated from each other as they headed for the woods of the Mohawk Park area. All roads were jammed with Negro people going in all directions. Some went to Sapulpa, some to Sand Springs, some crawled through sewers trying to get away. Hundreds of them remained in the woods, trying to find family members. Their homes were burned and they didn't know where to go, or what to do.

The national guard finally quieted things down on June 2.

As street car conductor Edgar Stevens drove the street car along Archer Street that morning, he took his camera. He showed the pictures to Mr. Page. Archer Street and much of the north side of Tulsa was in shambles.

Mr. Page was appalled when he heard what had happened. "Cap, we've got to help those poor homeless people," he said.

Mr. Page often said "we," when he meant I, but Mr. Breeding asked what he wanted him to do.

"I'd like to use you as a go-between," said Mr. Page. "I've got my kid's safety to think of. I don't want anyone retaliating. My kids could be caught in the middle if I took sides, but those poor desperate people have no one to help them. What we do must be done in secret. I can get help to them through a trusted Negro who use to work for me, but I need someone whom I can trust to get in touch with him. Everyone knows and respects you. I don't want anyone to know you helped, although no one would hurt you if they found out. They would go after me, because you'd just be doing what your boss told you to do. The Kids are mine, you see, and they could be caught in the middle if I went to find this man.

So Mr. Breeding acted as a go-between to get help to the victims of the grizzly battle.

Three hundred people on both sides had lost their lives, and there were countless injuries to both men and women.

On June 9th the grand jury was called. They ruled that the riot was caused by a certain group of Negro agitators, but indictments were handed down to 87 people, one of which was John Akerson, chief of police. Only one black man went to jail.

The woman who had claimed Dick Walden had assaulted her dropped the case against him, and he was let out of jail.

The records of this shameful incident were either misfiled or destroyed, including the military records.

Later a tragic mine disaster occurred in Henryetta, Oklahoma. Mr. Page gave aid to the families of those injured or trapped in the mine. He gave aid to all organizations who asked, but the most marvelous of all his charities was that which he dispensed personally as he listened to those who came to his office in a seldom-ending procession. There were sad and pitiful tales of suffering; victims of tuberculosis, who were given a chance to get well; wives and mothers whose husbands and sons were in trouble; destitute families. He built a hospital for unwed mothers, who even came from other states, where they could have a place of concealment during their travail. Those who were sick and those who were merely hungry came to him, and to each he gave aid.

As George Campbell grew Mr. Page continued to urge his great-nephew to get a good education. George took his advice. He studied hard and made good grades. Graduating from high school in Sand Springs, he went on to Oklahoma A & M college where he received a BA degree. But Mr. Page was partial to Wisconsin, his home state, and sent George to the University of Wisconsin.

"You become a teacher and I'll build a school for you," said Mr. Page. George studied hard but he also became very interested in sports. He became a wrestler with two years of national collegian honors. He was National Champion, winning honors in the New York NCAA Tournament.

In 1923, with the thought of providing more jobs for women such as the widows of the Colony, Mr. Page built the largest cotton mill west of the Mississippi and the only one in Oklahoma. It had 23,000 spindles and cost him $1,600,000

Commander Mills, as it was called, was built in the place where Sam Adams had lived, along Adams Road. Sam's old log cabin was moved to the little Indian cemetery.

The first person to work at Commander Mills was a widow, Mrs. May Lane. She came to Mr. Page's office seeking employment just as the big machinery arrived. The machinery was dusty, and dirty. It needed to be cleaned before it was installed. Mr. Page mentioned this when Mrs. Lane asked him for a job.

"I can do that," said Mrs. Lane. With a soft cloth and a bucket of water she began. She cleaned every machine in the huge plant. May Lane later became a matron at the Home.

When the mill was ready for service Mr. Page held a grand opening. He gave the first piece of cloth from the cotton mill to the girls' matron. "Here, Dobozy," he said, as he handed the large piece of unbleached muslin to her. "You and the girls make something pretty out of this."

Miss Dobozy tore the unbleached muslin into squares for a quilt. Circles of morning glories were appliqued on each block by any girl who wanted to earn a nickel for doing so. It made a beautiful quilt.

Mrs. Cheatham received bolts of the unbleached muslin and made new pajamas and underwear for the children. Sheets and pillow cases were also made. Later when a bleachery was added, things were made of the bleached muslin.

In 1923 a flood disaster drove people from their homes all along the seven miles between Sand Springs and Tulsa. Although builders knew that the river sometimes went out of its banks, they ignored the danger and built too close to it. That spring it seemed the rains would never cease. The river, as well as every creek, overflowed more than it ever had before. Flash floods swept homes down the river. Furniture floated in the raging waters where houses had been swept from their foundations. The highway and the railroad tracks washed out. Some people were trapped, surrounded by water.

Although the people from 65th Street to Tulsa were citizens of Tulsa, Mr. Page sent rescue boats out to gather in all the people along the seven-mile-line between Sand Springs and Tulsa. They were taken to the park where he fed and sheltered them.

The street cars went as far as they dared on the unstable tracks to take the people from boats to the park. Each day more tracks washed out as the flood waters rose higher, making rescue operations more dangerous.

One family who refused to leave for fear their belongings would be stolen, were later found clinging to the roof of their floating home, where they were rescued. Lives were lost of both people and animals during that flood.

Every building in the park was full of cots, and tents covered the grounds. For days Mr. Page fed and cared for hundreds of families while they waited for the waters to subside and their houses to dry out sufficiently for their return.

The family of D.O. Clark, who had been Mr. Page's barber, was among those victims. With an over zealous pride against accepting charity, Mrs.

Clark took her small brood back into the house while the thick mud that covered everything, was still wet. Mr. Clark stayed in town to work at his job during the time, but his family had to rely on the help of others. He didn't know that his family had gone back into the house while it was still wet and were scooping mud and water from the floor and furniture. The family's clothing and everything of value had been stolen, and the dresser drawers were turned upside down in the mud. The whole family got sick. Thirteen-year-old Jimmy, eldest of the children, who was also sick, got out of bed to go to relatives for help. The baby girl was very ill, and so was Mrs. Clark. She couldn't raise her head from the pillow to take care of the rest of the family. The baby died within a few days.

Discouraged, the Clarks moved out of their home, losing what they had paid into it. Many others suffered about the same fate during that flood, and Mr. Page helped all who came to him.

The cafe at the park where many Tulsa and Sand Springs companies served annual picnic lunches. Also where the flood victims were fed.

41

Almost Submerged

ALTHOUGH MR. PAGE DIDN'T BELONG TO ANY PARTICULAR CHURCH, HE believed that every family should take their children to church. They should teach their children that God was a friend in times of joy or sorrow; a friend whom they could talk to when things went wrong and they needed someone to know they were hurting. He believed firmly in God, the great creator, the emancipator, the lover of mankind, and he encouraged any minister who wished to proclaim the greatness of God.

When the famous evangelist Raymond Ritchey came to Tulsa and there was no building big enough to hold the crowds, Mr. Page had a large tabernacle built on Detroit Street. All the Home children attended the revival and enjoyed it very much. When the revival was over, Mr. Page let the building stay where it was for other preachers to use. The building was called Faith Tabernacle.

Uldine Utley, a twelve-year-old evangelist used the tabernacle next. It was under Uldine's preaching that Rev. Garvin, pastor of a Presbyterian church got the "spirit of the Holy Ghost," and started speaking in tongues. He was ousted from the church for making a spectacle of himself. This caused a split in the congregation. He and his followers went to the Faith Tabernacle to hold services.

Charles Page admired a man who let the Spirit lead him, whether it was a popular thing to do or not. In August of 1924 Mr. Page started building a permanent Faith Tabernacle at 1245 South Trenton Avenue in Tulsa, at a cost of $50,000, a lot of money for the time. The church was to be nondenominational where anyone, regardless of faith, could worship. When the church was finished and furnished, Mr. Page handed the keys to Reverend Garvin, at no cost either to him or to his members. It was Reverend Garvin's church for as long as he lived.

Mr. Page helped any church that needed assistance. In 1925, when he moved the railway offices to Sand Springs, the rooms above the Sand Springs railway station on Main and Archer streets were donated to the Lighthouse Mission. The place wasn't large enough to accommodate the many who came for help, so he rented an entire building at 116-118 Archer Street and let them use the second floor. It was a rooming house, and the rents collected from the rest of the building were donated to the mission.

Mr. Page had a doctor friend in Tulsa who had adopted a pretty little girl named Thelma Heartly. Thelma couldn't hear. There were no schools for the deaf anywhere near, so Mr. Page converted the old home his kids had lived in to be used as a school for the hearing impaired.

Always concerned for people, Mr. Page tried to help any way he could; sometimes in ways least expected. John Henry Black, a man from Bartlesville had three small children under six years of age. He came to Mr. Page asking for help. Mr. Page couldn't put him in the Colony, but he felt he should do something for the man. He gave him a temporary job taking care of his lawn, and feeding and grooming Jim. He let Mr. Black live in the servants' quarters over the garage. The children were afraid of Jim because he was bigger than they were. Mr. Page hired a woman who helped in the kitchen at the home to care for Mr. Black's children during the day. But this wasn't too satisfactory. The woman came after them each morning and took them to work with her at the Home. In the evening she brought them to the father. Mr. Page saw how frightened the little children were of Jim. They hid in the summer house while their dad fed Jim. He felt sorry for the poor little children being dragged around from place to place. He adored his daughter Mary, and knew he wouldn't like for her to be treated this way. He began to try to come up with something better for them.

A solution to his problem came one day when least expected. A young mother with two little girls came asking for a job and a place in the Colony.

"Cap tells me there are no more vacancies in the Colony," said Mr. Page. "But I know a man who needs a housekeeper and someone to watch after his three little children. Would you consider a job like that? It wouldn't pay much but it would be food and a roof over your heads."

"I would be glad to have the job." said the woman.

That evening Mr. Page talked to Mr. Black. He told him of the woman with two children to support and asked him if he would be interested in hiring a housekeeper if Mr. Page found him a job that paid enough to support both families. Mr. Black said he would appreciate it very much.

Mr. Page gave Mr. Black a job as a night watchman at the Oil Well Improvements Company, and things worked out well for all.

Mr. Page worked night and day to keep his many interests and his huge philanthropies in operation. He kept in touch with his various superintendents by telephone at night, as well as by day. While the rest of the city slept, Charles Page was sitting at his desk at home until long after midnight. Superintendents who could not find time to talk to him during the day called at night.

He always had something going. No sooner was one project finished than another began. Each project was so big it taxed his mental and physical vitality almost to depletion before they were completed. Doctors kept warning him that he was working too hard, that with his diabetic condition, overwork could be fatal. Mr. Page didn't really understand about diabetes and thought the doctors were just fussing over him unnecessarily. Anyway, he had to get more industry into the town, to secure the future of his Kids. So he worked on.

One evening he was sitting on his front steps. Jim, who was now seventeen years old, lay with his head on Mr. Page's lap, looking up at his master. Mr. Page was talking to him and stroking his head. He didn't see his great niece, Amy Gottry, open the gate and come in, until Jim stirred.

"Hello, Uncle Charley," said Amy. Mr. Page raised his head. He looked very tired.

"What can I do for you, Amy?" he asked, holding his hand out to her.

"I don't want anything," said Amy, as she sat down beside him. "I just came to see you."

"I'm sorry," said Mr. Page wearily. "I guess I'm so used to saying that, that it has become a habit."

"Uncle Charley," said Amy, "don't you get tired of hearing people's troubles and having people ask you for money?"

Mr. Page sighed, and put his arm around Amy. "Amy," he said, "I love to help people who really need it. But sometimes I am almost submerged trying to solve people's problems."

Mr. Page belonged to the Tulsa Chamber of Commerce. On Saturday December 18, 1926, as he prepared to attend a Chamber of Commerce meeting, his wife cautioned him. The temperature was below freezing outside, and he had a bad cold.

"Charley, please stay home and take care of yourself," she pleaded. "Driving fourteen miles there and back in a cold car could give you flu or pneumonia."

"Aw, Lucy, you worry too much." He kissed her. "I haven't been bad sick a day in my life. I'll be all right. Besides, I've been trying to get a steel mill for Sand Springs. The Chamber of Commerce can be a big influence in helping me get it. That's what the meeting is about this evening. I can't miss it. Think of all the jobs a steel mill would make for my kids!"

When he came home from the meeting he was shivering and his teeth were chattering. Lucy didn't have to coax to get him into bed. She doctored him as best she could, and called the doctor in the morning. Charles Page had the dreaded flu.

Unable to go to work by Wednesday, he called a business meeting in his home.

The flu grew worse. His body was too exhausted to fight the disease and he went into a diabetic coma. He rallied on Sunday evening to see his wife and daughter hovering over him.

"What day is it?" he asked.

"It's Christmas, Charley," said his wife, feeling hopeful since he had come out of the coma.

"Did my kids have a good Christmas?" he asked.

His wife kissed him assuringly. "Charley, they had a fine Christmas," she said. He smiled.

That night he went to sleep and slipped back into the coma. It was Monday, December 26, at 3:30 o'clock in the afternoon when the nurse tried to wake him to give him to give him some nourishment. His heart had dilated. By 3:55 he was dead.

1972. A prayer of thankfulness and dedication.
An annual practice by the Trustees and present residents of the Home.

42

A Time to Mourn

CHARLES PAGE IS DEAD AND TWO CITIES MOURN

SO READ THE *TULSA TRIBUNE*, DECEMBER 28, 1926. ALL OKLAHOMA news media carried the story. The man who had once been called foolish was now described with words of praise. His death came as a surprise, and the people were in shock as they stood around discussing his demise.

The *Tulsa Tribune* devoted several pages of pictures and tributes from his friends. Their columns were bordered with black. There were ballads and poems written by sophisticated editors and just grateful folks.

Dr. Clinton lauded Mr. Page as a man who dreamed dreams and then had the courage to make them come true. He described him well when he said, "He was one of the most resourceful men I ever knew . . . Charles Page didn't wait to amass wealth before he began to do good deeds.

"The wide reach of his numerous interests made him the object of organized attacks, but his remarkable resources and distinguished ability eventually won and silenced the tongues of those who did not understand him.

"He had rare courage, remarkable persistence and distinguished discernability to properly evaluate men and measures. No man was too low in the scale of social or human existence for him to deny that person the opportunity to be reclaimed for some useful purpose in society. No man was ever too greatly entrenched in power to intimidate or swerve him from the conviction that given purpose or plan which he had settled upon after mature deliberation should be carried through . . . No individual single-handedly has developed a greater industrial district than has Charles Page.

"By friend and foe he was respected as a fighter worthy of the numerous laurels he won in many a skirmish on life's battleground."

"INASMUCH AS YE HAVE DONE IT UNTO THE LEAST OF THESE, MY BRETHREN, YE HAVE DONE IT UNTO ME." Richard Lloyd Jones quoted this passage from the Bible, and added, "Charles Page gave all that he had.

"To many he was known as a builder," said Mr. Jones. "To some he was known as a wealthy land owner, or a capitalist. He was known as a man of achievement, but it is not one of these titles by which he will be remembered longest in the heart of the people. Tulsans will remember Charles Page as "the giver." But to the hundreds of little children who have been shielded by his love and sympathy, he will always be remembered as DADDY PAGE.

In answer to the many inquiries as to what the future would hold for the Sand Springs Home and the charities created by Charles Page, Judge Stuart issued this statement.

"The prime purpose and chief thought of Charles Page during his lifetime was the establishment and maintenance of the Sand Springs Home. All of his energies were directed to that purpose. The Sand Springs Home is a corporation. Its articles of incorporation state the purpose for which it was created. It is provided in said articles of incorporation that upon the death of Charles Page the Sand Springs Home shall be managed, conducted and maintained by trustees appointed during his lifetime, and provision is made for the substitution of another trustee in case one dies or resigns. In other words, it was Mr. Page's purpose to keep intact the organization of the Sand Springs home and its auxiliary charities, and the trustees who now take up its work will carry out to the letter the purposes of Charles Page. There will be no change in policy or in the conduct of the management of the home.

"Mr. Page, twenty times a millionaire, left an individual estate in addition to the many interests which he controlled, but which are owned by the Home," said Judge Stuart. "He provided for a permanent endowment for the home, the colony and all the other charities, including his private "pay roll" for needy ones in all parts of the country which is understood to be $3,000 a month or more."

Judge Stuart went on to explain that trusted friends and relatives had all been remembered in Mr. Page's will which would be filed within a few days.

Page after page of testimonials bore such titles as:

"CHARLES PAGE, BUILDER OF CITIES, FRIEND TO ALL;"

"DEATH LAYS HEAVY HAND UPON TULSA;"

"PAGE, UNASSUMING RICH MAN, CLOTHES COVERED WITH ASHES, HAPPIEST WITH CHILDREN;"

"LIFE OF CHARLES PAGE READS LIKE WORK OF FICTION;"

"CALLED UNCLE CHARLEY BY MANY;"

"GRIEF-STRICKEN CITIES PREPARE TO HONOR PAGE."

Gloom also settled over his home town of Stevens Point, Wisconsin, and other towns where he had lived during his youth. *The Carlton Minnesota Vidette* carried this article:

"Charles Page, a pioneer of Northern Minnesota, was one time chief of Police at Tower, later to become associated with the

Pinkerton Detective Agency, still later was an agent for a railroad company . . ."

With pride they told of his later life and some of his accomplishments and philanthropies.

Newsmen came from the east to get his story. They wanted to know of his early years. Surely something in his childhood had played a part in making this most unique man the way he was.

For this, they went to his family and friends. For the latter part of his story they went to his friend and cohort, Mr. Brinton Flint Breeding.

Tulsa city officials passed a resolution of respect and condolence, rarely accorded to an individual, honoring the memory of Charles Page in recognition of his service to the city and state. The resolution, in part, follows:

"WHEREAS. Charles Page is universally recognized as one of the most valuable citizens, not only of his home city of Sand Springs, but of Tulsa and the state at large . . .

. . . and an expression of its appreciation of him and his activities for the good of Tulsa and Tulsa county."

They ordered copies of the resolution be placed on the records of the city and copies sent to his bereaved family and to the daily presses of Tulsa.

Stanley Funeral Home of Tulsa had charge of the funeral, and as plans for the funeral were set, the news headlines read:

Grief Stricken Cities Prepare to Honor Page

Thousands to Bow in Tribute at His Bier

Body to Lie in State at Children's Home

Thousands came from near and far to pay their last respects. Funeral services for Mr. Page were held at 2:30 p.m. in the living room of the Home. Boy Scouts took turns as guards of honor, standing at attention from 9:00 a.m. to 1:00 p.m. on Thursday, while thousands, black and white, rich and poor, passed the bier in a procession of sorrow at their loss.

More than two hundred former Home children were there to mingle their tears with the one hundred and ten sisters and brothers still living in the Home.

Both Sand Springs and Tulsa suspended all services and business activities to join the sorrowing funeral entourage. The traffic was so heavy from all around that police captain Roy Bolton and a crew of highway patrol officers had to direct traffic along the highways to and from the funeral.

By the time of the funeral, the press of the crowd was so great that many were unable to get close to the door. The throngs filled the wide driveway and were jammed together halfway down the spacious lawns around the Home. With bowed heads, and weeping, they listened to the service through loud speakers. Four hundred chairs had been placed in the large living room, and people filled the standing space.

Church bells rang and industrial sirens gave a mournful wail, as all the wheels of industry in both Sand Springs, Tulsa and surrounding cities came to a halt for ten minutes in respect to the man who had contributed so much to their cities.

Funeral services were conducted by three ministers: Dr. Seth R. Gordon, President Emeritus of the University of Tulsa and former minister of the community church at Sand Springs; Rev Garvin of the Faith Tabernacle which Mr. Page had built, and the Rev. J.C. Hollyman of the community church of Sand Springs.

Several spoke of the greatness of this most unassuming man. Humble George Nye was among them. He had remained faithful to Mr. Page, testifying at every opportunity offered him as to what Charles Page had done for him.

Dr. Kennedy told of his association with Mr. Page and of Mr. Page's dream to help those less fortunate than he, and how he had helped the needy of Tulsa through the Salvation Army.

Rev. Charles W. Kerr, called Mr. Page the poor man's friend.

"Among many philanthropies of Charles Page," he said, "I shall always remember what he did, through the Salvation Army, in the early days of Tulsa. He made possible the opening of charitable work in our city and for years was their chief backer. Many poor and unfortunate will greatly miss this great man."

Mr. Breeding was so overcome with grief he couldn't speak at the funeral of his friend.

After the funeral rites in the Home, the cortege moved along the highway, down Second Street to Cleveland Street and into the Woodland Cemetery.

Six older boys of the Home bore the casket of their beloved Daddy Page, while forty-three honorary pallbearers, members of the advisory board of the vast Page interests followed close behind.

Behind the pallbearers marched his sobbing "Kids," all wearing black arm bands. The girls were dressed in dark blue woolen middies and pleated skirts. Behind the children of the Home, walked sixty-eight widows and their children.

Charles Page was laid to rest beside his brother, James. It was after six o'clock when the funeral was over and people went sorrowfully on their way.

Mrs. Page, and Mary, now fourteen years of age, sobbed bitterly. They didn't understand about diabetes. "The doctors gave him too many of those old insulin shots," cried Lucile.

Jim, the magnificent wolf-like Lorraine shepherd dog, friend and constant companion to Mr. Page for seventeen years, was perhaps the saddest of all, because he didn't understand.

Jim lay beside his master's chair with his head on his forepaws. His master had gone without him, and he refused to eat. Every time the door opened Jim stood up and waited to see if it were his master returning. Then with a sigh and eyes filled with sadness he lay his head on his paws, keeping his eyes on the door as he waited. Without food, Jim grew weaker. Too weak to rise when someone opened the front door, he merely opened his eyes. Jim was found dead, as he lay beside his master's chair, awaiting his return.

Epilogue

In 1929 Mrs. Page donated a beautiful library of Art Deco architectural design, to the city of Sand Springs in honor of Charles Page. Her many charitable deeds were unknown to most who knew her. She was inducted into the Oklahoma Hall of fame in 1958 for the gift of an entire library from one person.

A bronze statue of Charles Page by Lorado Taft, a well known sculptor from Chicago, was placed at the center triangle in the town of his creation. It was financed by the Home Interest, Mrs. Page and friends. The statue, an exact likeness of Mr. Page, is flanked by a widow with a baby in her arms, and two orphaned children. The statue was unveiled by his daughter Mary, with a reverential ceremony at 2:00 p.m. on November 20, 1930. The inscription reads, "IN AS MUCH AS YE HAVE DONE IT UNTO ONE OF THE LEAST OF THESE MY BRETHREN, YE HAVE DONE IT UNTO ME.

Mary Page married Calder W. Seibels of Columbia, South Carolina, in 1942 and they made their home in South Carolina. When Mary's husband died, she and her young son, John, came to live with her mother in Sand Springs.

After many years of living in the three story mansion that Mr. Page had built for them, Mrs. Page decided that she and Mary needed a smaller home without stairs to climb. A new twelve room cottage was built to the north of the the mansion. The beautiful crystal light fixtures, the black marble fireplace, the marble entry and many parts of the old mansion were used in the lovely new dwelling. Mrs. Page and Mary had just moved into their new home when the beautiful old mansion caught fire and burned to the ground.

Nothing was ever the same after Mr. Page's death. Nor could it be. Times change and things change, but the Trustees have done their best to carry out Mr. Page's wishes. After twenty years of service, J. Blan Loflin retired due to bad health, but other than that there has never been a trustee to quit his job. As one Trustee dies another takes his place.

Trustees who have served since the original board included:

L.L. Wiles — October 22, 1930 to September 26, 1949.

J.S. Babbitt — March 23, 1940 to August 30, 1965.

E.J. Doerner — October 2, 1947 to December 31, 1980.

H.C. Jones — October 4, 1948, to March 18, 1966
S. Neal Johnson — December 26, 1956, to February 7, 1983
Joe A. Williams — September 14, 1965 — still serving.
J. Blan Loflin — May 2, 1966, to 1986 — only one to retire.
J.C. Warner — September 27, 1974, to March 12, 1991
Bill J. Brown — January 15, 1981 — still serving.
Joe R. Manning — April 30, 1991, to November 4, 1991
R.A. Weese — November 4, 1991 — still serving.

Mr. Breeding remained faithful through the years, always remembering Mr. Page's words: "Cap we've got to give them lots of love. They are all victims of some tragedy, and they have no one but us." Having lost his mother at age six, Mr. Breeding understood that although the children had just about everything, the thing they would miss most was the love of a mother and father. He tried to fill that void, becoming a father figure after Mr. Page died.

"I love you," he would always say, and the children knew him to be sincere. These words endeared Mr. Breeding to the children. He retired in 1948 at the age of 72, with forty years of service, having been the father figure to over 2,000 orphans. Loved by all, he was a legend to the town, as well.

He was in his late 90's when he retired as chaplain, to say a prayer for guidance as the Home Trustees met each Monday morning. Rev. Archie Kinion, also a legend to the town, became chaplain when Mr. Breeding decided to retire.

Mr. Page had sent George Campbell to the University of Wisconsin, where he was at the time of Mr. Page's death. After he received his degree, he taught school in Anadarko, where he met and married Garnett Dietrich. They had one son, George IV, deceased, a daughter Lotsee E.L. (Spradling), and three granddaughters, Arron, Stacy, and Michelle.

George returned to Sand Springs where he became supervisor of the older Home boys who were being housed in a stone two-story building east of the Home. One snowy winter night in 1929, the building burned to the ground, and the boys barely escaped with their lives. Luther Ramer awoke and immediately alerted the boys. The building was near collapsing when George rammed his fist through the window and pulled the telephone out the window. He called Mr. Monsell and asked him to come for the boys who were bare foot in the snow. Someone discovered that Edward Chambers was missing. George rushed back into the building and carried Ed out the door just as the walls caved in.

More than fifty boys from the Home and Colony were in the military service during World War II. George conceived the idea of sending a mimeographed letter every month, signed "Love from home," to the boys stationed at different battle fronts. Copies were also mailed to the folks at home as an exchange from one to the other.

George attended the University of Tulsa law school and became a member of the Oklahoma Bar Association. He became a well-known trial lawyer, winning fame throughout the State of Oklahoma.

George's accomplishments as well as his charities are too numerous to mention. He helped many Tulsa County young attorneys get started. When he needed a secretary he hired one of the Home boys. It was 1947, and Lawrence Hinson had just returned from serving in the armed services of World War II when George asked him to 'help him out' until he could get himself a secretary. In 1988 Lawrence was still in George's office 'helping him out.'

George always took time to help where ever needed. He served on the Boy Scout Board and performed many other community services.

George owns a ranch of approximately 900 acres, known as the "Flying G. Ranch." He and his wife, Garnett, raise registered Polled Hereford Cattle for which they are known throughout the southern states.

For twenty years, the annual Fourth of July Fishing Derby for under privileged children was held at Campbell's ranch. The Tulsa District Judges judged the contest. All prizes for the one who caught the smallest fish were horses or registered Hereford cattle, donated by the Campbells. The children and their parents were given a weekend outing and refreshments donated by the Campbells. This continued for twenty years until it was discovered that parents were teaching children to cheat by tying minnows onto hooks with screen wire.

Mr. Breeding liked the "Letters from home" idea, and when the war was over, he continued the practice of writing a letter each month, to keep the Home folks and the former Home children in touch with each other. He received letters from former Home children all over the world. He continued this mail exchange until at age 91 it became too burdensome to write. Opal Bennefield Clark typed the last Home Letter from his original, on August 12, 1966.

The Breedings lived ten years in the little house he had built in 1909, adding rooms as needed. In 1920 they built a large two story bungalow, where they lived until 1961.

Mr. Breeding was 86 years of age, and his wife was 78 with failing eye sight when they decided that the upkeep of the large home was too much for them. They sold it and bought a place in Sand Springs, on the southeast corner of Tenth and Garfield.

The Breedings were happy living in Sand Springs among so many friends. However, having been served by the street car to go wherever he needed to go, Mr. Breeding had never learned to drive. But that didn't stop him from visiting friends. He was quite a walker, and the first walk he took was to visit former Home children. After his visit with Opal Bennefield Clark, she drove him home. After that, he called her almost every week, inviting her to go with him to visit shut-ins, former children of the Home, the Colony, and friends. Opal enjoyed the visits and the talk of old times, and began taking notes and recordings.

Mr. Breeding loved poetry and, having encouraged the children to memorize poems, had himself committed to memory over fifty long meaningful poems. Everywhere he went, he was asked to quote one of his poems, and he did. He only stayed thirty minutes at each visit and as he rose to go he would have everyone hold hands while he said a prayer. Then he would go on to visit the next person on his list for the day. One day after talking about old times, Opal asked if she could write a book about Daddy Page, Mr. Breeding and the Home.

"Don't write a book about me, Opal," he said, "Write it about Mr. Page. I only worked for him. He did it all. He was a very kind and sincere man. He liked people and wanted to help them. Everything that was done was his doing. I just did what he told me to do."

"You were more than just an employee," Opal insisted. "You loved us too, and we knew it."

"Well, that's true, but love was all I had to give." Then he quoted one of his favorite poems.

WHY WE LIVE

Our only purpose as we live
Is something of ourselves to give
To others as they pass near by,
But what give I?

The artist paints for all to see,
The singer makes a melody,
The rich upon cash gifts rely,
But what give I?

The picture's cold when paint is dry,
Songs and poems are heard then die.
There is no peace that wealth can buy,
But what give I?

I have no talent large or small.
I have no wealth; it seems that all
I have is love that will not die,
And this give I.

The art and riches fade away.
All tangible belongings stray,
I find that but this gift will live,
The love I give.   *Author Unknown.*

Later Mr. Breeding asked Opal how she was doing on her book. "I was afraid someone would laugh at my writing, and I decided I'd better let someone else do it," said Opal.

Mr. Breeding took her hand in his. "Opal," he said, "there are no doubt many people who could do a better job than you can, but they haven't. Many years have passed and very little has been written about Mr. Page. Don't worry about your inadequacies. A stream can only go as deep as its source. No one can expect more. When you do your best, you have nothing to be ashamed of. I'll help you all I can. So go ahead. Do it for him. But first ask Mrs. Page's permission. She will be glad for you to do it I'm sure. Just do the best you can and it will be appreciated."

"I think that would be wonderful," said Mrs. Page when Opal told her of her desires. "The people of Sand Springs are forgetting Charley and all he did for them," she said. "I'll be glad to help you any way I can."

Many people gave assistance, but they will be mentioned later.

Mrs. Lucile Ann Page died September 6, 1973, after a stroke and a long illness. She was 91. She had told her daughter, Mary, that she didn't deserve, or choose to be buried in her husband's mausoleum. She loved flowers and the out of doors. She asked to be buried just outside the door of Charles Page's tomb. Mary granted her wish.

After Mrs. Page died, Mary felt that the beautiful twelve-room home was too large for her. She sold it to Hurley Lane, a former Home boy, and his wife Jean. Hurley's mother had been one of the matrons of the Home.

Mary moved to Tulsa, sharing an apartment with Mable Ellis, with whom she lived for about ten years. She now resides in South Carolina, near her son John and his family.

Mr. Breeding died March 31, 1974, at the age of 98.

Mrs. Breeding died October 31, 1977. She was 94.

The Trustees still do their best to carry out Mr. Page's wishes, and there is a lot of good going on in Sand Springs. They have memorial services at Mr. Page's mausoleum on each Memorial Day, and on June 2nd, Mr. Page's birthday, they rededicate themselves to their task.

Nor have they forgotten that the Sand Springs Home is the only home the former Home children can remember. Every other year, the Trustees graciously gather the children together again with a homecoming dinner, on the Sunday nearest Charles Page's birthday. The hundreds who attend, come from near and distant places.

There are many success stories among Mr. Page's kids that would make him proud. His motto THINK RIGHT is still a guide by which they try to live.

Since Social Security, there are not as many children dependent upon the help of others, but there are always children who need the love and kindness of a good home. Children are still being loved and cared for in the Sand Springs Home.

Mr. Page got his steel mill. As of 1978 Sheffield Steel produced 423,930 tons of steel, and provided jobs for 478 people. Being the only steel producer in Oklahoma, Sheffield serves an area within the radius of 250 miles of Sand Springs.

The Kerr Glass company is still doing well. It produces an estimated 750,000 glass containers a day, and is presently employing 335 workers.

At present, according to Cherry Knowles, Cathy Mashburn and Allene Becou, of the Sand Springs city administrative offices, Sand Springs has 36 industries, 670 varied commercial enterprises, 13 schools, numerous pre-schools, 58 churches. The city of Sand Springs covers a distance of 18.937 square miles, and has a population of over 24,000 and keeps growing on both sides of the river.

There are a few sad notes too. It's always sad to see landmarks removed. But this happens with progress. The beautiful little hospital is gone. It couldn't meet the competition when so many larger hospitals were built in Tulsa. But there are several small medical clinics scattered throughout Sand Springs.

The old Widow's Colony outlived its usefulness, and a new Colony was built where the hospital once stood. Within the 95-acre Home grounds, 136 attractive two-bedroom brick cottages are clustered. Here, mothers with two or more children live rent free, with utilities provided, a quart of milk a day for each child, and a day nursery within the colony grounds where working mothers may leave their small children.

Yet these charities are not handouts. They are opportunities. A widow in the Colony is still expected to provide for her family and to keep the rules. The children are expected to attend school and maintain at least a "C" average so that they will be able to learn skills which will enable them to stand on their own two feet . . . without becoming dependent on welfare. Mr. Page's wishes were that children grow up with pride in self reliance . . . to become useful members of society.

A large, low-rent senior citizens' complex of apartments now occupies the spot in Squirrel Hollow where the original colony used to be. The creek, once so large a trestle had to be built over it to allow the street car to pass, has diminished considerably. But it still flows along, reminding this former Home girl of such times as when the boys found an abandoned buggy beside the stream and waded the water, pulling the buggy to give the girls a ride across "the raging waters" of Squirrel Creek.

During the depression in the thirties the park fell into disrepair and was torn down for insurance reasons. Instead of one large park, there are now twenty small parks scattered throughout the city. The park at what's left of Squirrel Creek, is called Brown's Park.

In the forties, homes were built on the old park grounds. As many of the centuries old oaks that could be spared, were left, and the area given the name "Oak Park." Ten or so years later "Oak Park Addition" was added north of Oak Park, and the town's boundaries keep stretching outward.

A few years ago, the Keystone freeway was built over the big spring which was presumed too weak to cause any damage. However, the legendary spring refused to die. It worked its way from under the tons of dirt and cement, threatening the highway. Pipes had to be inserted to set the spring free. The water was run off to the south side of the freeway to form a small stream.

The park lake is not as large as it was, due to progress and the building of a large golf club for the activity center. The sands washed into the upper springs that fed the lake, shortening its length to about half its size. But for every loss there are gains. The city now owns a recreation facility and a pool.

The people of Sand Springs are proud of their thriving city. Not many towns can boast of such a rich and unique history. They know full well that Sand Springs is a city built for the love of humanity, and they'd like to keep it that way.

Throughout the ages there have been men who felt some inner compulsion to give more than others in return for the privilege of being born into this world. They are called philanthropists, meaning literally, lovers of mankind. Charles Page was one of these. He had no bitterness because of his own deprived childhood. Instead, he tried to create a better world for others. He wanted for others what he couldn't have for himself.

He worked hard for what he got, but still contended, "it all belongs to God," and humbly refused to put his name on his many enterprises. His town has honored him however. There is now the statue, the library, a Charles Page High School, and the highway he built between Sand Springs and Tulsa that bears his name.

Charles Page received recognition in *Ripleys Believe It Or Not* as having the only known Widow's Colony, and for being at least fifteen years ahead of any other man known to take on the entire responsibility of an orphanage with no outside help. Even more unique, he built a town around his "kids," to maintain their support.

Charles Page proved that he kept his THINKING RIGHT, and that his dream was not the dream of a fool. He kept his vows to his mother, and to God, and saw his dream come true. He earned for himself a place in the pages of "WHO'S WHO", "WHO WAS WHO IN AMERICA," "THE AMERICANA," "THE TULSA HALL OF FAME," and publications too numerous to mention. But more than these he left a monument to all mankind.

The Tulsa waiting-station of the Sand Springs Railway Co.

The library and study hall of the Sand Springs Home.

Above: *Sarah Davis (now Barber). One of the original orphans brought from Cross & Anchor Home 1909.*

Below: *The new director Mike Nomura and Opal Clark with some of the children and directors. Photo taken by Bill Brown, S. S. trustee, May 1989.*

Last Street Car Run, Sand Springs Railway.

*Front addition to the Sand Springs Green House
made with varied colors of brick from Mr. Page's brick plant north of the lake.*

1962. *Semi Centennial celebration.* **L-R. Back Row:** *Blanch McCaskey; Josephine
Hughes; A. Neal Johnson; Mrs. Grant Picket;
Mr. and Mrs Jack Babbit; Cyril H. Jones and Dorothy Randal.
Seated in front: Mr. and Mrs. B. F. Breeding.*

George Nye, whom Mr. Page found sleeping in a piano box behind the stores, remained faithful to Mr. Page, and to God. He is shown next to the flag. Note the crate of live hens beside the baskets of food for the poor.

School superintendent C. C. Jelks and a group of children of Garfield School.

February 1912.
Mr. Page's oil well,
Elan Orcutt No. 1.

Below: *Aunt Fanny*
Brown, sister to Charles
Page's mother, was a
nurse. She took care of
Charles' invalid wife,
Lucy. Charles did much of
the cooking.

Charles Page's mother

Governor Trapp,
Charles Page,
and his dog Jim.

Charles Page, 1926.

*Mrs. Lillian Rawson, Governor Johnston Murray
and Mrs. Charles Page at the celebration of the widening of
Charles Page Highway, then called Sand Springs Road.
October 27, 1951*

Christmas 1922. *One of the truck loads of supplies from
Sand Springs Home, for the poor. This load goes to Drumright, Oklahoma.*

September 1942. *A group of the Home children around the Howitzer canon located on the front lawn of the Children's Home. The canon weighed 6,000 pounds.*

Home's graduating class 1952. **Front row L-R:** *Jo Ann Turner, Earline Thomas, Sam Miller, Deloris Coley, Irene Wright* **Back Row:** *Jess Phillips, Bob Barger, Jack Hughes, Joe Miles, Jerry Childs and Frank Knight.*

Marcus Haimes, of Sand Springs, formerly one of the Globe Trotters, had his own team of local boys called the Marcus Haimes players. Fred Westphall, Superintendent of Armco Steel, presents an award, while Ed. Dubie, high school athletic director, looks on.

One of the classes of children of the Garfield School. Mrs. Daughority, teacher.

Above: *1942 Home children's annual Halloween Weiner Roast.*

Below: *Followed by a party later in the evening.*

Section of Cold Storage of S. S. Home.
John Avery, butcher, showing meat and blocks of cheese.

George Campbell, "Cap" B. F. Breeding and T. H. Steffens hold
a plaque with names of World War II service men from Sand Springs.

1960. *A group of the Home Children and their attendants.*

Sand Springs Home Boys' Band 1928. Left to right, back row: *Earl Miller band instructor, Ray Ritchie, Homer McPeters, Edward Chambers, William McPeters, Morland Edger, Elsworth Page.* **Second row:** *Sam McGahey, Walter Chance, Oran Hoover, Additon O'Kelly, Raymond Stamps, John Kyler, Roy Hollis.* **Front row, L-R:** *Frank McPeters, Ted Nipps, Paul Dobbs, Tommy Logue, Billy Skinner, Harvey Logue, Kenneth Minson.*

1913. *Industry of Sand Springs. They made corn flakes cereal and got into trouble with the original makers of Corn Flakes. They changed their product to making flour.*

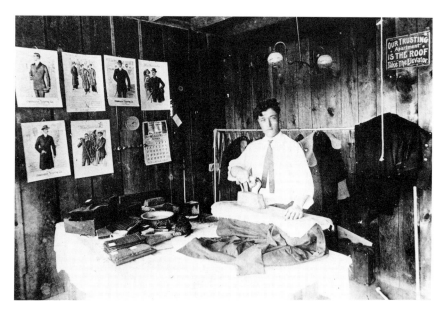

Burt Sutton and Sand Springs' first cleaning and pressing shop.
Note the pan of naptha used to spot clean.

Mary Page Seibels and her son John.
Tulsa Tribune 1946.

Gertrude and Haskell Bennefield
pose for a picture to be put into
the Home files. Taken about 1919.

Gertrude, Beulah and Opal Bennefield.
Taken 1919.

Early picture of the congregation of the Church of the Nazarene.

1960. *Picture of Broadway Baptist Fall's Creek group.*

May 20, 1950. *Side view of the Pleasant View School house built 1908.*